American Indian Wars

American Indian Wars

*A Chronology of Confrontations
Between Native Peoples and Settlers
and the United States Military,
1500s–1901*

Michael L. Nunnally

McFarland & Company, Inc., Publishers
Jefferson, North Carolina, and London

The present work is a reprint of the illustrated case bound edition of American Indian Wars: A Chronology of Confrontations Between Native Peoples and Settlers and the United States Military, 1500s–1901, *first published in 2007 by McFarland.*

LIBRARY OF CONGRESS CATALOGUING-IN-PUBLICATION DATA

Nunnally, Michael L.
American Indian wars: a chronology of confrontations between Native peoples and settlers and the United States military, 1500s–1901 / Michael L. Nunnally.
p. cm.
Includes bibliographical references and index.

ISBN 978-0-7864-5982-7
softcover : 50# alkaline paper ∞

1. Indians of North America — Wars. 2. Indians of North America — Warfare.
3. Indians of North America — History — Chronology.
4. Battles — United States — History. I. Title.

E81.N85 2010   973.04'9700202 — dc22   2007001912

British Library cataloguing data are available

©2007 Michael L. Nunnally. All rights reserved

No part of this book may be reproduced or transmitted in any form or by any means, electronic or mechanical, including photocopying or recording, or by any information storage and retrieval system, without permission in writing from the publisher.

Cover photograph: Warm Springs Indian scout who served in the U.S. Army, 1873, photograph by Eadweard Muybridge (courtesy California History Room, California State Library, Sacramento)

Manufactured in the United States of America

*McFarland & Company, Inc., Publishers
Box 611, Jefferson, North Carolina 28640
www.mcfarlandpub.com*

For my wife, Dawn,
and daughter, Robin

Acknowledgments

A small group of people were of great help to me in assembling this book. Special thanks to Elizabeth Cross, the Memphis and Shelby County Public Library, my wife Dawn, who traveled the history trail with me and never complained, Diane Merkel, editor of the *Little Big Horn Newsletter*, and Dusty DeStefanis. A very special thank you to Jeanne Cross, who served as my personal editor. I couldn't have done it without you.

TABLE OF CONTENTS

Preface

1

The Chronology

5

Appendix: American Indian Wars After 1890

157

Bibliography

161

Index

165

PREFACE

The goal of this chronology is to record the day-to-day, year-to-year violent struggles in America between Native Americans, the original inhabitants of the continent, and white Europeans, who came to claim the rich natural resources of North America. The basic conflict between these adversaries was the continuous encroachment of European settlers and a totally oppositional land-use philosophy: the European idea of land ownership versus the Indian concept of the land being loaned to man for his use by the Great Spirit. The conflict of these two philosophies led to violent encounters as each group attempted to dominate the issue. Interestingly enough, conflicts over land sharing had existed among Indian tribes before the arrival of white settlers. However, the settlers' increasing population pushed the Indians into all-out resistance as they saw their lifestyle threatened with extinction.

I became interested in the Indian wars as a child of the 1950s and 1960s, seeing the Western movies and magazine stories that described the Western mystique, an exciting American odyssey. Also, the vast scope and endurance of the Indian conflict became fascinating to me. This childhood fascination became an adult interest in researching the specifics of these ongoing battles. In my personal study I could find no one book that could gather the majority of Indian war information into one place. The books I used covered specific eras, regions, wars or tribes. My book was born of a need to draw all this information together. It is arranged chronologically as that seemed the most useful presentation for readers. I utilized microfilm, newspapers, magazines, journals, books and the Internet in my research.

Of the numerous sources used for this compilation, a few proved outstanding. *King Philip's War* by Eric B. Schultz and Michael J. Tougias and *Indian Wars in New England* by Rev. William Hubbard are two excellent books on King Philip's War and the Pequot War in New England. *West Texas Frontier* by Joseph McConnell and *Texas Indian Fighters* by A. J. Sowell are the definitive works on the Indian Wars in the Lone Star state. *The Creek War* by H. S. Halbert and T. H. Ball is an excellent book on that subject as is Steve Rajtar's *Indian War Sites*. *Great Western Indian Fights* by the Potomac Corral of the Westerners has some twenty-five accounts of the most well-known western battles and is the book which hooked me way back in 1973. Robert Utley's *Frontier Regulars: The United States Army and the Indian, 1866–1891* is another superior work. These books are but a few of the excellent sources I used in writing this book on the Indian wars. A number of informational websites on the Indian Wars are available, among them the Kentucky Historical Society and *www.forttours. com*, which has a number of entries from Joseph McConnell's excellent book, *The West Texas Frontier*.

In my study I found that the earliest accounts of Indian conflicts are the least well documented. Early settlers were more concerned about surviving their harsh pioneering life than thoroughly documenting the regular, almost daily, Indian attacks. When early historians mention these conflicts, they most often refer to the "Indians" generally without mentioning a specific tribe. Many Indians were unified in alliances, which made identifying the participants difficult. Any number of possible arrangements of tribes was possible. During the French and Indian War and other protracted conflicts, Indian tribes often flip-flopped in their allegiances, making complete accuracy in documentation impossible.

Although the American Civil War has been described as *the* defining war on the North American continent, many historians disagree with that statement. In an age of political correctness Americans should know the truth of their history, not a sanitized version of it. The real version can be found in first-hand accounts in newspapers, diaries, letters and government documents, but not generalizations in textbooks. One of my goals in writing this book is to rebut twentieth-century deniers, revisionists who seek to minimize the range and scope of this monumental conflict of wills.

The Indian wars began soon after European explorers set foot on the North American continent as two different and defined cultures faced each other in the vast arena of North America. While the American Civil War lasted four years, the struggle between white man and red man lasted well over four hundred years, and the scars remain prominent in the twenty-first century.

Starting in the 1500s and extending well into the 1880s America was a battlefield. As the English, Dutch and French began to invade the northeast coast, and Spanish explorers began their quest into Florida and the Southwest, tensions between whites and native peoples began to boil. The long-time inhabitants of the continent found their traditional lands and hunting grounds overwhelmed by a seemingly never-ending influx of people whose thirst for land was unquenchable.

By the time of the French and Indian War, tribes had begun warring on other tribes as sides were drawn for loyalty. French battled British as British battled colonists and Mohawks, Senecas, Ottawas and Chippewas battled with and against each other. This pattern continued as white settlers and explorers pushed their way westward. Arikara, Pawnee, Crow and other tribes, once enemies of the advancing whites, soon aligned themselves with their former enemies to battle Sioux, Cheyenne and Comanche. All the while, inter-tribal warfare continued to rage across the continent.

The Indians' ability to make war on this new European enemy was increased as the horse made its appearance on the plains. The Indian then had an edge as wild Spanish ponies gave him the mobility for warfare; horse and Indian became as one. The fear of Indian capture — of scalping, mutilation and torture — was foremost in the minds of the explorers and settlers. Another possible fate awaiting Indians' captives was enslavement with hard labor. Many women were forced to become wives or concubines of warriors. Fear of Indian capture was so intense that many settlers, explorers and soldiers "kept the last bullet for themselves" to avoid a gruesome fate.

As traditional Indian lands slowly diminished due to white encroachment and broken treaties, the American Indian found himself confined to reservations sometimes thousands of miles from his traditional homeland. As the twentieth century began, the American Indian fought for survival and his very identity in his own country.

This text is designed to be a chronology of actual events, not an editorial on the hundreds of years and thousands of incidents of conflict. Many attacks on both sides were not in any way part of an organized resistance but at times were just incidental occurrences that were part of daily life in America.

On both sides of this ongoing war, many participants were less than noble, and a few were downright criminals. This book does not address the morality of expansionism or its consequences, but it does document the reality and frequency of each side's participation. Most involved were not villains or heroes but everyday people responding to events and circumstances in which they found themselves. In so many accounts the dates given are contradictory. More than one date is sometimes given for the same event, and the same disparity is true of some actual battle sites. For instance, the actual site of the Sand Creek Massacre is still debated, and Sand Creek was a big battle. I have tried to resolve these factual conflicts to the best of my ability by referring to the historians who specialize in a specific era. The locations of many of these battles and skirmishes are lost to time, but many are marked with monuments and plaques which speak to us across time of the struggles between red man and white man.

The entries in italics provide background and additional historical information. The quotations in bold serve to show the philosophical differences between whites and Indians and are from primary sources.

The Chronology

> We did not ask you white men to come here. The Great Spirit gave us this country as a home. You had yours. We did not interfere with you. The Great Spirit gave us plenty of land to live on, buffalo, deer, antelope and other game. But you have come here; you are taking my land from me; you are killing off our game, so it is hard for us to live. Now, you tell us to work for a living, but the Great Spirit did not make us to work, but to live by hunting. You white men can work if you want to. We do not interfere with you, and again you say, why do you not become civilized? We do not want your civilization! We would live as our fathers did, and their fathers before them.
>
> — Crazy Horse [Source: 88]

Pre-Columbian Era

Recent archaeology suggests that Norse explorers arrive perhaps 200 years before Columbus on the shores of eastern Canada. Indian conflict may have driven the prospective immigrants away.

1400s

Christopher Columbus reaches San Salvador. John and Sebastian Cabot explore east coast of North America.

1500–1599

Spanish and European settlements are founded in North America. European diseases begin taking a toll among Indians as Spanish invaders begin enslavement in the southwest. Ponce de León's ships are driven off by Calusa arrows, and France lays claim to northeast Indian lands. Coronado explores the southwest as Acoma and Zuni Indians battle Spanish in New Mexico and Arizona. Yamasee Indians attack Georgia settlements. The horse is introduced to the American continent and changes the Indians' way of life and warfare.

1513

Juan Ponce de León arrives in Florida. Calusa and Ais Indians begin attacks on Spanish forces and slave traders.

June 3, 1513 — *Florida*

Ships commanded by Juan Ponce de León are attacked by Calusa Indians in twenty canoes. Several Indians and one crewmen are killed in one of the first violent encounters recorded between American Indians and Europeans. The Spanish ships are attacked in the harbor the next day and a number of arrows are fired at the ships, but no one is injured. Source: 87, 88

1517

April 18, 1517 — *Florida*

At Charlotte Harbor, ships commanded by Francisco Hernandez de Cordoba land to collect water. As they prepare to return to the ship, twenty-one crewmen are attacked by Calusa or Ais Indians, wounding six Spaniards and killing over twenty-three Indians. Source: 87

1521

July 1521—*Florida*

Over 200 men under Ponce de León land to establish a settlement near present-day Tampa Bay. The Spaniards are attacked by a large force of Indians. Caught totally by surprise, over twenty Spaniards are killed. Ponce de León is wounded by an arrow (perhaps poisonous) and dies several days later. Source: 87, 88, 5

1528

June 17, 1528—*Florida*

Under orders from the governor Spanish forces led by Cabeza de Vaca attack an Apalachee Indian village. The Spanish drive off the Indians, capturing a number of women and children, but release them later. The Apalachee return the next day and demand the release of one of their chiefs but soon attack. One Indian is killed. Source: 87

July 20, 1528—*Florida*

After leaving an Apalachee village Spanish forces are attacked while crossing a lake. Several soldiers are wounded, but the Indians are driven off by Spanish Dragoons. Source: 87

August 2, 1528—*Florida*

Indians attack the camp of Gov. Pánfilo de Narváez at the mouth of the Apalachicola River. No human casualties are reported, but one horse is killed. Source: 87

October 27, 1528—*Florida*

After being invited to sleep in a Panzacola (Pensacola) village, 242 Spaniards are attacked by 150 of the Indians in the middle of the night. Several soldiers are wounded, and the Indians are driven off. Source: 87

1539

September 15, 1539—*Florida*

While spending the night at the village of Napituca near the Suwannee River, over 300 Utinas Indians approach the forces of Hernando de Soto and ask for the release of their leader. The Spaniards attack and kill over thirty Indians. Source: 87

> "Think, then, what must be the effect of the sight of you and your people, whom we have at no time seen, astride the fierce brutes, your horses, entering with such speed and fury into my country ... things altogether new, as to strike awe and terror into our hearts."
> —Chief of Ichisi, 1540
> [Source: 88]

1540

June 2–4, 1540—*Mississippi*

Hernando de Soto's expedition is attacked by Natchez Indians led by Chief Quigualtam on the Mississippi River near present-day Vicksburg. Source: 87

July 7, 1540—*New Mexico*

Conquistadors under Francisco Vázquez de Coronado clash with Zuni warriors of the pueblo of Hawikuh. Coronado and his expedition are searching for the "lost city of gold" when they come upon the Zuni pueblo and decide to capture it. The Zuni rocks and arrows are no match for the Spanish firearms, and a number of Indians are killed. Source: 87

October 18, 1540, Battle of Maubila (Mobile)—*Alabama*

A 950-man Spanish force under Hernando de Soto is attacked by Maubila Indians under Chief Tuscaloosa. The Indians are out-weaponed, and 3,000 Indians are reported killed. Twenty Spaniards are also killed. Source: 87, 88

1541

January 1541— *Mississippi*

Chickasaws led by Curaca attack de Soto's camp, killing a number of his men. Source: 87

March 4, 1541— *Mississippi*

When Hernando de Soto demands 200 Indians to carry his baggage, the Indians attack his camp, killing 12 men, 57 horses and burning a number of huts. Source: 87

1564

French Fort Caroline is established in Florida.

1565

Florida

Spanish Commandant Pedro Menéndez de Avilés with over 1,500 men attack and burn down French Fort Caroline. Avilés then subjugates the Seloy tribe who control the area. Source: 88

1566

Florida

An expedition led by Avilés is attacked by Calusa Indians, at Mound Key, killing three Spaniards. Source: 87

November 1566— *South Carolina*

Spanish forces battle Indians at Spanish Fort San Juan and kill over 1,000 natives while losing only two wounded. Over fifty Indian homes are burned. (The garrison at Fort San Juan is massacred by natives in April 1584.) Source: 87

1568

April 13, 1568— *Florida*

French forces led by Dominique de Gourgues, with allied Timucuan Indians, attack and destroy Spanish San Mateo at present-day Jacksonville. (The Spanish had burned down the French Fort Caroline in the same area three years before and attacked a number of Timucuan Indians in the area.) Source: 87

1569

Florida

A Spanish landing party sent out by Pedro Menendez Marquez is attacked by Calusa Indians at Mound City. Source: 87

1572

Spring 1572— *Virginia*

A Kiskiack native youth had been kidnapped by Spanish officials and taken to Spain and Mexico where he was held for nine years. He returns in 1572 with Spanish soldiers and escapes back to his Kiskiack people. Angry over the youth's having been taken in the first place, Kiskiack natives attack a nearby mission and massacre all of the inhabitants. Spanish soldiers led by Pedro Menéndez de Avilés arrive to punish the Kiskiack Indians for the attack and massacre. When the Spanish find that the boy has already returned to his people, they open fire on the natives and then leave the area. The Spanish forces leave Chesapeake Bay for good. Source: 56

1576

South Carolina

When food supplies run low at Spanish Fort Santa Elena, the commander sends a detachment of twenty-one soldiers to the Escamacu native settlement to raid their food supply. The soldiers take the natives' provisions and head back toward Santa

Elena but are attacked by the pursuing Indians who kill all but one of the soldiers who escapes back to the fort. Source: 87

1584

April 1584—South Carolina

Fort San Juan is attacked by local natives, and the entire garrison is massacred. Source: 87

1585

July 1585—North Carolina

British soldiers burn the Indian settlement of Aquascogoc after discovering a silver cup has been stolen. Source: 56

1586

June 1, 1586—North Carolina

Local Roanoke Indians led by Chief Wingina grow increasingly resentful of the English settlers' inability to feed themselves during the cold winter months. Gov. Ralph Lane launches a surprise attack on the Indians in an attempt to obtain much needed stored food. The settlers' conditions worsen until salvation arrives in the form of Sir Francis Drake and a fleet of English warships. Source: 56

> "Your forefathers crossed the great water and landed on this island. We took pity on them, and they sat down among us. We gave them corn and meat. They gave us poison in return."
> — Sagoyewatha (Red Jacket), Seneca [Source: 88]

1590

New Mexico

A Spanish expedition led by Castano de Sosa has some cattle stolen by Plains Apaches near the Pecos River. Sosa and his men attack the Apaches, killing two. Source: 40

1593

New Mexico

A Spanish expedition led by Francisco Leyva de Bonilla and Antonio Gutierrez Humana sets out to explore the plains and is never heard from again. The expedition is assumed to have been killed by Indians. Source: 40

1597

Georgia

Yamasee Indians led by Don Juanillo attack several Spanish missions on the Georgia coast, killing Fathers Pedro de Corpa, Blas de Rodriguez Aunon, Badajoz, and Francisco de Velascola. In retaliation Spanish forces attack and burn several Yamasee villages. (Don Juanillo is killed by the Spanish in 1601.) Source: 87

1598

December 4, 1598— New Mexico

Pueblo Indians kill Juan de Zaldivar and twelve of his men after his demands for food angers the natives at Acoma Pueblo in western New Mexico. Source: 40, 98, 127, 133

1599

January 21, 1599, Acoma Massacre—New Mexico

The Acoma Pueblo is attacked by Spaniards under Vicente de Zaldivar to avenge the death of his brother the month before. The Spaniards kill over 800 natives and take over 500 prisoners. All males over twelve are sold into slavery. All males over twenty-five are sentenced to have one foot cut off. Source: 40, 87, 88, 127. Marker: Acoma Pueblo is located 40 miles west of Albuquerque, NM.

1600–1699

Champlain attacks Onondaga villages. Jamestown is founded in Virginia. Explorer Henry Hudson's ships are attacked by Manhattan Indians. French and Mimac war with Beothuk natives. The Spanish establish mission forts in the southwest. The Pequot War and King Philip's War ravage New England. Pueblo and Pima Indians battle with Spanish forces in the southwest.

1605

Maine

Violence between white settlers and Indian natives breaks out after Capt. George Waymouth kidnaps five natives living on Maine's coast. On Waymouth's planned return to England, the Plymouth forts' commander, Sir Ferdinando Gorges, refuses to let him take the captured natives with him. Source: 95

1606

OCTOBER 15, 1606 — *Massachusetts*

French ships under the command of Samuel de Champlain land at a Almouchiquois native village at Cape Cod. Five men go ashore and are attacked by the natives, killing four French sailors. Source: 87, 95

1607

Jamestown Fort is established in Virginia.

MAY 26, 1607 — *Virginia*

James Fort [Jamestown] is attacked by over 400 Powhatan natives led by Chief Wahunsonacock, killing two settlers and wounding fourteen. The colony at Jamestown will be attacked by Indians for years. Source: 56, 88. Marker: Jamestown Village, Jamestown, VA.

1607

FALL — *Virginia*

Capt. John Smith and several men attempt to buy corn from local Powhatans, but a fight soon develops when the whites refuse to trade their guns. Shots are fired, and the English withdraw. Smith is captured, taken to Wahunsonacock and soon adopted into the tribe. Source: 88

1609

JULY 29, 1609 — *New York*

French leader Samuel de Champlain, accompanied by Algonquin and Huron allies, defeats a Mohawk Iroquois raiding party on Lake Champlain. Source: 87, 98

FALL — *Virginia*

Powhatan Indians lay siege to James Fort, but a relief force soon arrives and the siege is lifted. Source: 56

1614

New Mexico

Spanish officials hang several Jemez Indian leaders after their killing of an Indian of the Spanish Cochiti Pueblo. Source: 40

1621

Fort Hill is established in Plymouth, Massachusetts.

1622

MARCH 22, 1622, JAMESTOWN MASSACRE — *Virginia*

Powhatan Indians led by Opechancanough begin attacks on settlements and plantations along the James River. Opechancanough begins a war to exterminate the English settlements from the area. On the first day of attacks at Jamestown over 350 colonists are killed from an area with a population of 1,200. At Martin's Hundred, 78 of 140 settlers are killed. The town of Henrico is destroyed. Source: 50, 56, 88

1623

Massachusetts

Miles Standish and eight other men attack local Indians who are planning to attack and destroy the town of Wessagusett south of Plymouth. Source: 87

1624

July 1624—Virginia

A raiding party led by Capt. William Tucker attack a Powhatan village, killing at least forty Indians. Tucker and his men attend peace talks with the inhabitants and offer them poisoned wine, which reportedly kills some 200 Indians. Source: 87

1632

November 1632—Delaware

Indians attack the farm of Gillis van Hoossett, killing him and another man. Indians kill some thirty-two colonists working in fields during this period. Source: 87

1634

Connecticut

Captain Stone and his seven men are killed by Indians near their boat on the Connecticut River. Source: 19, 87

1636

May 20, 1636—Connecticut

John Gallop and his sons are sailing off Block Island when they spot the ship of Capt. John Oldham, its decks full of Indians. Gallop rams the vessel, sending a number of the savages fleeing overboard. He finds Oldham's body with the head bashed in and cuts on the hands and feet where the natives were attempting to cut them off. He captures and binds four of the Indians and then throws them overboard. Source: 87

July 20, 1636, The Pequot War—Massachusetts

Trader John Oldham has been killed by Pequot Indians who claim Oldham cheated them. This incident sparks the beginning of the Pequot War in New England. A militia group is organized to punish Oldham's killers. Source: 6

July 1636—Massachusetts

A militia force, in retaliation for the murder of John Oldham, attacks the Pequot Indian village on Block Island, killing fourteen Indians and burning their village and crops. Source: 6

October 1636—Connecticut

Lt. Lion Gardiner sends five men to cut hay on an island near Lyme shore where they are attacked by Pequot natives. A man named Butterfield is reportedly killed and eaten by the Pequot. Source: 87

1637

February 22, 1637— Connecticut

Lt. Lion Gardiner and ten men are attacked by Indians about a half a mile from Fort Saybrook. Two of the men are killed and John Spencer and Lt. Gardiner are wounded. Source: 87

March 1637—Connecticut

Pequot Indians attack settlements around Fort Saybrook, killing several settlers. Source: 87

April 23, 1637—Connecticut

One hundred Pequot Indians ambush British forces near Wethersfield, killing six men, three women and a number of cows and horses. Two girls are taken captive but are later rescued by Dutch authorities. Source: 87

May 1637 — *Connecticut*

Allied Mohegan, scouting ahead of Capt. John Mason's Connecticut forces, kill seven Pequot Indians. Source: 87

May 25, 1637, Fort Mystic Massacre — *Connecticut*

A militia force led by John Underhill, Lt. Lion Gardiner and Capt. John Mason attacks a Pequot village on the Mystic River. The militia includes seventy-seven Englishmen and Mohegan led by Uncas. Only seven Pequots survive the dawn attack, which kills between 300 and 700 Indians, many of whom are burned alive. "It was a fearful sight to see them thus frying in ye fryer," eyewitness William Bradford wrote, "...but ye victory seemed a sweetie sacrifice." Source: 6, 88, 95, 98 (Quote 95)

May 1637 — *Connecticut*

Pequot Indians kill several settlers along the Connecticut River. Forces led by Capt. John Mason attack a small party of Pequot natives, killing men, women and children. Source: 87

July 28, 1637 — *Connecticut*

Two hundred Pequot Indians led by Sassacus surrender to English forces at Fairfield. Pequot leader Sassacus is turned over to Mohawks, allied with the English, who kill him. This event ends the Pequot War. Source: 87, 88

1639

New Mexico

Pueblo rebels begin a series of raids around the Pueblos, taking a large number of livestock and killing several mission Indians and friendly Apaches. Gov. Rosa is later charged with allowing the raids aimed at the missions and the Franciscans who have hindered Rosa's trading business. Source: 40

1640

New York

A party of Dutch settlers attack and kill several Raritan Indians on Staten Island over some stolen pigs. Source: 87

1641

September 1, 1641 — *New York*

Raritan Indians attack and burn the plantation of David de Vries and kill four workers. Source: 87

1643

February 25, 1643 — *New York*

Under orders from Gov. William Kieft, Dutch militiamen attack and kill over eighty Wappinger Indians on Manhattan Island. Source: 87

1644

April 18, 1644 — *Virginia*

Powhatan, Weyanock, Nansemond, Pamunkey and Chickahominies attack settlements and plantations along the James River, killing over 400 colonists. Source: 15, 56

1648

February 1648 — *Florida*

An Apalachino native rebellion breaks out at the mission San Antonio de Bacuqua near Tallahassee, killing three missionaries and burning seven churches. Friendly Apalachino help stop the rebellion, and the rebel leaders are sentenced to death or hard labor. Source: 87

1653

Wisconsin

Iroquois Indians attack the Potawatomi village of Mitchigami but are unable to capture it. A truce is called, and the Potawatomi offer the Iroquois some corn laced with poison. As the poison begins to take effect, the Iroquois attempt to flee but almost all are killed. Source: 87

1655

SEPTEMBER 15, 1655—*New York*

Five hundred Hackensack warriors attack New Amsterdam and Staten Island in retaliation for the murder of a squaw caught stealing peaches from the orchard of Hendrick Van Dyck. Sixteen settlers are killed, and forty-nine are taken captive. Source: 87

1656

Virginia

In an attempt to remove Rechahecrian Indian settlements along the James River 100 soldiers led by Col. Edward Hill attack and kill a number of natives, burning their villages. Source: 76

1657

New Mexico

Navajo warriors attack the Jemez Pueblo, killing nineteen of its inhabitants. In retaliation Spanish forces led by Don Juan Dominguez y Mendoza surprise the Navajos during a native ceremony, killing several and capturing 211. Many of the captured Navajos are sold into slavery. Source: 133

1658

MAY 1658—*New York*

Native warriors shoot and kill Herman Jacobsen and then burn the Adriaensen farm. Source: 87

SEPTEMBER 20, 1658—
New York

Over 500 Indians attack and kill settlers at Wiltwyck. A number of the captive settlers are burned at the stake. Source: 87

> "I was as much an Enemy to the English at their first coming into these parts as anyone whatsoever, and did try all ways and means to destroy them ... but I could in no way effect it ... therefore I advise you never to contend with the English, nor make war with them."
>
> — Passaconaway
> [Source: 51]

1659

New Mexico

An army of 40 Spaniards and 800 Indian allies attack Navajo natives along the Rio Grande River, killing a large number and capturing many who are sold into slavery by Gov. Bernardo Lopez de Mendizabal. Gov. Mendizabal is arrested in 1662 after his growing slave trade becomes a problem for Spanish officials. Source: 40, 133

1661

New Mexico

In an effort to suppress native religious beliefs Spanish forces raid a number of Pueblo villages, destroying hundreds of Kachina masks considered sacred to the Indians. Source: 88

1662

MAY 12, 1662—*New Mexico*

Spanish officials find Gov. Bernardo Lopez de Mendizabal guilty of violating treaties of some Apache tribes by capturing and selling them. His governorship is revoked by officials, but Mendizabal recovers it in several years. Source: 40, 133

1663

June 1663 — *New York*

Esopus Indians attack and burn the Wiltwyck settlement, killing several inhabitants. Source: 87

1669

June 1669 — *New Mexico*

Apache natives attack the Acoma Pueblo, killing twelve people including Spanish Capt. Don Francisco de Chaves. The Apaches take a number of Spanish and Indian captives along with sheep, goats, horses and cattle. Source: 133

1672

New Mexico

After continuing raids, Gov. Juan Francisco de Trevino appoints Don Juan Dominguez y Mendoza to lead a campaign against the Navajos. The Spanish force along with over 300 Pueblo Indians attack a number of Navajo settlements, killing six and recovering several captives. Navajo crops are burned, and thirty-five natives are captured and sold into slavery. Source: 133

1675

January 1675 — *Massachusetts*

John Sassamon (Wussausmon), a Christian Indian, warns the Plymouth colony that Wampanoag Indians are planning a revolt. When Sassamon is later found dead in Assawamsett Pond, Tisaquin, sachem, or chieftain, of the Assawampsetts, is found guilty of the murder and may have been hanged with two others of his tribe. Source: 19, 64

June 20–23, 1675, King Philip's War — *Massachusetts*

A small band of Pokanoket Indians cross the Kickamuit River and raid several farms in the English settlement of Swansea (Swanzy), burning two. The Indians are from the village of King Philip (Metacom) and the raid launches a bloody war in northeast America. (The colonial population has grown to around 40,000 while the Indian population has remained static: this growing number of whites leads to more tension between the two peoples.) Source: 19, 49, 64, 87, 88, 93, 94, 99

> "King Philip was a warrior bold, whose deeds are writ in records old; He through New England's woods did roam, and sorrow brought to many a home."
>
> — King Philip nursery rhyme [Source: 93]

June 23, 1675 — *Rhode Island*

John Salisbury shoots and kills a Pokanoket native. Source: 93

June 24, 1675 — *Massachusetts*

Pokanoket or Wampanoag warriors kill seven English settlers working in a field at Mattapoisett. The heads of the victims are displayed on poles at Kickamuit. At the town of Swansea, the war party ambush settlers returning from a worship service at a nearby church, killing one. Source: 51, 59, 93

June 25, 1675 — *Massachusetts*

At Fall River, Layton Archer and his son are killed by Wampanoag Indians. The Indians raid the settlement of Taunton. Edward Bobet is discovered hiding from the raiders in a tree and killed by the war party. Source: 51. Marker: Bobet marker located on Berkley St., Taunton, MA.

June 27, 1675 — *Massachusetts*

The settlement of Taunton is attacked by Wampanoag Indians. Source: 93

1675

New Mexico

Don Juan Mendoza is commissioned by Gov. Juan Francisco de Trevino to lead an expedition against the Navajo. Spanish forces led by Mendoza along with 300 Zia Pueblo Indians attack the Navajos, killing about fifteen. Thirty-five Navajo are captured and taken back as slaves. Source: 133

JUNE 28, 1675—*Massachusetts*

Troops under Col. Benjamin Church are ambushed while crossing a bridge near Miles' Garrison. Guide William Hammond is fatally wounded, and several others are also hit. Source: 50, 59

JULY 9, 1675—*Massachusetts*

The settlement of Middleboro is attacked and burned by Indians. The attackers are believed to be Wampanoag or Narragansett natives. Another outpost at Dartmouth is attacked and burned by warriors led by Totoson, sachem (chief) of the Mattapoisett Indians. Source: 59, 93. Marker: John Thomason's house burned in the attack is marked with a plaque on Rt. 5, about one mile north of the Middleboro line.

JULY 14, 1675—*Massachusetts*

Nipmuc Indians led by Chief Matoonas attack the settlement at Mendon (Mendam), killing five or six residents including the wife and son of Matthias Puffer. Source: 51, 64, 93, 94. Marker: Located at Providence Rd. and Hartford Ave., Mendon, MA.

JULY 19, 1675—*Massachusetts*

Militiamen engage Wampanoag Indians near Pocasset Swamp (near Taunton), and two of the militia scouts are killed. Source: 59, 93, 94

JULY 1675—*Virginia*

Doeg natives cross the Potomac River and attack the plantation of Thomas Mathews, killing the plantation overseer. In retaliation for raids against white settlements, a force led by Lt. Col. John Washington attacks Susquehannock natives near Fort Washington. When five chiefs come out to parlay, Washington's men kill them. Source: 87

JULY 1675—*Rhode Island*

Massachusetts forces under Capt. Mathew Fuller are ambushed by Wampanoag Indians on John Almy's farm at Tiverton. The militiamen retreat to a beach on the neck of land between Punkatees and Fogland Point. Two of Fuller's men are wounded, but none are killed. Source: 93

AUGUST 1, 1675—*Rhode Island*

English forces, aided by Mohegan Indians led by Oneko, attack the Wampanoag at Nipsachuck Swamp at present-day Smithfield, Rhode Island. Greatly outnumbered, 265 to 40, the Wampanoag Indians fight their way out and escape along the Blackstone River, losing twenty-three warriors and four chiefs. Source: 50, 59, 93, 94

AUGUST 2–4, 1675, WHEELER'S SURPRISE—*Massachusetts*

Capt. Thomas Hutchinson, Capt. Thomas Wheeler and a twenty-five-man militia along with Indian guides are ambushed three miles from Brookfield by Nipmuc Indians. Eight are killed, including Sgt. John Wheeler. The militia retreat to a house in Brookfield and are closely followed by the Nipmuc, who fire on the house for three days until troops arrive from Lancaster. Two of those killed are listed as John Eires and Richard Coy. Capt. Edward Hutchinson is wounded in the fight and dies of his wounds on August 19. Source: 51, 59, 64, 93, 94. Marker: Located on West Rd., Brookfield, MA.

August 22, 1675—
Massachusetts

Monoco (One-Eyed John) leads a force of Nashaway Indians against Lancaster, killing seven English settlers. Source: 59, 94

August 25, 1675, Battle of South Deerfield—
Massachusetts

Capt. Thomas Lathrop, Richard Beers and 100 soldiers engage Norwottock Indians at Hopewell Swamp in present-day Whately. Reinforcements under Capt. Samuel Moseley arrive, but the battle rages for another three hours. Forty Norwottock natives are reported killed. Source: 59, 93, 94

September 1, 1675—
Massachusetts

Deerfield is attacked by sixty Norwottock Indians who burn a number of buildings and barns and kill one settler. Source: 93, 94. Marker: Located on Rt. 9, Brookfield.

September 2, 1675—
Massachusetts

Eight men are killed and property burned at Northfield (Squakeag) by Pocumtuck and Nashaway Indians led by Monoco. The inhabitants of Northfield begin evacuating on September 3, but a number of residents refuse to go. Monoco is captured the following year and hanged in Boston on September 26, 1676. Source: 59, 93

September 4, 1675, Beers' Ambush—*Massachusetts*

Capt. Richard Beers and his men are ambushed on their way to help evacuate Northfield. The Pocumtuck and Nashaway Indians drive Beers and his men into a nearby ravine where he and several of his men are killed. The survivors of Beers' command retreat to Hadley. On September 6, Northfield is totally evacuated. Source: 51, 59, 64, 93, 94. Marker: Located on Rt. 63, Northfield, MA.

September 9, 1675—
Massachusetts

After hearing gunshots from the Thomas Wakely farm, George Ingersol investigates. "When I came to the place I found the house burnt down, and six persons killed ... their own son was shot through the body, and also his head dashed in pieces.... Wife was dead, her head skinned." Source: 51, 61, 93 (Quote 61)

September 12, 1675, Deerfield Evacuated—*Massachusetts*

Deerfield is attacked for the second time by Pocumtuck natives. Two homes are burned. The town is evacuated. Source: 51, 93

September 18, 1675, Bloody Brook Massacre—
Massachusetts

Capt. Thomas Lathrop (Louthrops) and seventy-nine men start on a slow march from Deerfield to Hadley after retrieving 3,000 bushels of corn from the deserted town, but they stop along the way. An Indian war party under Muttawmp falls on the unsuspecting militiamen, killing Lathrop, forty soldiers and seventeen teamsters. A force under Capt. Samuel Moseley dashes to the scene but is nearly overwhelmed and battles the Indians all day. Source: 19, 50, 51, 59, 93, 94. Marker: Bloody Brook Monument, 286 North Main St., South Deerfield, MA.

September 18, 1675—
Maine

The home of Capt. John Bonython is burned by Abenaki Indians at present-day Saco. Source: 93

> "To put to death men that have deserved to die, is an ordinance of God, and a blessing is promised to it."
> — John Eliot
> [Source: 51]

September 26, 1675 — *Connecticut*

John Pynchon's mill is burned by Indians at Suffield. Source: 93

September 28, 1675 — *Massachusetts*

Praisever Turner and Uzacaby Shakspeare are killed and scalped by Indians while cutting wood in Northampton. Source: 93

1675 — *New York*

King Philip's camp at Schaghticoke and the Hoosic River is attacked by Mohawk Indians, who are allies with whites, and over 350 of Philip's Wampanoag warriors are killed. Source: 51, 87, 93

October 1, 1675 — *Maine*

Richard Tozer's house at Newichawannock, present-day Berwick, is attacked by Abenaki Indians. Tozer escapes with fifteen others. Source: 93

October 5, 1675 — *Connecticut*

A combined force of over 300 Nipmuc and Agawam Indians attack and burn more than thirty-five homes and several mills at Springfield. They kill three men, including Lt. Cooper. A relief force under Maj. Robert Treat arrives on the west bank of the Connecticut River but is unable to cross in the face of enemy fire. Source: 51, 64, 87, 93

October 16, 1675 — *Maine*

Abenaki Indians return to Richard Tozer's house at Newichawannock and kill him and his son. A rescue party sent to Tozer's house is ambushed, and two men are killed. (Some accounts say Tover's son is kidnapped and released four months later.) Source: 51, 93

October 18, 1675 — *Maine*

Lt. Roger Plaisted and two his sons are killed by Indians near present-day Berwick. Source: 6, 93, 94

October 19, 1675 — *Massachusetts*

Warriors led by Muttawmp lure a scouting party led by Capt. Samuel Moseley into an ambush, killing eight of the ten-man party. The Indians then attack Hatfield but are driven off. Settlers demand protection from the army after repeated requests. "We are a distressed people," one settler writes. "We hear nothing since from our army." Source: 51, 59, 64, 94 [Quote 51]

October 26, 1675 — *Massachusetts*

Indians attack and kill three Springfield men who are transporting grain to Westfield. The Indians then burn several Westfield houses. Source: 51, 59

October 29, 1675 — *Massachusetts*

Settlers working in a field at Northampton are killed by Indians. Source: 87, 93

November 3, 1675 — *Massachusetts*

Twenty inhabitants of Scarboro are attacked by Indians, but a relief force drives the Indians off. Source: 51

December 15, 1675 — *Rhode Island*

Several soldiers are killed by Narragansett Indians under Stonewall John after peace negotiations go bad at Smith's Garrison. Source: 59, 93

December 16, 1675 — *Rhode Island*

A group of soldiers sent to Pettaquamscutt to look for soldiers discover a number of dead people at Bull's Garrison, presumed killed by Indians. Source: 59, 93, 94

December 19, 1675, The Great Swamp Fight — *Rhode Island*

The combined armies of Massachusetts Bay, Plymouth and Connecticut, totaling more than 1,150, attack a large fortified Narragansett village called Canonchet's Fort located in the Great Swamp. Completely overwhelmed, the Indians flee into the swamp, leaving over 600 dead on the field. More than eighty of the English troops are killed. Source: 19, 50, 59, 64, 93. Marker: Located off SR 2, South County Rd., South Kingston, RI.

1676

January 27, 1676 — *Rhode Island*

Pawtuxet is attacked by Narragansett Indians, and several buildings are burned and some livestock stolen. Source: 93

February 1, 1676 — *Massachusetts*

The farm and garrison of Thomas Eames is attacked by Nipmuc Indians. Eames' entire farm is destroyed including house, barn, corn, hay and cattle. Mrs. Eames and possibly three of the four children are killed. Source: 51, 64, 93. Marker: Located on Mount Wayte Ave., in present-day Framingham.

February 10, 1676, Attack on Lancaster — *Massachusetts*

Four hundred Nipmuc warriors under One-Eyed John (Monoco) attack Lancaster, killing or wounding fifty settlers including Rev. Joseph Rowlandson and capturing twenty-four settlers. Mary Rowlandson is taken captive. (She will later write *The Narrative of the Captivity and Restoration of Mrs. Mary Rowlandson* detailing her captivity among the Indians.) Six weeks later Lancaster is abandoned. Source: 6, 51, 64, 93, 94. Marker: Rev. John Rowlandson marker, Main St. and Whitcomb Dr., Lancaster, MA.

February 21, 1676 — *Massachusetts*

Three hundred Nipmuc and Narragansett Indians attack Medfield. Eighteen English settlers are killed, and several are kidnapped. Source: 59, 93, 94

February 25, 1676 — *Massachusetts*

Nipmuc Indians burn several buildings at Weymouth. Source: 51, 94

March 2, 1676 — *Massachusetts*

Groton is attacked by Indians, and some cattle are taken. Source: 93

March 9, 1676 — *Massachusetts*

Groton is attacked by several Indians. One Indian is killed, and one taken captive. Source: 93, 94

March 12, 1676 — *Massachusetts*

Mattapoisett Indians attack William Clark's garrison on the Eel River. Many of the men of the garrison are away at a meeting in Plymouth. Eleven women and children from two families are killed by Mattapoisett natives led by Totoson. Source: 51, 59, 64, 93

March 13, 1676 — *Massachusetts*

Groton is attacked by Nipmuc and Narragansett warriors led by One-Eyed John (Monoco). One settler is killed, and sixty-five homes are burned. The residents of Groton are evacuated to Boston. Along the way they are ambushed by Indians and two are killed. Source: 51, 59, 64, 93

MARCH 14, 1676—*Massachusetts*

Nipmuc and Narragansett Indians attack Northampton but are driven back by heavy fire from troops under Maj. Robert Treat and Capt. William Turner. Five colonists are killed, and ten houses burned. Source: 51, 64, 93, 94

MARCH 16, 1676—*Massachusetts*

Indians attack and burn Marlborough. Source: 93

MARCH 17, 1676—*Rhode Island*

Indians burn all but one house in abandoned Warwick. Source: 51

MARCH 26, 1676—*Rhode Island*

A force under Capt. Michael Pierce is ambushed with heavy losses by Narragansett Indians at present-day Central Falls. Pierce and fifty-five of his men are killed and sixty-three wounded. Source: 49, 50, 59, 64, 93. Marker: Located at Macomber Field on High St., Central Falls, RI.

MARCH 26, 1676—*Connecticut*

Simsbury is attacked and burned by Narragansett Indians. Source: 49, 93

MARCH 26, 1676—*Massachusetts*

Indians kill a man and a girl at Longmeadow. The war party captures a woman and two children but are pursued by the town's residents. They kill the two children and wound the woman. A second war party attacks Marlborough, setting fire to eleven barns and thirteen houses. Source: 51, 59, 94

MARCH 28, 1676—*Massachusetts*

Old Rehoboth is attacked by 1,500 Wampanoag and Narragansett Indians. Forty-five homes, twenty-five barns, two corn mills and one sawmill are burned. Source: 49, 87, 93, 94

MARCH 29–30, 1676—*Rhode Island*

Narragansett natives attack and burn over 100 buildings at Providence, including the home of Roger Williams. Source: 49, 93, 94

APRIL 3, 1676—*Rhode Island*

Capt. James Avery and a force of militia ambush a party of Narragansett warriors and capture Canonchet, Algonquin military leader. Source: 6, 49, 63

APRIL 9, 1676—*Massachusetts*

Indians burn a house and barn at Bridgewater. Source: 93

APRIL 10, 1676—*Massachusetts*

A woman and two small children are killed by Indians at Woburn. Source: 51

APRIL 11, 1676—*Rhode Island*

An English militia force led by Capt. George Denison and allied with Pequot, Mohegan and Niantic Indians attack Narragansett native settlements near Pawtuxet. Canonchet, the Narragansett chief, is captured and taken to Stonington, Connecticut, where he is told to swear allegiance to the British. He refuses and is shot by the Pequot, beheaded by the Mohegan and cut up and burned by Niantic Indians. His head is sent to Stonington, Connecticut. Source: 19, 49, 64, 87, 93

APRIL 15, 1676—*Massachusetts*

Chelmsford is attacked and burned by Indians. Source: 51, 93

APRIL 17, 1676—*Massachusetts*

Remaining structures in Marlborough are burned. A force under Capt. Samuel Brocklebank pursues the raiders and attacks them in their camp at night. Source: 51, 64, 93

APRIL 21, 1676—*Massachusetts*

Over 500 Algonquin Indians led by Muttawmp attack Sudbury, burning houses and buildings as the inhabitants retreat to several nearby garrisons. A relief force of a dozen men from Concord are ambushed, tortured and killed. A militia force of sixty from Marlborough are caught in a trap and retreat to Green Hill where most are killed, including Capts. Samuel Wadsworth and Samuel Brocklebank. Thirteen survivors of the attack escape to a nearby mill. Source: 49, 51, 59, 93, 94. Marker: Water-Row Rd., Sudbury, MA.

MAY 2, 1676—*Massachusetts*

Mary Rowlandson is ransomed. She was captured February 10 during an attack on Lancaster in which several of her children were killed. Source: 6, 51, 93, 94

MAY 5, 1676—*Massachusetts*

A force of settlers led by Capt. Daniel Henchman and forty "Praying Indians," (Indians who live peaceably with the whites) attack Wampanoag natives at Hassanamassett and kill eleven natives allied with King Philip. Source: 51, 59, 93

MAY 8, 1676—*Massachusetts*

Three hundred Indians under Tispaquin attack Bridgewater, putting the town to the torch, but a driving rainstorm extinguishes the fire. Source: 51, 93, 94

MAY 11, 1676—*Massachusetts*

The few buildings still standing at Bridger are burned by Indians. Sixteen houses are burned at Plymouth. Eleven houses burned at Halifax. Source: 59, 93, 94

MAY 19, 1676, BATTLE OF TURNER'S FALLS—*Massachusetts*

A force of 150 men under the command of William Turner launches a dawn attack on a Peskeompskut native camp, killing men, women and children. Warriors from a nearby camp arrive and launch a counterattack. In a running battle, the militia retreats in panic toward Hatfield. Turner and thirty-eight of his militiamen are killed. Source: 51, 59, 64, 93, 94. Marker: Monument located at intersection of Montague City Rd. and French King Hwy. Montague, MA.

MAY 20, 1676—*Massachusetts*

Scituate is attacked by Indians, and nineteen houses are burned. Source: 93

MAY 24, 1676—*Massachusetts*

A party of Indians fishing near Rehoboth are attacked and killed by Capt. Thomas Brattle and his troops. Source: 87, 93, 94

MAY 30, 1676—*Massachusetts*

Indians launch a retaliatory strike against Hatfield, killing seven, wounding five, burning twelve barns and stealing livestock. Source: 93, 94

JUNE 1, 1676, THE TALCOTT MASSACRE—*Massachusetts*

Five hundred troops under Capt. Daniel Henchman begin a march to rendezvous with 440 English troops under the command of Maj. John Talcott. Along the way Henchman's force attacks several Indian villages, killing several hundred natives. Source: 51, 93

JUNE 7, 1676—*Massachusetts*

Militia under Capt. Daniel Henchman attack natives fishing at Washaccum Pond, killing seven of the Indians and rescuing a small white boy who had been taken previously. Source: 51, 59, 94

JUNE 12, 1676—*Massachusetts*

Connecticut troops drive off an attack on Hadley by a large Indian force. Mohawks allied with the colonists attack the Wampanoag and Narragansett camp, killing a number of people including women and children. Source: 51, 59, 93, 94

JUNE 16, 1676—*Massachusetts*

Eight farmhouses are burned by Indians at Rehoboth, and a Capt. Pierce and four other people are killed. Source: 51, 93, 94

June 26, 1676—*Rhode Island*

Indians kill Hezekiah Willet at Mount Hope. Source: 51

June 30, 1676—*Massachusetts*

Over ninety Sakonnet Indians surrender to Maj. William Bradford under the condition that they will be allowed to live in peace with the whites. After the natives surrender, they are marched off to Sandwich as prisoners of war. Source: 93, 94

July 2, 1676—*Rhode Island*

Connecticut militiamen under the command of Maj. John Talcott attack Narragansett Indians on the Pawtuxet River, capturing or killing 171 warriors. Source: 49, 64, 93

July 3, 1676—*Rhode Island*

Narragansett Indians under Chief Potuck surrender at Warwick and are executed. Source: 64, 93

July 11, 1676—*Massachusetts*

Indians plan to attack Taunton, but Maj. Bradford is warned of the attack by a captive Negro and the Indians are easily driven away. Source: 93, 94

July 25, 1676—*Massachusetts*

Chief Pumham is killed and his Narragansett forces are defeated near Dedham by a force under Capt. Samuel Harding. Fifteen Narragansett natives are killed. Source: 19, 51, 59, 64, 93, 94

July 30, 1676, Bacon's Rebellion—*Virginia*

Tobacco planters led by Nathan Bacon are denied permission to attack the Susquehannock Indians who have been raiding the settlements. Bacon and his men attack Jamestown, killing a number of Indians at the settlement. Source: 19, 49

August 1, 1676—*Massachusetts*

King Philip's wife Wootonekanuska and son are captured and his uncle Unkompoin killed near the Taunton River. Source: 19, 51, 93, 94

August 6, 1676—*Massachusetts*

Twenty citizens of Taunton capture twenty-six natives at Lockety Neck. Weetamoo (known also as the Squaw Sachem) is found drowned, and her head is cut off and set upon a pole at Taunton. She had been closely allied with King Philip. Source: 6, 9, 19, 49, 64, 94

August 11, 1676—*Maine*

Abenaki warriors allied with Philip and led by Squando attack Cleve's Neck at Falmouth, killing or capturing thirty-four Englishmen. Source: 51, 93

August 12, 1676, Death of King Philip—*Massachusetts*

King Philip (Metacom) is killed at Mt. Hope. The Pokanoket leader's location is disclosed by one of Philip's men, Alderman. It is believed Philip had murdered Alderman's brother. The disgruntled Indian leads a colonial force under Benjamin Church to Philip's hideout where Alderman shoots and kills him. Philip is decapitated and the head sent to Plymouth. "Forasmuch as he had caused many an Englishmen's body to be unburied, and to rot above ground ... not one of his bones should be buried." Several of the settlers wish to hang Philip's nine-year-old son for his part in the war, but the Rev. James Keith intercedes, and the young boy is taken to Boston and sold into slavery. Source: 6, 49, 50, 51, 59, 64, 93, 94 [Quote 51]. Marker: Located at Anawan Rock, Rt. 44, Rehoboth, MA.

August 13, 1676—*Maine*

Richard Hammond's trading post on the east side of the Kennebec River (present-day Woolwich) is raided by Indians (possibly Abenaki natives under Squando), and Hammond is killed. Source: 93

AUGUST 14, 1676—*Maine*

An Abenaki woman asks to spend the night at the Arrowsic Garrison but opens the gates, letting warriors in who attack and kill many of the settlers. Source: 87, 93

AUGUST 15, 1676—*Massachusetts*

Talcott's troops hunt down and kill thirty-five Indians at Great Barrington. Source: 51, 93. Marker: Located on west bank of the Housatonic River near Bridge St., Great Barrington, MA.

AUGUST 28, 1676—*Massachusetts*

King Philip's war leader Anawan is captured in the Squannakonk Swamp and later executed. Source: 19, 49, 51, 93

OCTOBER 12, 1676—*Maine*

The garrison at Black Point under Capt. Henry Jocelyn is surrendered to Androscoggin natives led by Chief Mugg Hegone. Source: 93

OCTOBER 18, 1676—*Maine*

Mugg Hegone and his forces attack Wells, killing two people, but are driven off. Source: 51, 93

SEPTEMBER 3, 1676—*Maine*

Abenaki Indians attack a settlement on Munjoy's Island (present-day Peak's Island), killing seven settlers. Source: 93

1677

FEBRUARY 21, 1677—*Massachusetts*

A two-hundred-man force under Maj. Richard Waldron skirmishes with Squandro Indians near Falmouth. Source: 93

MARCH 1677—*Massachusetts*

Three Indians are arraigned at Plymouth for murdering John Knowles, John Tisdall and Samuel Atkins. The Indians were Timothy Jack (alias Canjuncke) Nassamaquat and Pompacanshe. Two are found guilty, and all three are sentenced, "to be sent out of the country speedily." Source: 51

MAY 14–16, 1677—*Maine*

Indians under Mugg Hegone lay siege to Jocelyn's Garrison at Black Point. The three-day siege is lifted when Chief Mugg Hegone is shot and killed by Lt. Bartholemew Tippen. Source: 6, 93

JUNE 29, 1677—*Maine*

Two hundred and forty new recruits under the command of Capt. Benjamin Swett and Lt. James Richardson pursue some Indians and are caught in an ambush. Swett, Richardson and sixty militiamen are killed. Source: 6, 93

SEPTEMBER 1677—*Massachusetts*

Indians attack the town of Hatfield, killing a number of men working in nearby fields and taking twenty prisoners. The Indians burn a number of homes. Source: 87

1678

JULY 12, 1678—*New Mexico*

Fifty mounted Spanish soldiers and 400 Pueblo allies led by Don Juan Dominguez y Mendoza attack several Navajo settlements, destroying Navajo crops, capturing two women and thirteen horses. Source: 133

NOVEMBER 26, 1678—*New Mexico*

Spanish forces led by Mendoza attack Navajo settlements, burning homes and corn crops. Source: 133

DECEMBER 28, 1678—*New Mexico*

Navajo natives attack the Acoma Pueblo, killing several of the inhabitants. The raid is a retaliatory attack against the Spaniards for previous raids on Navajo settlements. (Juan Mendoza had promised further action against the Navajos.) Source: 133

1679

Fort Miami is established in Michigan.

1679—*Georgia*

Creek, Cherokee and Westo Indians attack the Spanish mission at Saint Katherine's Island (Santa Catalina). Source: 87

1680

AUGUST 10–16, 1680—*New Mexico*

In 1674 forty-seven Tewas Indians were accused of casting spells on local missionaries who had died. In 1675 Spanish officials hanged four and sentenced the forty-three others to prison or to be sold into slavery. One of the freed natives, Pope (Popay), vowed revenge. Five years later 2,500 Pueblo Indians of Taos, Santa Clara, Picuris and Santa Cruz, led by Pope, attack the Spanish settlement of Sky City, killing 380 Spaniards and twenty-one priests. Surviving Spaniards flee to El Paso del Norte. The large horse herd left behind spreads across the west. Source: 87, 88, 133. Marker: Sky City is located 12.5 miles southwest of the junction of I-40 and SR 23.

1682

Fort Prudhomme is established by French Traders in Tennessee. Fort St. Louis is established in Texas.

1686

1686—*South Carolina*

Yamasee Indians, encouraged by local Scots immigrants, attack and destroy a Christian Timecho native village and mission. Over fifty Timecho natives and one friar are killed while twenty-two are taken prisoner. In retaliation 153 Spanish soldiers attack, plunder and burn the Scots town of Port Royal. The Scot population flees to English Charles Town. The Spaniards plan to attack Charles Town, but their ships are damaged in a hurricane. Source: 76

> "You think that the Axe-Makers are the eldest in the country and the greatest in possession. We Human Beings are the first, and we are the eldest and the greatest."
> —Sadekanaktie, Onondaga
> [Source: 88]

1688

JULY 1688—*Maine*

Near Yarmouth soldiers run into a group of Indians who have white captives. Gunfire breaks out, killing some on both sides, and the Indians withdraw. Source: 87

1689

1689—*Texas*

Karankawa Indians attack Fort St. Louis and kill all the defenders except some young children. Source: 87

AUGUST 21, 1689—*Maine*

Thomas Gyles and his three sons are attacked by Indians at Pemaquid Point while working in a field. Gyles is killed, and his sons are taken captive and held for six years. The Pemaquid settlement is attacked in the summer of 1689 by 500 French and Indian raiders and burned to the ground. A number of its residents are killed or taken prisoner. Source: 64, 87, 95

1690

FEBRUARY 9, 1690—*New York*

French soldiers and allied Indians attack the Dutch settlement at Schenectady, killing over sixty people and capturing thirty. Source: 15, 64

March 18, 1690—*Maine*

French and Indian forces attack Salmon Falls, killing about thirty settlers and taking a number captive. Source: 64, 87

1691

January 25, 1691—*Maine*

Popish warriors attack the town of York, killing over 50 settlers and taking over 100 captives. Rev. Shubael Dummer is killed, and his wife is taken captive. She dies later while being held prisoner. Source: 64, 87

1692

February 1692—*Maine*

Abenaki Indians, encouraged by French Jesuit priests, attack the settlements at York and Wells. Source: 64, 87

June 10–11, 1692—*Maine*

Indians attack Wells but are driven off. Source: 64

1693

December 29, 1694—*New Mexico*

An expedition of over 800 soldiers, settlers and priests march to Santa Fe on March 16. Expedition leader Don Diego Jose de Vargas informs local Indians that they are occupying Spanish property and must vacate. Don Diego finally grows tired of negotiating with the Pueblo Indians and attacks the natives on the December 29, killing seventy of the leaders and sending over 400 into slavery. Source: 98

1694

March 4, 1694—*New Mexico*

Spaniards under orders from Gov. Don Diego de Vargas attack the Tewa Pueblo of San Ildefonso, killing fifteen natives. Source: 87

April 17, 1694—*New Mexico*

Spanish forces and allied Keresan Indians led by Gov. Don Diego de Vargas attack and capture the Indian settlement of La Cieneguilla, killing several inhabitants. Source: 87

July 18, 1694, Oyster River Massacre—*New Hampshire*

Over 250 Indians and French forces led by de Villies attack the residents of the Oyster River Plantation (Durham), killing a great number. The home of Ann Jenkins is attacked, "...shot at my husband ... struck him three blows on the head with a hatchet and run him three times with a bayonet ... then killed my husband's grandmother and scalped her ... plundered then set the house on fire." Forty-nine women and children are taken captive, but a number are later killed by the Indians. Source: 26, 64, 87 [Quote 26]. Marker: Rt. 4, Durham, NH.

July 21, 1694—*New Mexico*

The Jemez Pueblo Indians with allied Navajos attack the Pueblo of Zia, killing four of its inhabitants. A command led by Gov. de Vargas attacks the Jemez village only to find it abandoned. The Jemez natives, in fear of retaliation of the Zia, flee to a mesa to the north. Vargas follows and attacks them there, killing 84 and taking 361 prisoners. The villages are also burned. Source: 133

July 27, 1694—*Massachusetts*

The township of Groton is attacked by Indians. Twenty settlers are killed and more than a dozen carried away. Source: 64

1694—*Massachusetts*

Abenaki Indians, encouraged by the French, attack Groton and several other settlements nearby. Source: 87

1696

1696—*New York*

French and Indian forces numbering over 1,000 men attack and burn an Onondaga village, killing a great many. Source: 87

JUNE 4, 1696—*New Mexico*

The pueblos of Taos, Jemez, San Ildefonso, Namble and San Cristobal stage a rebellion against Spanish rule and kill five padres and burn the missions. Twenty-one soldiers and settlers are reported killed. In fear of retaliation from Spanish authorities, the Pueblo Indians seek refuge with Zuni and Hopi Indians to the west. Source: 98, 133

OCTOBER 1696—*New Mexico*

On July 30, 1696, Gov. Diego de Vargas hears reports that large numbers of Pueblo Indians and their families are fleeing to the "land of the Apaches." Vargas organizes an expedition to punish the refugees. De Vargas' forces attack the Pueblo and Apache refugees, killing a number and capturing eighty-four. The captives are divided among the soldiers and settlers. Source: 40

1697

AUGUST 1697—*New Mexico*

Gov. de Vargas leads a expeditionary force to attack the Acoma pueblos but decides not to attack after hearing the Acoma's allies, the Apaches, are nearby. Source: 133

1698

MARCH 1698—*Arizona*

The Sobaipuri Mission known as Santa Cruz de Quiburi is attacked by several hundred Apache, Jocome and Jano Indians, but some 500 Pima Indians arrive to support the mission's defense. A truce is called, and it is agreed that ten warriors from each side will fight each other to determine who will win. The Pima warriors are victorious and continue to attack the Apaches and their allies, killing over fifty warriors. Source: 87

JULY 1698—*Massachusetts*

Deerfield men track Indians who have attacked Hatfield Meadows and carried away some prisoners. The men ambush a raiding party, killing one Indian and rescuing several captives. Source: 64

1699—*Florida*

While on a buffalo hunt in northern Florida, Francisco de Florencia and forty Chacatos Indians attack a trade party of Indians, killing sixteen of twenty-four. Source: 87

1701

Fort Pontchartrain is established in Michigan.

1702

Fort Louis is established in Alabama.

MARCH 20, 1702—*Florida*

Backed by the British, Lower Creek, Yuchi and Cherokee attack a Timucuan town and burn the mission at Santa Fe. Source: 87

1702—*Florida*

In retaliation for the attack on the Timucuan town, 800 Apalachee Indians and Spanish soldiers attack settlements along the Apalachicola River. Source: 87

1702—*Georgia*

English forces led by Capt. Antonio with friendly Creeks from Achito (Columbus) attack Spanish forces and 800 Indian allies under Capt. Francisco Romo Uriz. The English defeat the Spanish and capture or kill over 600 of the defenders.

Source: 120. Marker: Georgia 97, just south of Georgia 311 at Bainbridge, GA.

FALL 1702—*Florida*

Creek Indians and British militiamen led by Gov. James Moore from South Carolina attack Spanish St. Augustine. Source: 87

1703

1703—*Massachusetts*

A raiding party of French, Abenaki and Mohawk attack Deerfield, killing the settlers and burning the town. The Indians take over 100 captives. Source: 88

1703—*Maine*

Abenaki natives attack Casco, nearly wiping out the small settlement. Source: 87

AUGUST 1703—*Maine*

Abenaki Indians along with French allies attack the settlement of Wells, killing, burning and taking a number of captives. Source: 88

1704

JANUARY 14, 1704—*Florida*

British and Creek forces led by James Moore attack the Ayubale Mission, killing twenty-five Apalachee Indians. Over eighty-four Apalachee natives are captured and taken to South Carolina. Source: 5, 24. Marker: Located on private property on site of Mission of San Pedro.

JANUARY 15, 1704—*Florida*

Spanish troops with over 400 allied Indians led by Capt. Ruiz Mexia counterattack forces under James Moore who had attacked Ayubale Mission the day before. Mexia's force kills seven Englishmen and over 100 of their native allies. A counterattack by Moore's army kills a number of the Spanish soldiers, including Father Juan de Parga. The Spanish and their allies are routed, and a number are killed and wounded. Over 325 Spaniards are captured, including Capt. Mexia. Source: 24, 87

FEBRUARY 29, 1704, MASSACRE AT DEERFIELD—*Massachusetts*

Three hundred French Canadians, Caughnawaga and Abenaki Indians led by Hertel de Rouville attack the town of Deerfield, killing forty-eight men, women and children and taking over 111 prisoners to Canada. Many of the prisoners are killed by their Indian captors on their way to Canada. Source: 26, 41. Marker: Old Deerfield has preserved twelve buildings and a gravestone for the 48 killed. Off U.S. 5 and SR 10, Old Deerfield, MA.

APRIL 25, 1704—*New England*

A party of men led by Caleb Lyman along with several friendly Indians attack an Indian encampment of the Connecticut River, nine days from Northhampton. Lyman writes, "When we came to look over the slain, we found seven dead ... six of whom were scalpt." Source: 14

1705

1705—*Alabama*

The Chickasaw natives had sold a number of Choctaws as slaves to the English, and the Choctaws vowed revenge. After having visited French Fort Mobile, the Chickasaws, in fear of retribution from the Choctaws, ask Commandant Bienville for an escort through Choctaw country on their way home. Bienville, a French escort and the Chickasaws travel through the Choctaw country but are soon surrounded by the Choctaws who invite Bienville and the Chickasaws back to their village. Once back at the village Choctaw warriors attack and kill all of the Chickasaws and wound Bienville. He and his men are allowed to return to Fort Mobile. Source: 35

1706

Fall 1706 — *Louisiana*

Chitimacha Indians kill a priest near the Jean François Buisson de Saint-Cosme Mission. The Indians are hunted down and sold into slavery. Source: 87

1707

1707 — *Florida*

Tallapoosa Indians attack and burn Pensacola, laying siege to the Spanish fort, but are unable to take it. Source: 87

1708

August 29, 1708 — *Massachusetts*

Indians attack Haverhill, burning several houses and killing Mrs. Rolfe and Mr. Wainwright. Source: 26

1709

May 1709, Attack on Mobile — *Alabama*

Over six hundred Alibamon Indians attack Mobile, burning the town and capturing thirty women and children. A counterattack by French soldiers, supported by Tahome and Mobilian Indians, kills thirty-four Alibamon natives and burns down their village. Source: 87

1711

September 10–11, 1711 — *North Carolina*

Two explorers, Christopher Von Graffenried and John Lawson, are captured by Tuscarora natives in Bath County. Lawson is killed by the Indians, possibly by being burned alive. Von Graffenried is held for several weeks and released. Source: 114

September 22, 1711 — *North Carolina*

Tuscarora Indians led by Chief Hancock kill over sixty English settlers and seventy Palatine Indians along the Roanoke and Chowan Rivers in Bath County. A number of Indians from other tribes, including Marmusekit, Wetock, Bory, News, Pamptego, Cor and Trent Indians, assist the Tuscarora in the attack. When the Saxapahaws refuse to join the raid, the Tuscarora attack them and kill sixteen. The Tuscarora Indians kill over 130 settlers and 60 to 70 Palatine and Swiss Indians. Source: 76, 114

October 1711 — *North Carolina*

In retaliation for the raids on Bath County a fifty- to sixty-man force led by Capt. William Brice march toward Bath Town to punish the Tuscarora but are attacked by over 300 Indians and driven back to the Trent River. Source: 114

1712

January 28, 1712 — *North Carolina*

In retaliation for attacks in October, American forces commanded by Col. John Barnwell along with allied Yamasee, Apalachee, Yuchis, Cusabo, Santee, Cherokee, Wateree, Congaree, Catawba and Waxhaw Indians attack a Tuscarora fort and burn several Tuscarora settlements, killing at least ten natives. Source: 15, 24, 76, 114

March 6–7, 1712 — *North Carolina*

American militia with allied Indians attack Hancock's Fort, driving off some of the Tuscarora defenders on March 6. The next day the Tuscarora natives turn over several captives and agree to peace talks on March 19, but never show up. Source: 76, 87, 114

March 29, 1712—*North Carolina*

When Tuscarora natives fail to appear for peace talks March 19, American forces commanded by Col. Barnwell return to Hancock's Fort, but with so few men Barnwell decides not to attack the fort. Source: 76, 87, 114

April 8, 1712—*North Carolina*

After a ten-day siege by 153 Americans and 128 Yamasee allies, Tuscarora Indians surrender Hancock's Fort and hand over a number of captives to Col. John Barnwell. Source: 76, 87, 114

Summer 1712—*Michigan*

French forces with Missouria and Potawatomi Indians attack and destroy a Mascouten village and kill fifty. Source: 87

December 1712—*South Carolina*

After ravaging the countryside and killing a number of settlers, Tuscarora Indians are attacked by a force of 40 militiamen and 800 Indian allies under Col. James Moore. Two hundred Tuscarora warriors are killed and 800 captured on the Tar River. Source: 87, 114

1713

March 20–23, 1713, Fort Neoheroka Massacre—*North Carolina*

American soldiers led by Col. James Moore along with 350 Cherokee and Yamasee allies led by Col. Maurice Moore attack the Tuscarora at Fort Neoheroka. The whites and Indian allies overrun the fort, killing and scalping over 300 and burning another 200 alive in the fort. Over 392 Tuscarora are captured. Over fifty-six soldiers are killed or wounded while Indian allies lose over thirty-five. This defeat ends the Tuscarora War in which over 1,400 Tuscarora Indians are killed and some 1,000 are taken prisoners and sold into slavery. Source: 15, 76, 114

1714

Fort St. Stephens and Fort Toulouse are established in Alabama. Fort St. Jean Baptiste is established in Natchitoches, Louisiana.

Spring 1714—*South Carolina*

Alexander Long and Eleazar Wiggan, with help from Middle Cherokees, attack the Yuchi village of Chestowee and kill several natives and burn the houses. The Yuchi take refuge in a nearby house and kill their own women and children before killing themselves. Source: 76

1715

Fort Michilimackinac is established in Michigan.

April 15, 1715—*South Carolina*

Yamasee natives attack Fort Royal, burning homes and torturing and killing about ninety of its inhabitants. A force of Yamasee with allied Apalachee, Catawba and Creek Indians attack and burn St. Bartholomew's Parish. Several traders are tortured by wood splinters inserted under the skin and set on fire. The splinters burn for several days, prolonging the torture. Source: 15, 76

April 1715—*South Carolina*

A temporary fort built by the Colleton County militia is attacked by Yamasee natives, but the militia manage to drive them off near Salkehatchie. Source: 76

June 1715—*South Carolina*

Four hundred Cherokees appear at the homestead of John Herne. Herne feeds the natives and talks peace with them. They kill him with a tomahawk. A ninety-man militia pursues the Indians but is ambushed and loses twenty-six men, including Capt. Thomas Baker. Source: 76

June 1715—*South Carolina*

A large force of natives approach the garrison of Benjamin Schenkingh and propose a peace plan. The whites agree and lay down their arms but are attacked and killed with knives and tomahawks. The garrison is plundered and burned to the ground. Source: 76

July 19, 1715—*South Carolina*

A native raiding party believed to be Yamasee Indians is ambushed at a plantation near Ponds by 120 militiamen led by Capt. George Chicken. The militiamen kill forty natives, wound several and rescue four whites taken prisoner previously. Source: 76

July 1715—*South Carolina*

Savannah, Yuchi and Apalachee Indians attack the settlement of New London but are repelled by the garrison there. In their retreat they attack the nearby Stono River Plantation, burning over twenty buildings and the Edisto River Bridge. Source: 76

Fall 1715—*South Carolina*

As Yamasee Indians continue their raids near Combahee, forces led by Col. Fenwick attack them near the Jackson home and kill nine natives and take two prisoners. Fenwick then joins his men with forces under Capts. Stone and Burroughs and ambushes natives on Dawfuskey Island. Thirty-five Indians are killed in the fight. Source: 76

1716

Fort Rosalie is established in Mississippi.

August 1, 1716—*South Carolina*

Creek and Yamasee Indians attack Port Royal, killing Maj. Henry Quintyne, Thomas Simons and Thomas Parmenter and scalping a Dr. Rose who recovers. Source: 76

1716—*Colorado*

Comanche and Ute natives attack Taos, Tewa Pueblos and Spanish settlements. A force under Capt. Cristobal de la Serna attacks a Ute village, killing several Indians. Source: 87

1716—*Mississippi*

Natchez Indians kill four Canadian traders at Fort Rosalie. Gov. Cadillac sends a force under Jean-Baptiste de Bienville to punish those responsible. Source: 142

1717

Fort St. Francis is established in Wisconsin. Fort Ouiatenon is established in Indiana.

1719

Fort de Chartres is established in Illinois. Fort St. Pierre is established in Mississippi.

October 12, 1719—*Florida*

In retaliation for raids on South Carolina settlements, British and Indian forces led by Col. John Barnwell attack Spanish towns around St. Augustine. The Spanish mission at Tuloomata is burned. The raiders also burn a deserted Apalachee house. A Spanish company attacks the raiders and lose fourteen of their men. Source: 87

1720

June 1720—*South Carolina*

A Yamasee war party attacks St. Helena, kills one settler and takes a number of prisoners, including a Mr. June and twelve slaves. Source: 76

August 14, 1720—*Nebraska*

A 120-man force of Spanish soldiers under Gen. Don Pedro de Villasur, with

Indian allies, attempts to make peace with Pawnee Indians. The Pawnees surround the force and at dawn attack and kill almost all, including Villasur. Only fourteen soldiers make it back to Santa Fe. Source: 87

1721

APRIL 1, 1721—*Texas*

Juan Blanco, a Negro Texas militiaman, is killed by Apaches northeast of the San Antonio mission and buried at Valero. Source: 82

1722

Fort Miamis is established in Ohio.

1724

AUGUST 23, 1724—*Maine*

Capt. Jeremiah Moulton leads a force of eighty Massachusetts Bay militiamen and Mohawk allies against an Abenaki native village. A Jesuit missionary, Sebastian Rasles (Rale), and seven Abenaki chiefs are killed in the attack. Father Rasles was believed to have encouraged raids by the Indians on English settlements. Two militiamen and one Mohawk are also killed. (Some sources state this event occurred in 1725.) Source: 87

1725

FEBRUARY 20, 1725— *New Hampshire*

Capt. John Lovewell leads a force of New England militia against Indians near Wakefield. It is believed to be the first time white settlers take human scalps for bounty. Source: 87

MAY 8, 1725—*Maine*

Forty-four militiamen and frontiersmen led by Capt. John Lovewell battle Indians at Pigwacket. Lovewell and over a third of his men are killed. Source: 14, 87

1726

Fort Niagara is established in New York.

SEPTEMBER 1726—*South Carolina*

Yamasee Indians attack and kill John Edwards at his home on the Combahee River. Source: 76

1727

JUNE 1727—*South Carolina*

Indians, possibly Yamasee, kill English settlers John Sparks and William Lavy. Source: 76

JULY 23, 1727—*South Carolina*

Yamasee natives attack the trading post of Mathew Smallwood, killing him and Albert and John Hutchinson, John Annesley and Charles Smith. The war party then attacks the other nearby settlements, killing Henry Mishoe and Hezekiah Wood and taking ten slaves. A pursuit party led by Capt. John Bull catches up with the raiding party and kills six Yamasee Indians and a Spaniard. Source: 76

SEPTEMBER 1727—*South Carolina*

The homestead of Alexander Dawson is raided by fugitive slaves and Indians, possibly Yamasee, who kill several of the white settlers and children. A number of whites captured during the Yamasee Wars end up in Spanish St. Augustine, Florida. Source: 76

1728

MARCH 9, 1728—*Florida*

South Carolina militia and Chickasaw allies led by Capt. John Hunt, Capt. William Peter and Col. John Palmer attack a Yamasee village near St. Augustine, killing over thirty Indians and burning the town. The Spanish finally drive the English and Indian forces off. Source: 87

1728—*Texas*

A Ziaguan Indian listed as a vaquero and known as Carlos is killed by Apaches "one quarter league" from Valero at San Antonio. Source: 82

1729

1729—*Louisiana*

A small slave army under the direction of Louisiana Gov. Étienne de Périer attack and destroy a Chaoucha native village. Source: 87, 134

NOVEMBER 28, 1729, FORT ROSALIE MASSACRE—*Mississippi*

Natchez Indians attack French Fort Rosalie, killing over 237 French inhabitants including Commandant De Chepart and Father du Poisson, whose deaths anger the Quapaw natives. French and Quapaw wage all-out war on the Natchez Indians, who they believe have been encouraged by the British. The Natchez Indians attack Fort St. Pierre on the Yazoo River, near present-day Redwood. Source: 87, 136, 142. Marker: Natchez National Historical Park, 1 Melrose-Montabello Pkwy., Natchez, MS.

> "When the French arrived at these falls, they came and kissed us ... They never mocked at our ceremonies, and they never molested the places of our dead. Seven generations of men have passed away, and we have not forgotten it."
> — Chippewa chief
> [Source: 88]

1730

1730—*Louisiana*

French Gov. Périer of Louisiana sends over 1,400 troops and friendly Choctaw Indians from New Orleans to punish the Natchez Indians for the massacre at Fort Rosalie in November of the preceding year (at present-day Natchez, Mississippi). The retaliatory force attacks the Natchez natives in Louisiana and drives them into present-day Catahoula Parish where they stay for a short time. The Natchez Indian tribe is eventually driven to the brink of extinction. Source: 136

AUGUST 17, 1730—*Illinois*

Five hundred French soldiers join a confederation of Illinois, Kickapoo Potawatomi and Mascouten Indians to besiege the Fox Indians along the Illinois River. (The Foxes have fled Wisconsin and are pursued by a number of French allied tribes.) Source: 87

SEPTEMBER 9, 1730—*Illinois*

The besieged Foxes ask the French for leniency but are denied. They attempt to break out but are pursued by the French soldiers and their native allies. Over 250 Fox warriors are killed, plus women and children. A little over sixty escape back toward Wisconsin. Source: 87

1730 MISSOURIA MASSACRE— *Missouri*

A friendly Missouria native village near Fort Orleans is attacked and overwhelmed by Sac Indians, who kill over 300 Missouria Indians. Source: 87

1730—*Texas*

Apache Indians attack the Spanish garrison at El Alamo in San Antonio, killing fifteen soldiers and stealing a herd of cattle. Source: 32

1731

1731—*Mississippi*

After the Natchez Indians massacre French settlers at Fort Rosalie in 1729, French and Choctaw Indians wage a war to exterminate them. The Natchez settlement is attacked in 1731 by the French and Choctaws, and most of the tribe is killed. Some of the 300 survivors are sold into slavery, and others escape to join the Creek and Cherokee tribes. Source: 87, 142

1736

Fort Frederica is established in Georgia.

MARCH 25, 1736, BATTLE AT CHUCALISSA—*Tennessee*

French and Quapaw warriors set out to exterminate the Chickasaw natives and attack the village of Chucalissa on the Mississippi River near present-day Memphis. The village is defended by over 500 warriors and twenty Englishmen, and they soon inflict heavy casualties on the French and Indian forces, killing over 100 and driving them off. Source: 87. Marker: Chucalissa Indian Village is located off Hwy. 61 and Mitchell Rd. in Memphis, TN.

APRIL 14, 1736—*New Mexico*

Settlers at the Paraje del Rio del Oso in the Chama district complain to local officials that Ute natives have killed their livestock. Source: 10

MAY 26, 1736—*Mississippi*

French and Indian Allies attack the Chickasaw town of Ackia (at present-day Tupelo) but are soon overwhelmed and driven from the field, suffering 24 killed and 53 wounded. Source: 87, 142. Marker: Ackia Battleground National Monument, Tupelo, MS.

1740

MAY 1740—*Florida*

Gen. James Oglethorpe with British, Cherokee, Yamacraw and Creek Indian forces attacks and burns Fort St. Francis de Pupa near St. Augustine.

1740—*Georgia*

British and Creek Indian forces attack and defeat Spanish forces along the Flint River. Source: 87

1742

JULY 7, 1742—*Georgia*

A Spanish force from Havana numbering some 1,300 men attacks Fort Frederica on St. Simons Island. A military force and several hundred Creeks led by Gen. James E. Oglethorpe ambush and rout the Spanish at Bloody Marsh. Source: 87

FALL 1742—*Georgia*

Spanish and Yamasee forces attack and burn the trading post at Mt. Venture, killing several Creek Indians. Source: 87

1744

The Fort at No. 4 is established in New Hampshire.

> "We know our lands are now become more valuable. The white people think we do not know their value."
>
> — Canasatego, Onondaga
> [Source: 88]

1745

Fort Sandusky is established in Ohio.

SPRING 1745—*Maine*

King George's War. French and Indian forces attack and burn Waldoboro. Source: 87

JUNE 30, 1745—*Texas*

On the night of June 30, 1745, the mission San Antonio de Valero (the Alamo) and the town of San Antonio are attacked by a force of Ypandi and Natage Apache Indians. They are spotted attempting to set fire to one of the complexes, and an alarm is raised alerting the Spanish soldiers who put up a stout resistance. The Apache force consists of approximately 350 men, women and children who attack at three different locations and nearly overrun the Spanish defended mission. The mission is saved by 100 mission Indians who attack the Apaches from the rear. The Apache force is driven off and later makes peace with the Spanish officials. Source: 82. Marker: The Alamo is located in downtown San Antonio, TX.

August 23, 1745—*New England*

Lt. Gov. Spencer Phips, acting governor in the absence of Gov. Shirley, declares war "against the Eastern and Canada Indians" because the "Norridgewack and Penobscot tribes, and other Indians of the eastern parts ... are now broke out into open rebellion," and committed acts of hostility and murder. Source: 27

September 5, 1745—*New England*

Near George's Fort Lt. Proctor and nineteen men skirmish with a war party in which two noted chiefs—"Col. Morris" and "Capt. Samuel" (as they are called) from the Penobscot tribe—are killed. Source: 27

October 2, 1745—*Mississippi*

Choctaw warriors from the village of Blue Wood attack an English convoy, killing two. A civil war breaks out among the Choctaws, some backing the French and some backing the English. Pro-English Chief Red Shoe is among those killed. Source: 87, 142

November 16, 1745—*New York*

Three hundred French and 200 Indians led by French Priest Francis Piquet attack the Dutch settlement at Saratoga killing and scalping thirty people. Houses, barns and sawmills are burned to the ground and cattle killed. A number of slaves are taken. No casualties are reported among the French and Indian forces. Source: 126

November 28, 1745—*New York*

French and Abenaki Indians attack and burn settlements at Saratoga. Over 100 settlers are killed or captured. Source: 87

1746

April 19, 1746—*Maine*

Gorham Town. Twenty Indians led by French officer Ensign de Niverville fire on three field workers, killing a Mr. Briant. The Indians then go to Briant's house and kill and scalp four of his children. Three people are taken captive, including Mrs. Briant. Source: 27

April 20, 1746—*Massachusetts*

Thesaotin, a chief of the Saulk, returns to his village after a raid near Boston with several white scalps. Source: 27

April 22, 1746—*Massachusetts*

Moses Harvey is shot at as he is traveling between Northfield and Deerfield, the ball passing through the brim of his hat. The garrison at New Hopkinton is attacked, and several people are taken prisoner. Source: 27

April 23, 1746—*New Hampshire*

The garrison of Upper Ashuelot is attacked by a force of about 100 Indians. John Bullard and Daniel McKenny's wife are stabbed to death. Nathan Blake is taken captive but is released the following year. Six houses and one barn are burned in the attack. Source: 27

April 26, 1746—*New Hampshire*

Joshua Holton is killed and scalped by Indians on the road between Lunenburg and Northfield. Source: 27

May 2, 1746—*Massachusetts*

Soldier Seth Putnam is shot and killed by Indians outside of Garrison Number Four. Maj. Josiah Willard and two soldiers fire on the Indians, killing two. Source: 27

May 4, 1746—*New Hampshire*

At Contoocook a party of Indians fire upon five white men and a slave named Caesar, killing him and Elisha Cook. They take Thomas Jones prisoner, and he later dies in captivity. Source: 27

May 4, 1746—*New York*

An Indian trying to get into the fort at Upper Ashuelot is shot in the abdomen and dies. Source: 27

May 6, 1746—*New Hampshire*

Indians attack some farmers at Falltown, wounding John Buck. The Indian chief's arm is broken by a shot fired by Timothy Brown or Robert Moffet. The two are taken prisoner but released the following year. Source: 27

May 7, 1746—*New York*

Christian Tedder is taken captive by Indians at Schenectady but dies a year later. Source: 27

May 9, 1746—*Massachusetts*

Indians fire on and wound John Miles and Sgt. John Hawks while they are riding horses near Fort Massachusetts. Miles makes a run toward the fort, but Hawks, after falling from his horse, fights off the Indians until help arrives from the fort. Source: 27

May 10, 1746—*New Hampshire*

Mathew Clark, his wife, daughter and three soldiers are attacked by Indians. Clark is killed and scalped, his wife and daughter are wounded, but one of the soldiers fights off the five attacking Indians. Source: 27

May 10, 1746—*New York*

Six settlers are killed in sight of Albany; two are slaves. Source: 27

May 10, 1746—*Massachusetts*

Gatienoude, an Iroquois of the Five Nations, is killed and scalped by the English while raiding near Orange. Source: 27

May 13, 1746—*New York*

Three men belonging to the garrison of Saratoga are attacked while fishing near the fort. Indians kill William Norwood's son, take another captive and the third man escapes. Source: 27

May 15, 1746—*New York*

Indians attack the settlement at Kinderhook and burn the houses and barns of Tunis Van Sluyck and Peter Vosburgh. Their cattle are killed, but the two men escape to a nearby garrison. Simon Groot and two of his brothers are killed and scalped three miles from Schenectady. Source: 27

May 1746—*New York*

Fourteen well-armed men sent out to bring in corn from a deserted farm are attacked by Indians at Norman's Creek, eight miles from Schenectady. Source: 27

May 21, 1746—*Maine*

At Broad Bay Indians attack and burn the houses and kill cattle. Some of the settlers are killed; several are taken captive. Source: 27

May 22, 1746

Thirteen men are attacked near St. George's Fort by Indians who wound three of the men and carry off one. The captain of the fort loses no time in pursuing the war party and captures one of the Indians whom he takes back to the fort and scalps. Source: 27

May 24, 1746—*Massachusetts*

Capt. Paine and a mounted force are ambushed near Garrison Number Four. Gunfire from the fort drives the Indians off. Several soldiers are killed. Source: 27

May 25, 1746—*Maine*

At Sheepscot, Indians ambush two men, killing one and wounding the other, who kills an Indian with a hatchet. Source: 27

May 27, 1746—*Massachusetts*

Eight Iroquois of Sault St. Louis attack a settlement near Orange, killing and scalping six settlers. Source: 27

June 1746—*New Mexico*

Comanche Indians attack Pecos, killing and scalping twelve inhabitants in the area. Source: 40

June 6, 1746—*Massachusetts*

At Westcot's Field at Long Creek twenty-five soldiers are attacked and driven from the field by seven Indians who kill and scalp two of the soldiers. Source: 27

June 11, 1746—*Massachusetts*

A work force is attacked near Fort Massachusetts by a party of Indians who scalp Elias Nims and wound Gershon Hawks. Gunfire from the fort kills several Indians, and the rest withdraw. Source: 27

June 16, 1746—*Massachusetts*

Joseph Swett is shot and killed by Indians near Blanchard's settlement. Source: 27

June 19, 1746—*Massachusetts*

At Garrison Number Four Capt. Phinehas Stevens and Capt. Josiah Brown with a force of fifty militiamen march out of the garrison, but a nearby dog's barking alerts the men to an ambush. The Indians open fire on the patrol, mortally wounding Jedidiah Winchell. A number of Indians are killed in the skirmish, and the rest withdraw. Source: 27

June 22, 1746—*Maine*

At Sheepscot seven field workers, three men, two women and two children are killed, and one girl is taken captive. Source: 27

June 24, 1746—*Vermont*

Twenty Indians attack Bridgman's Fort, killing William Robbins and James Barker. One Indian is killed in the fight. Source: 27

June 27, 1746—*New Hampshire*

Indians attack five men working in a field near Rochester. The men are chased to a nearby house, but the Indians break through the roof, killing Joseph Heard, Joseph Richards, John Wentworth and Gershom Downs. Source: 27

July 3, 1746—*New Hampshire*

An Indian ambush is discovered and routed at Col. Hinsdale's Mill in Hinsdale. Source: 27

July 10, 1746

A party led by Capt. Rouse is attacked by 200 Micmac Indians under the command of French leader M. Croisille de Montesson as they come ashore at St. Johns Island. Twenty-eight of Rouse's party are killed or taken to prison in Quebec. Source: 27

July 28, 1746—*Massachusetts*

David Morrison, a young boy of Colerain, is carried away by Indians and never seen again. Source: 27

August 3, 1746—*Massachusetts*

Garrison Number Four is alerted to a large force of Indians by barking dogs. The warriors besiege it until the following day. Ebenezer Phillips is killed, along with his cattle, and several buildings are burned. Source: 27

August 6, 1746—*New Hampshire*

Thirty Indians who had come to Winchester waylay six people on the road, firing on them, killing and scalping Joseph Rawson and wounding Amasa Wright. Source: 27

August 9, 1746—*Massachusetts*

Philip Greely is killed at North Yarmouth by Indians. Source: 27

August 11, 1746 — *New Hampshire*

At Northfield young Benjamin Wright is shot while bringing cows home. He stays on his horse until he gets to town but dies that night. The Indians then ambush five soldiers on a nearby road. Source: 27

August 20, 1746, Fort Massachusetts Massacre — *Massachusetts*

An 800-man French and Indians force, commanded by Gen. Rigaud de Vaudreuil, arrives at the gates of Fort Massachusetts, demanding surrender. The fort's tiny garrison of twenty-two men is no match for Vaudreuil's army, and the fort surrenders in twenty-four hours. Sgt. John Hawks, commanding the fort, asks that they not be turned over to the Indians, to which Vaudreuil agrees. The small garrison surrenders and is turned over to the Indians, who kill most of the defenders. Source: 27

August 22, 1746 — *Massachusetts*

Ten men on the road from Deerfield to Colerain are fired on by Indians. Constant Bliss, a soldier, is killed and scalped. The Indians find and drink a quantity of rum and are found sleeping near the fort, where they are killed. Source: 27

August 25, 1746 — *Massachusetts*

At Deerfield Indians kill and scalp Eleazar Hawks, a hunter. Also killed are several men and a young boy, Simeon Amsden, who is beheaded. A girl, who is struck by a tomahawk blow, "which was sunk into her head," recovers. Two Indians are killed. Source: 27

August 26, 1746 — *Maine*

A soldier is killed by Indians at New Casco. Richard Stubs is taken captive, and John McFarland's plantation is burned to the ground. Source: 27

September 6, 1746 — *Maine*

Joseph Gordon is killed by Indians at Saco. Source: 27

October 20, 1746 — *Maine*

James Anderson is killed by Indians at Sheepscot. Source: 27

November 10, 1746 — *New Hampshire*

A Mr. Estabrook, traveling on a road, is ambushed and killed by Indians. Source: 27

1747

January 31, 1747 — *Massachusetts*

Colonial Gov. William Shirley lays out a plan to drive the French and Indian forces out of Nova Scotia. A 700-man force under the command of Col. Arthur Noble marches north but is ambushed by French and Indian forces. Col. Noble, several officers and seventy men are killed. Source: 27

March 30, 1747 — *Massachusetts*

Forty Indians set fire to Shattuck's Fort, but the soldiers and settlers manage to put out the flames. The Indians are driven off, and one is shot. Source: 27

March 31, 1747 — *Vermont*

Capt. Eleazer Melvin and some of his company hear of the attack on Shattuck's Fort and march in pursuit of the Indians. After crossing the river they are ambushed near Great Meadow, losing one man. Melvin and his men then proceed to the deserted Shattuck's Fort and burn it down to "prevent the Indians the gratification of doing it." Source: 27

April 3, 1747 — *New York*

British Col. Johnson sends a company of Mohawks to scout the French forces at Crown Point. After obtaining the information they need, the Mohawks fire on the French garrison, killing five of the twenty soldiers. Source: 27

APRIL 7, 1747—*Massachusetts*

Garrison Number Four, in possession of thirty men under the command of Capt. Phinehas Stevens, is attacked by a force of French and Indians. After refusing to surrender, the fort is showered by fire arrows, and the French make several unsuccessful assaults on the garrison. Source: 27

APRIL 10, 1747—*New York*

Indians attack Kinderhook where they surprise a party of eleven at work, killing two of them and taking the other nine captive. They burn the house and barn of John Van Alstine and escape unmolested. Source: 27

APRIL 13, 1747—*Maine*

Nathaniel Dresser is killed by Indians at Scarborough within two hundred yards of a garrison. Source: 27

APRIL 14, 1747—*Maine*

Indians capture William Knight near Portland. The same week they kill a Mr. Eliot and his two sons near Portland. Source: 27

APRIL 15, 1747—*Massachusetts*

Nathaniel Dickinson and Asahel Burt are killed and scalped by Indians at Northfield. The Indians move on to Winchester, in present-day New Hampshire, and two Ashuelot River towns and burn all three places. Source: 27

APRIL 15, 1747—*Maine*

Three men weighing hay in a barn at Saco are attacked and killed by Indians. Source: 27

APRIL 21, 1747—*Massachusetts*

About fifty Indians attack the homestead of Mr. Foster, killing him and taking his wife and six children captive. Source: 27

APRIL 25, 1747—*Maine*

Fifty or sixty Indians attack the blockhouse at Saco. The fighting continues all day, and the Indians finally withdraw after two are killed. Source: 27

APRIL 27, 1747—*Maine*

Three people are attacked at Damariscotta. Two women are killed and scalped, and Capt. John Larman is taken captive. Source: 27

MAY 2, 1747—*Massachusetts*

Indians kill two women near Falmouth. Source: 27

MAY 4, 1747—*Maine*

A man is chased into the center of the town of Wells and killed by Indians. Source: 27

MAY 5, 1747—*New York*

A Mr. Hinkley is killed by Indians at New Meadows Neck. Source: 27

MAY 21, 1747—*New Hampshire*

Two men returning from a grist mill between Amauskeeg and Suncook are fired on by Indians. One man named Starkee is killed; the other escapes with bullet holes in his hat and coat. Source: 27

MAY 22, 1747—*Maine*

At Pemaquid a party of fourteen men who have come ashore from a whale boat and a canoe are fired upon by Indians. The men flee except for Capt. John Cox, who stands his ground and is killed outright while the others are pursued. Nine are killed and four are taken captive. Source: 27

MAY 23, 1747—*New Hampshire*

At Rochester, Samuel Downs is ambushed and shot in the hip. Source: 27

MAY 25, 1747—*Massachusetts*

A party of five scouts and a squad of soldiers, sent out by Maj. William Williams of Stockbridge, are ambushed while clearing the road for wagons. A Stockbridge Indian is killed, and two soldiers are wounded. Source: 27

JUNE 1, 1747—*New England*

Chief Kinitigo, an English ally, and six of his men return to Mohawk Castle after a raid against French forces near Montreal. They bring in seven prisoners and three scalps taken at St. Pierres. Source: 27

JUNE 7, 1747—*New Hampshire*

A party of Indians fires on three boys. Men at work in a nearby field come to the boys' aid and drive the Indians off. Source: 27

JUNE 15, 1747—*Massachusetts*

Two thousand French and Indians attack Fort Saraghota, killing sixty settlers. A relief party led by Col. Schuyler drives the Indians off. Source: 27

JUNE 20, 1747—*Canada*

A militia force of 102 men under the command of Lt. Chew starts toward Canada on a raiding party but are ambushed, losing fifteen killed and forty-seven wounded. Lt. Chew and the rest of his men are captured and sent to Crown Point. Source: 27

JULY 28, 1747—*New Hampshire*

At Penacoock a party of Indians shoot some cattle and are pursued by fifty men, but escape. Source: 27

JULY 31, 1747—*Maine*

At Mount Swag, Ebenezer Hilton, Joseph Hilton and John Boynton are killed by Indians. Source: 27

AUGUST 21, 1747—*New Hampshire*

Mrs. Charles McCoy is carried off by Indians at Epsom. In raids on nearby settlements Robert Beard, John Folsom and Elizabeth Simpson are killed by Indians. Mrs. McCoy is later returned. Source: 27

AUGUST 26, 1747—*New York*

At Northampton Elijah Clark is killed and scalped as he is threshing grain. Source: 27

OCTOBER 16, 1747—*Massachusetts*

Several men, along with Maj. Willard and Capt. Alexander, engage Indians led by a Frenchman. The Frenchman is shot, and the Indians desert him, but Capt. Alexander sends him to Boston where he recovers. Source: 27

OCTOBER 19, 1747—*Massachusetts*

Settler John Smead is killed and scalped on the road from Northfield to Sunderland. Source: 27

OCTOBER 22, 1747—*New England*

Forty Indians carry off Jonathan Sartle at Bridgman's Fort. Source: 27

NOVEMBER 14, 1747—*Massachusetts*

Twelve men are ambushed near Number Four Garrison. Nathaniel Gould and Thomas Goodale are killed and scalped. The men with Gould and Goodale escape. Source: 27

1748

JANUARY 1748—*New Mexico*

A force of seventy men and friendly Jicarilla Apaches sent by Spanish Gov. Joaquín Codallos y Rabal attack Comanche lodges on the Jicarilla River, killing several. The attack is in retaliation for a number of Comanche raids in the area. Source: 40

MARCH 29, 1748—*Massachusetts*

Between Fort Dummer and Colerain, Lt. Sergeant and four men on a wood cutting expedition are ambushed by Indians, mortally wounding Moses Cooper who dies that night. Joshua Wells is killed outright, and Lt. Sergeant is killed in the retreat to the fort. No help comes from the fort because of a measles outbreak and a lack of snowshoes. Source: 27

APRIL 27, 1748—*New England*

Indians take Job Philbrook and Samuel McFornay captive. They are presumed to have been taken to Canada. Presbury Woolen, taken in the same raid, is released and returns in October. Source: 27

APRIL 30, 1748—*New Hampshire*

Near Suncook, Robert Buntin, in company with James Carr and his son, are attacked by Indians. Carr is killed trying to escape. Source: 27

MAY 1, 1748—*New Hampshire*

Mrs. Jonathan Hodgdon is attacked while on her way to milk cows. When her screams won't cease, the Indians kill her with a hatchet. "Mr. Hodgdon heard her cries, and was near enough to see the fatal blows dealt, as he was powerless ... he fled to the garrison." Source: 27

MAY 3, 1748—*Maine*

Several persons are killed by Indians at Brunswick, including Capt. Burnet. Source: 27

MAY 8, 1748—*New York*

Twelve Indians ambush and kill Noah Pixley near Southampton. Source: 27

MAY 10, 1748—*Maine*

A young woman named Morell is seized near her home and is killed and scalped. Source: 27

MAY 21, 1748—*Massachusetts*

Sgt. Elisha Chapin and several men stumble upon an ambush party, who turn and flee. Chapin and his men open fire, killing one Indian who is then scalped. Source: 27

MAY 25, 1748—*New York*

Eighteen men led by Capt. Eleazer Melvin on a scouting expedition near Lake Champlain spot two canoes full of Indians near the bank. At a place near Crown Point Melvin's men open fire on the unsuspecting warriors, who make their way to the shoreline and take cover. Soon Melvin and his men find themselves surrounded, and a heavy gunfire is poured on them. Six of Melvin's party are killed, and the rest of the men fight their way out and flee the area. Source: 27

JUNE 16, 1748—*New Hampshire*

Between Col. Hinsdale's Fort and Fort Dummer, Indians ambush a party of thirteen men. Joseph Richardson, Nathan French and John Frost are killed, three escape and the rest are taken captive. Source: 27

JUNE 26, 1748—*Massachusetts*

A scouting expedition from Garrison Number Four under Capt. Humphrey Hobbs discovers it is being followed by a war party of 150 warriors. Hobbs and his small forty-man force dig in for an attack, which is not long in coming. The warriors charge en masse toward the small party but are staggered by the first volley. The whites load and fire rapidly as the Indians continue their assault on Hobb's determined little force. They battle for over four hours until a shot from Capt. Hobbs drops the Indians' war chief, and they withdraw. The expedition loses four killed and a number wounded. Source: 27

JULY 5, 1748—*Massachusetts*

At Lunenburg, John Fitch, his wife and five children are taken captive by Indians. Two of Fitch's work hands are killed. Source: 27

JULY 14, 1748—*Massachusetts*

Between Fort Hinsdale and Fort Dummer, a company of seventeen men led by

Sgt. Thomas Taylor is attacked by approximately 100 Indians. Only four men of the seventeen escape the carnage. Source: 27

July 18, 1748—*New York*

While out hunting for stray horses near Schenectady, Daniel Tol, Dirk Van Vorst and a slave discover a war party. Tol and Van Vorst are both shot while the slave escapes toward town. The shots are heard at Maalwyck, two miles away, and a force of seventy men under the command of Lt. Darling goes in search of the Indians. The whites encounter the Indians near the woods and fire a volley at them, which stuns them momentarily, but they recover and deliver a volley of their own. The Indians then charge the whites, and the fight becomes hand-to-hand. Lt. Darling and twelve of his men are killed while five are taken prisoner. Source: 27

July 23, 1748—*Massachusetts*

At Northfield, Aaron Belden is killed and scalped by Indians. Source: 27

July 1748—*Florida*

After running aground near Cape Florida, an English ship carrying logs from Honduras is attacked by sixty Indians in canoes. Eleven men on the ship are killed. Source: 87

August 23, 1748—*Maine*

Two men are killed by Indians near the Sheepscot River. Source: 27

October 1748—*New Mexico*

A Ute and Comanche camp on the Chama River is attacked by forces led by Gov. Rabal. Rabal's forces kill over 107 natives and capture 200. Source: 87

October 20, 1748—*New England*

Capt. Jedediah Prebble and Capt. Gorham row ashore from the *Anson*, resting in the St. John's River, and are fired on by Indians, killing three of the men in the boat. The landing force fires on the Indians, and they withdraw. Source: 27

1750

1750—*Georgia*

In the escalating war between Creeks and Cherokees, Creeks led by Malatchi attack and burn the trading post near the lower Cherokee towns of Echoi and Estatoe. Source: 87

1751

Spanish Fort Presidio San Sabá is established in Texas.

November 1751—*New Mexico*

Forces under Gov. Tomás Vélez Cachupín attack a Comanche camp near Santa Fe, killing over 100 natives. Source: 87

1752

Summer 1752—*Ohio*

French forces along with allied Ottawa and Chippewa attack a British trading post at Pickawillany in western Ohio, killing an English trader and thirteen Miami native defenders. The Miami leader, La Demoiselle is captured and "made a broth" of by the Ottawas and Chippewas. Source: 87, 104

1752—*South Carolina*

After a party of Cherokee and Savannah Indians kill a Chickasaw man and two women, the Chickasaws retaliate by killing ten Cherokees and taking their scalps. The feud soon escalates, and, by April, Northern Cherokees ally themselves with the Chickasaw natives. Source: 76

1754

May 27–28, 1754—*Pennsylvania*

Lt. Gov. Robert Dinwiddie sends a force of forty Virginia militiamen and

Seneca Indians led by Lt. Col. George Washington into the Ohio Valley to build a military road through the region. Scouts report a French camp in the area, and Washington attacks in the early morning, killing nineteen French soldiers and capturing twenty-one. Source: 1, 30, 50, 52, 104. Marker: Located on Jumonville Rd. near Mount Summit.

1754—*South Carolina*

Indians, possibly Savannahs, attack and kill sixteen settlers in York County. Source: 76

August 27, 1754—*New York*

French and Indian allies attack the settlement of Hoosick, killing about twenty people. Source: 87

1755

May 1755—*Pennsylvania*

While building a road eighteen-year-old James Smith is captured by Caughnawagas, a branch of the Mohawks. Smith is treated well, but others are not as fortunate. "About sundown I beheld a small party coming in with about a dozen prisoners, stripped naked, with their hands tied behind their backs," Smith wrote, "... their faces and their bodies blacked. These prisoners they burned to death on the bank of the Allegheny River opposite the fort [Fort Duquesne]." Smith escapes from the Caughnawaga town in 1759. Source: 28

July 8, 1755—*West Virginia*

Shawnees led by Black Wolf attack the settlements of Draper's Meadows, killing several people including Col. James Patton and Bettie Draper's baby. At the Muddy Creek settlement fifty whites are attacked by a Shawnee war party led by Hokolesqua. The Shawnees kill all of the men and several women and children. Source: 30

July 9, 1755, Braddock's Defeat—*Pennsylvania*

Twelve hundred British and colonial troops under Gen. Edward Braddock are attacked by 900 French and Indian forces while traveling to Fort Duquesne. The French and Indian forces led by Capt. Pierre de Contrecoeur fire into the British columns for two hours. Braddock chooses not to fight with concealment or irregular lines, and his forces are decimated. Aide-de-camp George Washington has two horses shot out from under him. Gen. Braddock is mortally wounded and carried from the field. In one of the most devastating defeats of the war, Braddock loses over 900 killed while French commander de Contrecoeur loses sixteen killed. Traditional European fighting tactics are called into question by Native Americans allied with the British. The Iroquois Indians have grave doubts about the British ability to fight, and they consider backing the French who have adapted the Indians' fighting style. Source: 1, 30, 50, 88, 104. Marker: Fort Necessity National Battlefield, U.S. 40, Farmington, PA.

1755—*Georgia*

Battle of Taliwa. In a continuing war between Cherokees and Creeks, Cherokee forces defeat the Creeks in northern Georgia. Nancy Ward, wife of Cherokee Chief Kingfisher, gains fame for her fighting ability in the battle. Source: 87

September 8, 1755—*New York*

Six hundred French Canadians and 700 Iroquois Indians ambush a British column near Lake George. After intense fighting the Iroquois withdraw leaving the French on their own, and the British drive them from the field. British Col. Ephraim Williams is killed. Source: 52. Marker: Rt. 9 and Montray Rd., Queensberry, NY.

1756

Fort McCord is established in Pennsylvania. Fort Frederick is established in Maryland. War is officially declared between France and Great Britain over ownership of the Ohio Territories, beginning the French and Indian War, sometimes known as the Seven Years' War, 1756–1763. Various dates are applied to the length of this war because of differences of historical opinions.

MARCH 27, 1756—*New York*

French and Indian forces led by Lt. de Lery attack Fort Bull, storming the walls and killing most of the defenders. The French burn the fort and its supplies. Source: 52

JULY 3, 1756—*New York*

A British force of 300 soldiers is ambushed by some 700 French and Indian allies near Oswego. The British force led by Lt. Col. John Bradstreet surprise the French by a counterattack that kills a great number and drives the French and Indians from the field. Source: 52

JULY 30–AUGUST 2, 1756—*Pennsylvania*

Delaware Indians led by Capt. Jacobs attack, capture and burn Fort Granville. Source: 87

AUGUST 14, 1756—*New York*

French and Indian allied forces attack the British Forts Ontario and Oswego, capturing over 1,000 British troops. Source: 1, 15, 52. Marker: Fort Ontario State Historic Site is located in Oswego, NY.

SEPTEMBER 3, 1756—*Georgia*

Tuckabatchee Creek warriors steal a number of horses near the town of Ogeechee and are pursued by the inhabitants who kill three of the Indians, but finally a cease-fire is called, and the Indians withdraw peaceably. Source: 87

SEPTEMBER 8, 1756—*Pennsylvania*

Three hundred soldiers under Col. John Armstrong attack the Delaware village of Kittanning. Delaware Chief Jacob is trapped in his house and burns to death. The Indians lose forty killed while Armstrong loses eighteen soldiers killed. Source: 87

1757

JULY 21–24, 1757—*New York*

French and Indians fire on British barges harbored in Lake George. Some of the English merchantmen attempt to swim to safety but are captured, killed, cooked and eaten by the Indians. Source: 1

JULY 1757—*New York*

Frenchmen and Indians attack Fort Edwards, killing all thirty-two English defenders. Source: 87

AUGUST 3–9, 1757, SIEGE OF FORT WILLIAM HENRY—*New York*

French forces lay siege to Fort William Henry. After four days the British agree to surrender terms, including safe passage, but as they march away from the fort, the rear guard of New Hampshire militiamen is attacked by Abenaki and Potawatomi Indians who kill over 200 soldiers. Two hundred white prisoners are carried off by Indians. Source: 1, 15. Marker: Lake George, NY

NOVEMBER 1757—*New York*

French and Indians attack and burn the German colony of Palatine. Source: 87

1758

JANUARY 1758—*New York*

In deep snow an Indian war party pursues a party of British soldiers whose escape is hindered by a lack of snowshoes. The Indians catch up to and kill the soldiers. Source: 87

March 13, 1758 — *New York*

French forces led by Sieur de Langy attack forces under Maj. Robert Rogers west of Lake George in deep snow. Rogers' men are driven back up the slopes followed by the French and Indian forces. Some of Rogers' men are captured and beheaded. Source: 87

March 16, 1758 — *Texas*

Over 2,000 Comanche attack and burn the San Saba Mission on the San Saba River, killing eight people including Father Alonso Giraldo de Terreos and Father Santiesteban. Source: 32

July 6–8, 1758, Battle of Ticonderoga — *New York*

On July 6, over 15,000 British soldiers cross Lake George and move toward French occupied Fort Carillion on Lake Champlain. French Gen. Louis Montcalm orders the bridges over the river burned to slow the British advance as French forces withdraw to the woods and open fire on the advancing English, killing Gen. Howe. The British continue their advance the next day as French forces fight from their rear guard to halt the British advance. An all-out frontal assault on the eighth of July, led by British Regulars, Highlanders and Royal Americans, suffers heavy casualties, and the British are driven from the field with over 400 killed and 1,200 wounded. Source: 1, 15, 32. Marker: Fort Ticonderoga is located one mile northeast of Ticonderoga on SR 74.

September 14, 1758 — *Pennsylvania*

British troops with Indian allies attack Fort Duquesne but are routed by Ottawa, Potawatomis and French defenders. Source: 30, 88

October 12, 1758 — *Pennsylvania*

Over 400 French soldiers with 150 Indian allies under the command of Charles Phillipe d'Aubry attack British forces at Loyalhannon Creek. A party of sixty Rangers led by Col. Burd is driven back by the French and Indian forces. Source: 87

1759

Spring 1759 — *Pennsylvania*

Indians attack and burn the Dunkard Creek settlement. Source: 30

1759 — *West Virginia*

Mingo Indians attack the Decker's Creek settlement, killing all of the settlers. A tracking party led by Col. John Gibson and men from Fort Pitt catch up with ten Mingo natives led by Little Eagle, who is killed and beheaded. Source: 30, 35

June 8, 1759 — *New York*

The New York *Mercury* reports, "two of our boats were attacked on their way up the Mohawk's River, by a party of the enemy ... scalped a woman, and carried off a child and a servant ... the woman lived 'til she got into Schenectady, tho' in great agony." Source: 122

July 2, 1759 — *New York*

A small wood cutting detachment is attacked by Indians near Lake George. "They were surprised in sight by a party of the enemy, consisting of about 240, who killed and scalped six, wounded two, took four prisoners, and only four of the whole party escaped.... They butchered our people in a most shocking manner, by cutting pieces of flesh out of their necks, thighs and legs." Source: 123

July 13, 1759, Siege of Fort Niagara — *New York*

British forces commanded by Sir William Johnson lay siege to Fort Niagara. Johnson's force includes over 900 Seneca and Iroquois allies. A French relief force is attacked three miles from the fort by troops under Lt. Col. Eyre Massey and Capt. James De Lancey and allied Seneca. The French and their native allies are routed and over 500 are killed. The fort surrenders to the British on July 26. Source: 1. Marker: Fort Niagara State Park is located off SR 18F in Youngstown, NY.

AUGUST 1759—*Texas*

A Spanish retaliatory force searches for Comanche that attacked the San Saba Mission the year before. The expedition under Col. Don Diego Ortiz Parrilla consists of 139 soldiers, 241 militiamen, 120 Tlaxcaltecan and mission Indians and 134 Apaches. Parrilla's force mistakes a Tonkawa village for a Comanche village. The attack kills about sixty Tonkawa warriors, and 150 women and children are taken prisoners. Source: 32

OCTOBER 1759—*Texas*

Spanish forces under Col. Don Diego Ortiz Parrilla attack the Taovaya village on the Red River. The village contains several thousand natives including Comanche, Red River Caddoan, Wichita and some Osage Indians. Greatly outnumbered, Parrilla's men and native allies flee the area. In a running battle Parrilla's force loses nineteen killed and fourteen wounded. Parrilla is court-martialed by Spanish authorities. (Some accounts place this action across the Red River in present-day Oklahoma.) Source: 32

1759—*South Carolina*

A party of Cherokee chiefs and leaders arrive at Charles Town (Charleston) for peace talks but are arrested by Gov. William Henry Lyttleton of South Carolina who sends them to Fort Prince George. The Cherokee natives begin a series of retaliatory raids on settlements from Virginia to Georgia. The Cherokees lay siege to Fort Prince George and eventually kill the post's commander. The soldiers retaliate by executing their Indian prisoners in the fort. A number of nearby settlements are burned, and fourteen whites killed. Source: 56, 76

1760

FEBRUARY 1, 1760— *South Carolina*

The white settlers of Long Canes are attacked by Cherokee Indians as they plan to evacuate to Augusta. Fifty settlers are killed, and a number of loaded wagons are taken. Source: 76

FEBRUARY 16, 1760— *South Carolina*

When Lt. Cotymore leaves Fort Prince George for a parlay with Indians, he is ambushed and killed. The soldiers in the fort open fire with a cannon, and one Indian is killed. Cherokee prisoners held in the fort are executed in revenge. Source: 76

MARCH 6, 1760—*South Carolina*

Fort Ninety-Six is attacked by Cherokees but well defended by twenty-eight Englishmen who drive the Indians off and scalp some of the dead. Source: 76

JUNE 1, 1760—*South Carolina*

An army of over 1,200 soldiers, including a battalion of Highlanders and four companies of Royal Scots under the command of Col. Montgomery, sweeps through and burns the Cherokee towns of Little Keowee, Estatoe and Sugar Town. Sixty Cherokees are killed, and a number of orchards and cornfields are destroyed. Source: 76

JUNE 27, 1760—*North Carolina*

Over 1,200 British troops under Col. Montgomery attack the Cherokee towns at Echoe (present-day Franklin) but are forced to withdraw because of heavy fire from the Cherokee warriors. Twenty soldiers are killed, and seventy-six are wounded. Source: 76, 87

AUGUST 1760—*New Mexico*

Comanche Indians attack a fortified ranch house near Taos, killing a number of men and capturing fifty-six women and children. Source: 87

AUGUST 1760—*Tennessee*

A force of British soldiers and allied Chickasaws attack and burn fifteen Cherokee towns in east Tennessee. Source: 15, 56

1761

JUNE 10, 1761—*North Carolina*

Over 2,000 British troops under Col. James Grant march from Fort Prince George and attack and defeat Cherokee Indians at the Cherokee settlement of Echoe. Grant loses over fifty men killed, but the Cherokees are forced to negotiate for peace. Source: 76, 87

DECEMBER 27, 1761— *South Carolina*

Creek Indians living in a Lower Cherokee village attack and kill fourteen settlers in the Long Cane region. The Creeks say they are angered by the encroachment of the "Virginians," as they have termed the frontiersmen and settlers coming into the area. Source: 87

1763

FEBRUARY 10, 1763

The Treaty of Paris is signed, ending France's claims east of the Mississippi River and south of Canada. French troops are withdrawn, and many northeast tribes allied with the French are angered by the capitulation. The Indians lose a major ally and source of armament in the French. The tribes are left to battle the growing British colonies by themselves and feel abandoned by the French.

MAY 7, 1763—*Michigan*

Chippewa Indians, under the direction of Chief Pontiac, attack and kill four men of a twelve-man expedition on Lake St. Clair east of Detroit. Source: 87

MAY 9–12, 1763, SIEGE OF DETROIT—*Michigan*

Ottawa Indians under Pontiac attack settlements around Fort Detroit, killing a number of settlers and firing on the schooner *Huron* anchored on the Detroit River. The Indian force consists of Ottawa, Chippewa, Ojibway, Huron, Mississauga and Potawatomi natives who lay siege to the fort until October. Fur trader Alexander Henry is captured by Chippewas at nearby Fort Michilimackinac. Henry observes a celebration event the Indians hold in honor of the destruction of the forts. Henry writes of Chief Wawatam, "After about half a hour he returned, bringing in his dish a human hand and a large piece of flesh. He did not appear to relish the repast, but told me it always had been the custom, among all the Indian nations when from war, to make a war feast from among the slain." Source: 28, 87, 88 [Quote 28]

MAY 16, 1763—*Ohio*

Chief Pontiac sends a force of Ottawa and Huron to capture Fort Sandusky. The Indians are allowed to enter the fort to negotiate with its commander, Ensign Christopher Pauli. During the negotiations the Huron seize Pauli and kill about fifteen soldiers with him. Pauli is taken back to Detroit as a prisoner but later escapes. Source: 87. Marker: Located on SR. 6 and Freemont Ave., Sandusky, OH.

MAY 25, 1763—*Michigan*

Potawatomi Indians under Chief Pontiac attack Fort St. Joseph, killing eleven and taking a number of captives who are held for over two years. Source: 87. Marker: Fort site is located at the corner of Fort and Bond St., Niles, MI.

May 27, 1763—*Pennsylvania*

Shawnee, Delaware and Mingo led by Pucksinwah lay siege to Fort Pitt (present-day Pittsburgh). The garrison under the command of Capt. Simeon Ecuyer is infected with smallpox, and blankets from the fort are given to the Indians. The disease kills a great number of the natives. The Indians continue harassing the fort until August 1, when a relief party arrives and the Indians withdraw. Source: 30, 35, 52, 56

May 28, 1763—*Michigan*

Flat-bottom boats with ninety-six men under the command of Lt. Abraham Cuyler are attacked by Pontiac's warriors as they come ashore twenty-five miles east of Detroit. The whites retreat to their boats and flee with a number of wounded. Source: 87

June 1, 1763—*Indiana*

Pontiac's War. Miami, Weas, Kickapoo and Mascouten Indians force the surrender of Fort Ouiatenon. Source: 87

June 2, 1763, Attack on Fort Michilimackinac—*Michigan*

Fort Michilimackinac on Michilimackinac Island, commanded by Capt. George Etherington, is attacked and captured by Sauk and Chippewa Indians. The fort, defended by thirty-five soldiers, loses seventeen killed and fifteen taken prisoner. Source: 87. Marker: Fort Michilimackinac living history, Mackinaw City, MI.

June 4, 1763—*Pennsylvania*

Fort Ligonier under the command of Lt. Archibald Blane is attacked by warriors. Source: 93. Marker: U.S. 30 in Ligonier, PA.

June 16, 1763—*Pennsylvania*

Seneca and Shawnee Indians attack Fort Venango, killing the entire garrison. The fort's commander, Lt. Gordon, is slowly roasted by the Indians. The fort is burned and never rebuilt. Source: 104. Marker: 8th and Elk St., Franklin, PA.

June 18, 1763—*Pennsylvania*

Shawnee and Seneca natives attack and burn Fort LeBoeuf. The small garrison of eleven soldiers under the command of Ensign George Price escapes and flees to Fort Venango but find it burned down. Source: 87. Marker: Fort LeBoeuf Museum, 31 High St., Waterford, PA.

June 21, 1763—*Pennsylvania*

Two hundred Seneca, Ottawa, Huron and Chippewa Indians attack a blockhouse, and after agreeing to let the defenders go free, attack and massacre all but three who escape. Source: 87

June 23, 1763—*Michigan*

The sloop *Michigan* is attacked while anchored in the Detroit River by Chief Pontiac's warriors. The ship's cannons open fire on the attackers, killing fourteen and wounding a number of Indians. Source: 87

July 31, 1763, Battle of Bloody Run—*Michigan*

A force of 247 men under Capt. James Dalyell march toward Pontiac's camp but are ambushed on a bridge crossing at Parent's Creek. Caught in a cross-fire, the soldiers are driven back toward the fort, suffering over twenty-two dead and twelve wounded. Source: 87

August 1, 1763—*Pennsylvania*

The siege of Fort Pitt, begun May 27, is relieved when a relief force of 460 under Col. Henry Bouquet arrives. The Shawnee, Delaware and Mingo warriors withdraw. Source: 30, 52, 56. Marker: Point State Park, 101 Commonwealth Place, Pittsburgh, PA.

AUGUST 5, 1763, BATTLE OF BRUSHY RUN—*Pennsylvania*

Delaware, Mingo, Huron and Shawnee Indians attack a supply troop headed for Fort Pitt. Eight officers and 116 soldiers are killed. Native losses are estimated at twenty-two. The troops, weakened by the attack, reach the fort four days later. Source: 1, 15, 30, 52. Marker: Brushy Run Battlefield, located on Brushy Run Rd., Jennette, PA.

SEPTEMBER 2, 1763—*Michigan*

Chippewa and Ottawa warriors under Pontiac attack the ship *Huron* anchored in the Detroit River. The Indians fight their way on deck and fight hand-to-hand with the crew. The crew suffer fifteen killed, including Capt. Horsey, but finally drive the warriors off. Source: 87

SEPTEMBER 14, 1763—*New York*

At a place on the Niagara River known as Devil's Hole, over 400 Seneca Indians attack and kill soldiers unloading supplies. A relief column later finds over seventy soldiers' bodies, including officers. A relief force coming to the soldiers' aid is ambushed, and five officers and sixty-seven men are killed. Source: 104

OCTOBER 20, 1763—*New York*

On their way to attack Detroit, British troops under Maj. John Wilkins are ambushed by Indians who kill eight men. Source: 87

DECEMBER 14, 1763—*Pennsylvania*

Twenty Christian Susquehannock natives are attacked by a civilian mob led by the Paxton brothers and a Presbyterian minister. Six of the Indians are killed. The natives are under the protection of the Pennsylvania government after having survived an earlier attack. On December 27, the mob follows the natives to a workhouse and massacres them all. Source: 56, 87

1765

MAY 1765—*Pennsylvania*

Warriors led by Chief Pontiac attack Indians with Indian agent Maj. George Croghan killing several. Pontiac believes the Indians with Croghan are Cherokees, enemies of Pontiac's alliance. Croghan survives the attack and later begins new peace talks with Pontiac. Source: 87

1768

SEPTEMBER 1768—*New Mexico*

Spanish soldiers along with sixteen settlers and Ute warriors attack an entrenched Comanche war party and kill twenty-one. Source: 87

"Sir: I send you by one of our runners the child we will deliver, that you may know ... I do not make war on women and children. I am sorry to say that I have those engaged with me ... who are more savage than the savages themselves."

— Joseph Brant, Mohawk [Source: 88]

1769

APRIL 20, 1769, DEATH OF PONTIAC—*Illinois*

At the French village of Cahokia on the Mississippi, Ottawa Chief Pontiac is tomahawked and killed by Peoria Indian Black Dog who was said to be avenging an earlier insult to his uncle Makachinga. (Pontiac had been successful in uniting a number of tribes in their war against the British. A smallpox epidemic and the arrival of winter during this alliance eventually ended Pontiac's native unification attempts.) Source: 25, 99

1770

Fort Savannah is established in Georgia.

1771

SEPTEMBER 18, 1780 — *Texas*

A Comanche war party attacks Laredo, Texas, driving the settlers off. Many of the settlers return and rebuild a town (Nuevo Laredo) on the Mexico side of the Rio Grande River for better protection. Source: 32

1772

SPRING 1772 — *West Virginia*

Adam Stroud, his wife and five children are killed by Cherokee Indians on their farm near the Gauley River. A volunteer force led by William White and William Hacker arrives at a nearby Delaware village, and, believing them responsible for the Stroud killings, kills about twenty of the native inhabitants. Source: 30

1773

OCTOBER 9, 1773, DANIEL BOONE'S SON KILLED

Daniel Boone's son James and several others are killed in Powell Valley, VA, by Shawnee natives. Source: 35

1774

Fort Henry is established in West Virginia.

APRIL 25, 1774 — *West Virginia*

A militia company led by Capt. Michael Cresap travels down the Ohio River and attacks a Mingo camp at Captina Creek, killing three Indians. Source: 30

APRIL 30, 1774 — *Ohio*

Jacob Greathouse and his men welcome ashore a party of Cayuga and Mingo Indians near the mouth of the Yellow River on the Ohio River. Greathouse asks the warriors to discharge their weapons at a nearby target which they do. Greathouse's men hidden in the bushes open fire on the natives, killing almost all. Chief Tachnechdorus's sister is stabbed to death in the ambush. Tachnechdorus (also known as John Logan) begins a series of raids on white settlements in retaliation for the death of his sister on the Yellow River. Source: 30, 56

AUGUST 1774 — *New Mexico*

One hundred Comanche Indians attack Pecos, killing seven. The next day Spanish forces pursue and attack the warriors, killing over forty Indians. Source: 87

OCTOBER 10, 1774, BATTLE OF POINT PLEASANT — *West Virginia*

Three thousand troops under the command of John Murray Dunmore, colonial governor of Virginia, attack and defeat 1,000 Indians at Point Pleasant, south of the Ohio River. The Indians, led by Cornstalk (Hokolesqu), include Delaware, Shawnee, Wyandot, Seneca, Cayuga and Mingo. The Indians are completely overwhelmed and withdraw north of the Ohio River. A number of troops are killed, including Col. John Field. Source: 30, 56, 104. Marker: Point Pleasant Monument State Park, 1 Main St., Point Pleasant, WV.

1775

MAY 1775 — *New Mexico*

Comanche Indians attack the Pecos settlement, killing three settlers. Source: 87

1775 — *New Mexico*

Fifteen hundred troops under the command of Hugh O'Connor attack Gileno Apache natives near the Gila River, killing over 138 warriors and capturing 100 women and children. Source: 87

NOVEMBER 1775 — *California*

Eight hundred Ipai and Taipai Mission Indians, tired of the brutal punishment inflicted for the slightest offense, burn down the San Diego mission and kill Father Jamie. Source: 87, 95

1776

JULY 4, 1776

The American colonies declare their independence from Britain on July 4, 1776. The event has very little immediate effect on the Native Americans, many already at war with the colonies. The growing military might of the united colonies becomes an issue that the Indians will have to contend with in the coming years, and some tribes realign themselves with the new continental government.

JULY 14, 1776 — *Kentucky*

Indians capture and carry off the daughters of Daniel Boone and Col. Calloway near Fort Boonesborough. Boone and a pursuit party catch up with the raiding Indians on the sixteenth, retaking their daughters and killing two Indians. Source: 35

JULY 15, 1776 — *South Carolina*

Cherokee and Creek Indians attack a number of settlements from southern Virginia all the way to northern Georgia. One hundred and two British soldiers with native allies attack the blockhouse at Robbin's Creek. The forty-man American force drives the attackers off and kills and captures a number of the British force. Source: 31, 76

JULY 20, 1776, BATTLE AT ISLAND FLATS — *Tennessee*

Warned by scouts that a large force of Indians is nearby, Tennessee militiamen led by Capt. James Thompson attack Chickamauga and Cherokee Indians at Island Flats. The 170-man militia kills thirteen Indians and wounds Cherokee leader Dragging Canoe. "We killed about thirteen on the spot ... There were streams of blood everywhere ... The Indians attacked us with the greatest fury. Had only four men wounded." Source: 31, 76, 97, 110 [Quote 110]

JULY 21, 1776 — *Tennessee*

Cherokees led by Chief Old Abram attack Fort Caswell under the command of John Carter, wounding several soldiers. The Cherokees besiege the fort for over two weeks but finally withdraw. James Cooper and Samuel Moore leave the fort and are attacked. Cooper escapes, but Moore is captured and burned alive a short distance from the fort. Source: 31, 110

AUGUST 1, 1776 — *South Carolina*

A continental force of 300 soldiers march to the Seneca town on Oconore Creek looking for British forces they know are allied with the Seneca and Cherokee natives. The American force under the command of Maj. Andrew Williamson attacks and drives the Cherokee and British forces across the river. The town is burned, and the corn crop is destroyed. Source: 31, 76

AUGUST 4–12, 1776 — *South Carolina*

An American force under Maj. Andrew Williamson continues its campaign against the Cherokee middle towns. On August 4, the Cherokee towns of Sugar Town, Soconee and Keowee are burned. Williamson's force also destroys the Cherokee towns of Estatoe and Tugaloo on August 8. Brass Town, Tamasse, Cheowee and Eustaste are burned and destroyed on August 11 and 12. Source: 31, 76

SEPTEMBER 1776 — *North Carolina*

Over 2000 soldiers with Catawba native allies begin a large sweep from Swannanoa

Gap down Rutherford's Trace, burning and destroying British allied Cherokee villages. By September 18, over thirty-six Cherokee towns have been burned and destroyed. On their return the American troops, led by Gen. Griffith Rutherford, are attacked near a mountain pass and avoid a complete disaster when Lt. Hampton rallies the troops who drive the Cherokee forces off. Source: 76, 87

DECEMBER 25, 1776—*Kentucky*

At Limestone Creek (near Maryville) a small party led by attorney John Gabriel Jones is attacked on Christmas Day by Indians led by Chief Pluggy (Plukkemehnotee). The Indians overwhelm the whites, killing Jones and William Graden and taking four prisoners. Source: 87

1777

MAY 17, 1777—*Florida*

American forces led by Col. Samuel Elbert attempt to capture St. Augustine but are driven off by British and Indian forces near the Duval/Nassau county line. Source: 5. Marker: U.S. 1 south of Callahan, FL.

MAY 31, 1777—*Kentucky*

Indians attack McClelland's Station at Limestone Creek defended by Brig. Gen. George Rogers Clark and his men. In the battle Chief Pluggy is killed along with defender George McClelland. Source: 87

JUNE 25, 1777—*New York*

A Capt. Madison is killed by Indians while hunting pigeons near Fort Stanwix. Source: 1. Marker: Fort Stanwix National Monument, Rome, NY.

1777 DAVID CROCKETT'S GRANDFATHER KILLED—*Tennessee*

David Crockett, grandfather of the legendary frontiersman, is killed along with some of his family members by Chickamauga Indians on Crockett Creek near present-day Rogersville. Source: 110

JULY 27, 1777—*New York*

Three young girls are attacked by Indians while picking berries. Two of the girls are killed; the other girl is wounded but escapes. Source: 87

AUGUST 3–22, 1777—*New York*

American Fort Stanwix is besieged by 1,300 British forces under the command of Col. Barry St. Leger on August 3. An American relief force of 700 to 900 led by Gen. Nicholas Herkimer is sent to relieve the besieged fort. Herkimer's soldiers are ambushed by British and Iroquois allies, killing over 500 Americans and Onieda Indians in hand-to-hand fighting. Source: 7, 104. Marker: Oriskany Battlefield, six miles east of Rome, NY.

SEPTEMBER 1, 1777—*West Virginia*

A party of soldiers led by Capts. Meason and Ogle leave Fort Henry to retrieve the bodies of several settlers killed by Indians but are ambushed by over 200 Mingo, Wyandot, Delaware and Shawnee natives. Ogle, Meason and most of their small twenty-four-man force are killed. The Indians then attack Fort Henry, setting several buildings on fire and killing some livestock. The Indians withdraw during the night. Source: 30, 31

SEPTEMBER 22, 1777—*West Virginia*

Sixty-five men led by Capt. William Foreman are sent from Fort Henry to the nearby Tomlinson garrison at the Grave Creek settlement to check on its status there. Finding everything fine, they start back but disagree over the route to be taken. The majority choose to follow Foreman through a dangerous area called "The Narrows" where they are ambushed by

Wyandot Indians. Twenty-three are killed, and some are never found. Source: 30, 31

SEPTEMBER 25, 1777—*West Virginia*

The Bendure homestead is attacked by Wyandot natives who wound John Bendure and carry off his wife and daughters. They are never seen again. Source: 30

SEPTEMBER 1777—*Kentucky*

Indian chief Chiungalla, angered over the death of Pluggy (May 31, 1777) at Limestone Creek, leads a force of Indians and British against Fort Boonesborough and several settlements near by. The settlements are well fortified and sustain little damage. Source: 87. Marker: Fort Boonesborough State Park, 6 miles north of I-75 on SR 627, Boonesborough, KY.

1778

MAY 30, 1778—*New York*

Mohawks led by Joseph Brant (Thayendanega) raid the settlement of Cobleskill where they are attacked by Schoharie militiamen who are no match for the Mohawks and lose over twenty killed. Source: 31, 104

JUNE 18, 1778—*New York*

The village of Springfield is attacked by Mohawks led by Joseph Brant. The Indians burn the settlement along with its barns and drive off 200 head of cattle. Source: 31, 104

JULY 3, 1778, WYOMING MASSACRE—*Pennsylvania*

American forces ambush British troops led by Col. John Butler as they march into the Wyoming Valley in northern Pennsylvania. The Americans are then attacked by a large force of Iroquois Indians, and in a running battle many of the Americans are tomahawked to death. The American death toll is estimated as high as 400. British casualties are believed to be three killed and eight Iroquois wounded. Source: 104. Marker: Located 5 miles from Wilkes-Barre, PA., on SR 11.

JULY 18, 1778—*New York*

Joseph Brant leads Mohawks on a raid against Andrustown. Source: 31

SEPTEMBER 7–20, 1778, SIEGE OF BOONESBOROUGH—*Kentucky*

French Capt. Antoine Dagneaux de Quindre with eleven soldiers and over 400 Shawnees demand the surrender of Fort Boonesborough, led by Daniel Boone. Boone and sixty Kentucky sharpshooters hold the fort for almost two weeks. The siege is lifted on September 20, when the French and Indian forces withdraw. During the siege thirty-five Shawnees are killed by Kentucky sharpshooters. Source: 31, 88

SEPTEMBER 17, 1778—*New York*

Four American scouts run headlong into a raiding British and Indian force led by William Caldwell and Joseph Brant. Three of the scouts are killed, but the fourth, John Helmer, is chased by the warriors for over twenty miles and finally reaches Fort Herkimer where he warns the Americans of the attack. The settlers in the area retreat to Forts Herkimer and Dayton. They watch as their homes, barns and mills are burned by the British and Indian invaders. Source: 31, 104, 140

OCTOBER 6, 1778—*New York*

In retaliation for the burning of Andrustown and German Flats, American militiamen attack the Mohawk town of Unadilla, burning homes and killing a number of Mohawks. Source: 31, 104

NOVEMBER 11, 1778, CHERRY VALLEY MASSACRE—*New York*

The garrison at Fort Alden in Cherry Valley is surprised by an attack of British troops along with Seneca and Cayuga native allies. American commander Col. Ichabod Alden and several others are caught outside the gates and killed. The Seneca and Cayugas leave the main attack to pillage nearby homes, leaving British commander Walter Butler's forces weakened, and he halts the British attack. Over thirty-one Americans are killed, and seventy-one are taken prisoners. Source: 31, 104, 140. Marker: Marker and tombstones are located at Fort Alden, NY.

DECEMBER 17, 1778—*Indiana*

Fort Vincennes is surrendered to British Lt. Gov. Henry Hamilton and a war party of Kickapoo. Source: 87

1779

Grant's Fort is established in Kentucky. Fort Nashborough is established in Tennessee and Fort Warren in Vermont.

JANUARY 23, 1779—*Ohio*

Capt. Clarke and fifteen of his men are attacked near Fort Laurens by Wyandot and Mingo Indians who kill two of the soldiers. Clarke and his men return to the fort, which is attacked by increasing numbers of Indians. A messenger sent from the fort is captured and taken to the British in Detroit. A party sent out from the fort on February 23 is attacked, and several are killed. The siege is lifted March 28, when reinforcements arrive. Source: 30. Marker: Located on Tuscarawas CR. 102, Bolivar, OH.

MARCH 30, 1779—*Pennsylvania*

While rebuilding his father's house which had been burned by Indians the year before, Moses Van Campen and several others are attacked by Indians on Fishing Creek. "On the 30th of March, we were surprised by a party of Indians," Van Campen wrote. "My father was lunged through with a war spear, his throat was cut and he was scalped, while my brother was tomahawked, scalped, and thrown into the fire before my eyes." Van Campen is released in a prisoner exchange in November 1783. Source: 28

APRIL 20, 1779—*New York*

Five hundred and eighty troops and militia from Fort Stanwix and under the command of Col. Goose Van Shaick attack and burn three Onondaga villages, capture thirty-eight women, and children and kill twelve warriors. Source: 31

APRIL 26, 1779—*Pennsylvania*

One hundred Seneca and Mingo Indians attack American Fort Hand on the Kiskeminetas River. The fort, under the command of Capt. Samuel Moorehead, loses several men killed, including Sgt. Philip McGraw. Delaware natives attack the homestead of George Sykes, carrying off his wife and six children and burning his cabin down. Source: 30

APRIL 1779—*Tennessee*

Commander Shelby of Virginia attacks Chickamauga Indians under Dragging Canoe at Chickamauga Town, killing over forty Indians. "I also enclose you a letter from Colonel Shelby stating the effect of his success against the seceding Cherokees and Chickamauga." Thomas Jefferson wrote, "The damage done them was killing a half a dozen, burning eleven towns, 20,000 bushels of corn." Source: 110

1779—*Tennessee*

Chickamauga Indians attack Bolton's Station in Greene County, killing two men. Four Indians are reported killed. A pursuit party is formed, but the Indians escape. Source: 110

MARCH 28, 1779—*Ohio*

The siege of Fort Laurens is lifted as 500 U.S. troops under Gen. McIntosh arrive. Source: 87

July 30, 1779 — *Ohio*

U.S. forces led by Col. John Bowman travel from Kentucky into Ohio and attack the Shawnee village at Chalahgawtha while over 1,000 of their warriors are away. The town located on the Little Miami River is burned, and over 100 horses are taken. The Shawnee warriors pursue and catch up with Bowman's forces and ambush the soldiers on their way back to Kentucky, killing thirty and wounding sixty. Source: 30

August 1779 — *Colorado*

Spanish Gov. Don Juan Bautista de Anza leads a force along with friendly Utes against Comanche, raiding and killing traders in the area. Anza and his men attack and kill a large number of Comanche and recover a number of goods. The Ute, fearing retaliation by the Comanche, leave for their nation. Source: 40

August 25, 1779 — *Pennsylvania*

A war party of Seneca and Wyandot Indians attack forces under Col. Daniel Broadhead at the Allegheny River but are driven off by heavy gunfire. As the Indians escape down the trail, they run into a well-planned ambush led by Capt. Samuel Brady, who shoots and kills Chief Bald Eagle. Source: 30. Marker: Pennsylvania 68, 1.3 miles east of Brady at Lookout.

August 29, 1779, Battle of Newton — *New York*

Over 4,000 U.S. troops led by Maj. Gen. John Sullivan attack the Iroquois town of Newton, which is defended by Mohawk Indians and British troops. After an artillery bombardment on the town, Mohawk Indians counterattack, attempting to drive the American forces back, but heavy firing sets them to retreat. U.S. troops burn the town. Source: 1, 31, 104. Marker: Joseph Brant Museum located at 1240 North Shore Blvd. E., Burlington, ON.

August 30, 1779 — *Colorado*

Spanish Gov. Juan Bautista de Anza leads over 800 Spaniards, Pueblo, Ute and Jicarilla Apaches and attacks a Comanche camp along Fountain Creek near present-day Pueblo, killing eighteen warriors and capturing thirty-four women and children. Source: 87

September 1779 — *Pennsylvania*

American forces under the command of Col. Daniel Broadhead sweep up the Allegheny River, burning a number of villages along the way. Seneca and Muncey Indians traveling on the river are seen by an advance scout of Rangers under Capt. Samuel Brady. Brady has a decoy lure the Indians ashore at the mouth of Brokenstraw Creek and then ambushes them, killing fifteen including Chiefs Dahgahgahend and Dehguswaygahent and wounding fourteen. The soldiers scalp the dead and take the wounded back to Fort Pitt. Source: 30. Marker: Located in Buckaloons Park near U.S. 62 east of Irvine, PA.

1780

Fort Mackinac is established in Michigan.

March 8, 1780 — *Kentucky*

Richard Callaway is killed by Indians near Fort Boonesborough while building a ferry boat. Source: 132

March 14, 1780 — *Alabama*

A militia force under Capt. John Donelson is fired on near the settlement at Muscle Shoals, wounding five men. Source: 87

May 26, 1780 — *Missouri*

Over 300 British soldiers and 900 Indian allies attack St. Louis. Fernando de Leyba, the Spanish governor, has been warned of the attack, and the recently installed cannons drive the attackers off. Source: 87

June 20, 1780, Kentucky Massacres—*Kentucky*

One hundred and fifty British troops and 1,000 Indians led by Capt. Henry Byrd (Bird) and Col. Alexander McKee attack Ruddle's Station and Martin's Station, slaughtering over 200 men, women and children of the 470 settlers. The British send a number of the prisoners to Detroit while many are given to the Indians to be murdered. Source: 87, 132. Marker: At Falmouth, KY, U.S. 27, in front of Shell Refinery.

July 14–17, 1780—*West Virginia*

Hugh McIver and his wife are killed in their cabin on the Greenbrier River on July 14 by Shawnee Indians. On July 15, warriors attack the home of John Pryor, killing him and taking his wife and daughter captive. On July 16, thirty Shawnees attack several cabins upstream from the Little Levels settlements, killing Thomas Drennon, Jacob Smith and Henry Baker and capturing their families. William Griffith and his family are taken captive by Indians on July 17. Source: 30

July 1780—*Tennessee*

Chickasaw Indians kill Nathan Turpin at Renfroe's Station in eastern Tennessee. Source: 97

Summer 1780—*Ohio*

Brig. Gen. George Rogers Clark leads a military force of 800 into the Ohio region to drive the British and their Indian allies out. They burn the Shawnee town of Chillicothe and kill a number of Indians. Source: 31, 87

August 8, 1780—*Ohio*

Shawnee Indians abandon the town of Chillicothe after it is burned by U.S. troops and flee to the fortified town of Piqua. Forces under Gen. George Rogers Clark attack the town, burning a number of houses. Clark's limited supplies force him to halt his campaign and return to Kentucky. Source: 31, 87

1780—*Illinois*

American forces attack Saukenuk, the capital of the Saulk nation. Because of the Saulk alliance with the British, the town is burned to the ground. Source: 87. Marker: Hauberg Indian Museum, Black Hawk State Historic Site, Rock Island, IL.

September 18, 1780—*Texas*

Over eighty Comanche Indians attack a military outpost at San Antonio, killing three soldiers. Source: 87

1780—*Texas*

Spanish forces under Brig. Gen. Ulvade, including Comanche and Wichita Indians, attack Apaches in a canyon on the Nueces River, killing all of them. This victory eliminates the Apaches as a problem in southern Texas. Source: 32

Fall 1780—*Tennessee*

Indians kill David Gower and Patrick Quigley at Mansker's Station. Source: 110

December 16, 1780, Battle of Boyd's Creek—*Tennessee*

North Carolinians and Virginians under the command of Lt. Col. John Sevier attack Cherokee forces at Boyd's Creek and inflict heavy casualties. Sevier's campaign kills twenty-nine Cherokees and destroys over 1,000 Cherokee homes. Cherokee Chief John Watts' brother is killed. Source: 110

1781

January 11, 1781—*Tennessee*

Chickasaw Indians attempt to gain access to Freeland's Station near Fort

Nashborough in the middle of the night. The garrison is aroused and puts up a defense. Captain Gower, his son Abel and James Randolph Robertson are killed in the first attack. A relief party from nearby Fort Nashborough drives the Chickasaws off. Source: 110, 143. Marker: Fort Nashborough Historic Site, downtown Nashville, TN.

February 12, 1781—*Illinois*

Sixty-five Spanish soldiers led by Capt. Eugene Poure, along with sixty Ottawa, Potawatomi, Chippewa, Siggenauk and Naakewoin Indians, attack British traders along the Saint Joseph River. Two traders are killed, and eight are taken prisoner. Their goods are divided among the warriors. Source: 87

April 1781—*Tennessee*

A party of men under Capt. James Robertson is attacked outside of Fort Nashborough by Chickamauga Indians under Dragging Canoe. The Indians withdraw after dogs from the fort run them off. Source: 110, 143

1781 Battle of Pensacola—*Florida*

A Spanish force of over 4,000 men led by Bernardo de Galvez attacks Pensacola but is defeated by 1,500 British soldiers with 500 to 2,000 Choctaw and Creek natives. Over 7,000 Spanish reinforcements arrive, and Gen. John Campbell surrenders the town. Source: 87

1781—*Ohio*

A force of 150 soldiers and 134 militia under Col. Daniel Broadhead burn the Delaware town of Coshocton. A number of Delaware natives are reportedly killed after they surrender. Source: 31

1781—*Kentucky*

Chickasaw Indians led by a Scotsman, Colbert, attack Fort Jefferson, killing a number of settlers. The Indians finally withdraw, and the fort is abandoned for good. Source: 132. Marker: 1 mile south of Wickcliffe, on U.S. 51.

1781—*Kentucky*

Miami Indians attack and kill over sixty settlers on their way to Squire Boone's Painted Stone Station. A militia burial party on the way to bury the dead is attacked by Huron Indians led by British Capt. McKee. Sixteen of the twenty-five militiamen are killed. Source: 132. Marker: U.S. 60, Eastwood, KY.

July 18, 1781—*California*

At Mission La Purísima Concepción near Fort Yuma, Spanish padres, settlers and soldiers are massacred by Yuma Indians. Among the killed are Father Garcés, Capt. Rivera and the men in his command. At San Pedro y San Pablo de Bicuner down river, all of the inhabitants are massacred. Source: 87

1781—*Kentucky*

Indians attack and burn Grant's Station. They then attack Strode's Station and kill two settlers. Source: 35, 132. Marker: 1 mile west of Winchester, U.S. 60.

October 12, 1781—*Ohio*

Brady's Rangers ambush a large war party of Seneca and Mingo Indians at Beaver Creek, killing ten. The small Ranger force of thirteen flees toward Fort McIntosh pursued by the warriors, but the Rangers stop and ambush the Indians again, this time stopping their advance. Capt. Samuel Brady is the only Ranger taken captive. He is made to run the gauntlet and then escapes, hotly pursued by the warriors, but hides in an old log and makes his way back to Fort McIntosh. Source: 87

October 19, 1781

British General Cornwallis is defeated at the Battle of Yorktown, leading to the end of

Britain's claim on America. Many Indian tribes are left without British support in their war on the American colonists. The formal surrender ending the Revolutionary War, the Treaty of Paris, is signed in 1783.

OCTOBER 30, 1781—*Texas*

After raiding near the Villa of San Fernando, Comanche Indians are attacked by a Spanish force from San Antonio de Béxar Presidio. Ten Comanches and two soldiers are killed. Source: 40

1782

JANUARY 1782—*South Carolina*

As Cherokee attacks increase, a campaign begins to destroy their towns. In January American forces led by Gen. Andrew Pickens attack and destroy a number of rebuilt Cherokee towns, kill forty natives and take forty prisoners. Source: 76

MARCH 10, 1782—*Ohio*

Pennsylvania militiamen led by Col. David Williamson pursue and overcome a Delaware war party at a Moravian Mission. The militiamen slaughter over ninety men, women and children in retaliation for the death of Jane Wallace and her infant child whose bodies had been found impaled on a sapling. The militiamen reportedly pack their ninety captives into several cabins and kill them with mallets and tomahawks. Natives begin retaliatory raids on nearby settlements. Source: 1, 30, 31. Marker: Gnadenhutten Monument is located on U.S. 36 about ten miles east of I-77.

JUNE 4–5, 1782, THE BATTLE OF SANDUSKY—*Ohio*

Army and militia forces led by Col. William Crawford are ambushed by over 600 Wyandot and Delaware Indians led by Monakuduto, Wingenund and Punoacan Indians on the upper Sandusky River. The soldiers retreat to a ravine where they battle all day on June 4, but a large number of them desert that night. Crawford and his men begin a retreat while they skirmish with the natives along the way. A number of Crawford's men are killed, and he, along with Dr. John Knight, is captured on June 11, by the Delawares. Col. Crawford is tortured and burned at the stake. "Colonel Crawford besought the Almighty to have mercy on his soul," Knight wrote. "He continued in all extremities of pain for an hour. At last being almost spent, he lay down on his belly. They then scalped him." Source: 1, 28, 30 [Quote 28]

JUNE 6, 1782—*Ohio*

The remnants of Crawford's forces under the command of Col. David Williamson are attacked by Indians as they linger at the Olentangy River. Maj. John Rose urges Williamson to find cover for the men, but the Indians catch them out in the open, killing three and wounding eight. Source: 30

JULY 13, 1782—*Pennsylvania*

Hannastown is attacked and burned by over 100 Senecas and sixty French Canadians who travel down the Allegheny River. Source: 30

AUGUST 14–15, 1782—*Kentucky*

British troops and Indian allies, about 500 total, attack the settlement of Bryant's Station, which consist of forty cabins, for three days. The settlers lose all their livestock. Source: 35, 87

AUGUST 19, 1782—*Kentucky*

A group of settlers and militia led by Daniel Boone set out from Bryant's Station near Lexington in pursuit of a raiding war party but are ambushed by Indians led by Simon Girty. The small force fights its way out and withdraws. Source: 35, 132. Marker: 5 miles north of Lexington at Bryan Station Park, KY.

August 19, 1782, Battle of Blue Licks—*Kentucky*

British and Indian allies fresh from their attack on Bryant's Station ambush 183 Kentuckians led by Col. Richard Todd near Blue Licks, killing seventy-two. The Kentucky militia includes Daniel Boone, whose son Israel is killed along with Todd in the battle. Source: 87, 132, 135. Marker: Blue Licks Battlefield State Park, U.S. 68 between Paris and Maysville, KY.

Fall 1782—*Georgia*

Battle of Savannah. Creek forces led by Emistesigo attempt to fight their way into Savannah to relieve British forces there, but Emistesigo is killed, and the Creeks negotiate a peace with Gen. Anthony Wayne. Source: 87

September 1782—*Tennessee*

Two hundred and fifty Tennessee militiamen led by John Sevier attack a Cherokee town at the base of Lookout Mountain. The Cherokee led by Dragging Canoe and Chief Skyuka, relocate to nearby Long Island, Crow Town, Nickajack and Running Water but keep up their raids on settlements in the area. It is believed that Siever's Cherokee scout John Watts led the soldiers away from the villages. Source: 31, 76

September 11–13, 1782—*West Virginia*

Indians along with British soldiers attack Fort Henry at Wheeling, West Virginia. The invading force had been seen prior to the attack, and the fort is prepared. Indian forces try unsuccessfully to scale the walls of Fort Henry and lose a number killed before withdrawing. Source: 30, 31

November 10, 1782—*Ohio*

One thousand Kentucky militiamen under Gen. George Rogers Clark capture the Shawnee town of Chillicothe. Source: 87

1783

The Treaty of Paris is signed ceding all British lands between the Appalachian Mountains and the Mississippi River to the new U.S. republic. Because they have supported Britain during the war, many tribes are also compelled to cede their lands to the U.S. government.

April 17, 1783—*Arkansas*

A force of 100 whites and Chickasaw Indians led by English trader James Colbert attacks Spanish Fort Carlos. Capt. Jacob Dubreuil, commander of the fort, sends Spanish troops and Quapaw natives on a counterattack, driving Colbert and his men off. Source: 139, 149

1783—*Minnesota*

Two hundred Dakota Indians attack a French and Ojibway outpost on the Crow Wing River, killing several inhabitants. Source: 87

September 1783—*Tennessee*

Cherokees and Creeks led by Cherokee Chief John Watts and Doublehead attack the Cavitt's Station blockhouse near Knoxville, killing all of the men, women and children there. Seven hundred soldiers under Lt. Col. John Sevier track the Indians as far as the Ustanali settlement in Georgia, which they burn. Source: 76

1784

July 1784—*Texas*

A Spanish force led by Francisco Amangual on its way to attack raiding Taovayas and Wichita runs into a large Comanche war party on the Guadalupe River. The battle lasts eight hours, and ten warriors are killed. Source: 87

1786

May 1786, Abraham Lincoln killed—*Kentucky*

Abraham Lincoln, grandfather to the future president, is attacked and killed by Indians on his farm in present-day Jefferson County. Source: 132. Marker: Marker and grave located 1 mile east of Eastwood, KY, U.S. 60, 460.

October 1786—*Indiana*

Forces under Col. Logan attack and destroy a Shawnee village on the Wabash River, killing ten warriors and twelve others including Chief Moluntha. A total of thirteen villages are destroyed. Source: 87

1787

April 11, 1787—*Kentucky*

Indians attack a homestead in Bourbon County, killing a number of women and children. A tracking party led by Col. John Edwards catches up with the raiders and kills two Indians. Source: 35

1788

October 17, 1788—*Tennessee*

Gillespie's Station is attacked by Chickamauga and Cherokee Indians led by Maj. Ridge. All of the male defenders are killed, and Col. Gillespie's daughter is stabbed to death. Cherokee Indian John Watts saves the lives of twenty-eight women and children. Source: 138

October 1788—*Kentucky*

Bland Ballard, his wife and three children are killed by Indians near Tyler's Station. His son Maj. Ballard kills six of the attackers and survives the attack. Source: 132. Marker: Tick Creek Massacre, U.S. 60 at Cross Keys Rd., Shelby City, KY.

1789

March 1789—*Pennsylvania*

Indians attack the homestead of William Thomas and Joseph Cambridge, killing them and Cambridge's entire family. Source: 30

March 1789—*West Virginia*

Indians attack and kill eight settlers near Clarksburg. Indians attack Kennedy's Bottom, killing Maj. William Bailey and capturing five members of the Jason Quick family. Source: 30

1789—*Kentucky*

John Tanner is captured by Indians at Elk Horn settlement in Kentucky. "As we were landing ... a young woman came towards me crying and struck me on the head," Tanner wrote. "Some of her friends had been killed by whites." Tanner lives with the Ottawa, Ojibway and Chippewa until returning to the white world in 1817 but returns to the Indians after murdering an Indian agent's brother. Source: 28

1790

February 1790—*Kentucky*

A flat boat is attacked by Shawnee natives on the Ohio River. Several people are killed, and Charles Johnston is taken prisoner. Among the dead are John May and Dolly Fleming. Johnston said, "I had not been seated long when the scalps of Mr. May and Miss Fleming ... were set before me at the fire to dry." Source: 28

April 1790—*West Virginia*

Wyandot Indians attack the sugar farm of John Martin at King's Creek, killing him, capturing five children and taking them to Half King's Town on the Upper Sandusky River. Source: 30

April 1790 — *Kentucky*

Hannah Barnett and two of her children are killed by Indians near Barnett's Station in present-day Ohio County. Barnett's ten-year-old daughter is carried off by the Indians. Source: 132. Marker: 2 miles east of Hartford on Barnett's Station Rd. off Kentucky 69

May 1790 — *West Virginia*

The home of Robert Purdy is attacked by Indians. Mr. Purdy and his infant son are killed in bed. Mrs. Purdy is knocked unconscious, and, when she comes to, discovers her daughters have been taken captive. Source: 30

May 29, 1790 — *West Virginia*

Rebecca Van Buskirk is captured by natives but is soon killed when her husband and several men chase the abductors. Source: 30

> "When your army entered the country of the six nations, we called you ... Town Destroyer; and to this day when that name is heard, our women look behind them and turn pale."
> — Cornplanter, Seneca, 1790 [Source: 88]

Summer 1790 — *West Virginia*

Shawnees attack Tackett's Fort while John and Lewis Tackett and their mother are harvesting turnips. The Indians take the three captive and kill George McElhany. Source: 30

1790 — *Texas*

Spanish commandant Brig. Gen. Ugalde leads a force, which includes 140 Comanche natives, against Mescalaro, Lipan and other Apaches west of San Antonio. The Apache suffer a number killed, including twenty-eight warriors, twenty-eight women and one child. Source: 87

July 1790 — *Ohio*

The homestead of John Carpenter is attacked by Indians while he works in a field on Short Creek. Carpenter is wounded but hides in a nearby cornfield. The nearby home of George McCoy and his wife is attacked, and they are killed. Also killed nearby is David Cox and Thomas Van Swearingen. Source: 30

September 27, 1790 — *West Virginia*

Thirteen-year-old Henry Johnson and his eleven-year-old brother John are captured by two Shawnee Indians while bringing in some cows. That night the boys pretend to sleep but take the natives' rifle and tomahawk, killing one of the Indians and injuring the other. Source: 30

October 22, 1790, Maumee River Ambush — *Indiana*

Little Turtle and Blue Jacket lead the Miami and Shawnee in an ambush of over 1,400 regular soldiers under Brig. Gen. Josiah Harmar at Maumee River, killing over 183 Americans. Encouraged by the victory, Blue Jacket and his warriors start raiding settlements in January along the Ohio River. Source: 87

December 11, 1790 — *Ohio*

A deer hunting party is attacked in the middle of the night on Indian Wheeling Creek by a party of Mingo and Wyandot Indians who kill thirteen of the fourteen hunters. David C. Whitaker, one of the hunters, pretends to be dead as the warriors make their way around the bodies. Throwing his blanket over the nearest Indian he runs for safety barefoot through the snow. He finally makes his way to Fort Henry. Source: 30

1791

Fort Grenville, Fort Recovery and Fort Jefferson are established in Ohio.

January 2, 1791—*Ohio*

Indians attack and kill twelve defenders at the Big Bottom Settlement on the Muskingum River. Source: 35, 87

January 1791—*Ohio*

Dunlap's Station is attacked by 300 Potawatomi, Miami, Delaware and Shawnee Indians, killing several settlers. Surveyor Abner Hunt is captured and burned to death. Source: 87

March 17, 1791—*Kentucky*

Soldiers and their families returning from Pittsburgh are attacked while traveling in keelboats down the Ohio River by Shawnee Indians near Maysville. Capt. Kirkpatrick is killed along with six men. Twenty-one other settlers who were left behind are found dead a month later, killed by Indians. Source: 87

1791—*Kentucky*

Jinney Adams is killed by Chief Thunder near Fort Paint Lick. Source: 132. Marker: Hwy. 52, Paint Lick, KY.

April 16, 1791—*Kentucky*

Three Shawnees are ambushed and killed near Snag Creek by Ben Whiteman's militia. Thirty-two horses are recovered. Source: 87

May 1, 1791—*Pennsylvania*

Susan, Elizabeth, Christina and Catherine Crow are attacked by Delaware Indians while bringing cows in from a pasture. The girls attempt to outrun their captors and are all killed except Catherine, who hides in a nearby hollow tree until rescued by her father. Source: 30

November 4, 1791, Little Turtle's Victory—*Ohio*

While camped on the Wabash River about 1,400 American soldiers and militiamen under the command of Maj. Gen. Arthur St. Clair are attacked by 1,000 Indians led by Little Turtle and Blue Jacket. The whites retreat across the river and try to throw up a defense, but the Indians swarm over them. In hand-to-hand fighting Blue Jacket's Shawnees attack and massacre the artillerymen as over 500 soldiers flee toward the woods. In one of the most devastating defeats in American history over 832 soldiers and civilians are killed and 270 wounded. Fort Recovery is built on this site. Source: 1, 30, 50, 56, 104. Marker: Fort Recovery State Memorial is located on SR 49 and SR 119, Fort Recovery, OH.

December 20, 1791—*Ohio*

Feeling that Fort Harmar is too far away (24 miles) to give protection against Indian raids, settlers begin work on a new fort. Shawnee Indians under Blue Jacket attack the uncompleted fort at Big Bottom, killing eleven men, a woman and two children. Source: 30, 87. Marker: Big Bottom State Monument, SR 266, Stockport, OH.

> "The whole white race is a monster who is always hungry, and what he eats is land."
> — Chiksika, Shawnee
> [Source: 88]

1792

February 25, 1792—*Tennessee*

Four miles from Nashborough Indians attack and kill three members of the Thompson family and take three captive. Source: 125

March 10, 1792—*Ohio*

After having been forced by the British to relocate to a site on the Sandusky River, Delaware natives are attacked on the way by militiamen under Col. David Williamson. Over ninety Delaware natives are killed for their support of the British. Reports say the Delaware were unarmed. Source: 1, 30, 87. Marker: A reconstructed

Schoenbrunn Village is located on SR 259, New Philadelphia, OH.

JUNE 26, 1792—*Tennessee*

Creek, Cherokee and Chickamauga Indians attack Zeigler's Station in Sumner County, killing three, wounding four and taking twelve prisoners. Source: 125

SEPTEMBER 30, 1792—*Tennessee*

Buchanan's Station is attacked by Lower Cherokees, Creeks and Shawnees led by John Watts, but they are driven off. Source: 76

DECEMBER 22, 1792—*Tennessee*

Chickamauga Indians attack the home of Mr. Richardson while he is away, killing Mrs. Richardson, Mrs. Foster, Miss Schult and two children. The Chickamauga war party is led by Little Nephew and Towaka. Source: 143

1793

MARCH 9, 1793—*Tennessee*

James and Thompson Nelson are killed and scalped by Indians on the Little Pigeon River in the Smokey Mountains. Source: 143

APRIL 1, 1793—*Kentucky*

Morgan's Station is attacked while the men are off in the fields. Nineteen women and children are taken prisoners. Twelve of the prisoners are later killed by the Indians. Source: 132. Marker: 2 miles east of Mt. Sterling, KY.

JUNE 7, 1793—*Georgia*

A Cherokee raiding party kills a Mr. Gilliam and his son. In retaliation, fifty-six men led by Capt. John Beard attack the nearby Cherokee town of Echota, killing a number of Indians including Scantee, Fool Charlie and others. (The date June 12 is also given for this engagement.) Source: 87, 97

JUNE 19, 1793—*Tennessee*

The *Knoxville Gazette* reports, "In the night a large party of Indians came into Wear's Cove, on Little Pigeon Creek, and cut down much corn, stole ten horses and killed another, killed two cows and three hogs, which they skinned." Source: 143

JULY 1, 1793—*Tennessee*

After his three brothers are killed by Creek Indians near Nashville, Abraham Castleman and several men track the war party to their Nickajack River camp and ambush them, killing several Indians. Source: 143

JUNE 21, 1793—*Tennessee*

Militiamen led by Lt. Henderson track the warrior party that raided Wear's Cove on June 19, kill two Indians and retake several horses. Source: 143

SEPTEMBER 25–26, 1793— *Tennessee*

Cherokees and Creeks led by John Watts attack Cavett's Station near Knoxville. After talking with Watts, the defenders are guaranteed safe passage if they surrender. They surrender and are killed by Doublehead. Source: 97

OCTOBER 17, 1793—*Ohio*

Seven miles from Fort St. Clair 250 Shawnees led by Blue Jacket attack an army supply train guarded by 100 mounted riflemen, killing over fourteen soldiers. Source: 1, 30

DECEMBER 2, 1793—*Ohio*

A Shawnee raiding party that has stolen a number of horses is tracked by Simon Kenton and his men who catch up with them at Holt's Creek: six Shawnees are killed about thirty-two miles from Maysville. Source: 30

1794

Fort Adams and Fort Wayne are established in Ohio.

April 9, 1794 — *Tennessee*

Chickamauga raiders led by Bench are ambushed near Stone's Gap, killing him and two others. Bench and his warriors are responsible for over forty murders in the area. Bench is shot and killed by Lt. Vincent Hobbs, and his scalp is sent to Virginia where Bench had also committed a number of atrocities. Hobbs is awarded a silver-mounted rifle from the Virginia legislature for his actions. Source: 97

April 22, 1794 — *Tennessee*

The homestead of William Casteel near Knoxville is attacked by Cherokee Indians. Casteel, his wife and four small children are killed. Casteel's ten-year-old daughter is tomahawked a number of times but eventually recovers. Source: 97

May 5, 1794 — *Tennessee*

Peter Pearcified is killed by Indians near Wear's Cove in eastern Tennessee. Source: 143

May 14, 1794 — *Tennessee*

A pursuit party led by Joseph Evans, Thomas Sellers and James Hubbart track the murderers of Peter Pearcified, killed in Wear's Cove. They attack the raiding party at night, killing four Indians while they sleep. Source: 143

June 5, 1794 — *Alabama*

Cherokees from the Chickamauga towns attack a boat near the Tennessee River at the Muscle Shoals settlement, killing a number of people. The Cherokees then flee to Arkansas. Source: 87

June 30, 1794 — *Ohio*

Indians led by Blue Jacket attack Fort Recovery but are driven off by heavy fire from the fort. Source: 1, 66. Marker: Fort Recovery site located on SR 49 west of Dayton, OH.

August 20, 1794, Battle of Fallen Timbers — *Ohio*

Gen. "Mad" Anthony Wayne leads over 2,000 soldiers and over 1,000 Kentucky militiamen cavalry under Maj. Gen. Charles Scott in a military attack against Chief Black Wolf and 2,000 Indians, including Shawnee, Ottawa, Chippewa and Potawatomi under Chief Blue Jacket, on the Maumee River. Black Wolf's centerline breaks, and the soldiers dislodge Indians on each side. The Indians make a stand but are hard pressed by Wayne's forces and driven back by a series of bayonet charges, which leads to hand-to-hand fighting. The chief of the Ottawa is killed, and the Indians retreat, losing over fifty killed. Thirty-one soldiers are killed. The Indians retreat to Fort Miamis (Miami) five miles away and request help from the British but are denied and withdraw to the western shore of Lake Erie. Source: 15, 30, 50, 56, 104, 119. Marker: Fallen Timbers Battlefield, SR 24, west of Maumee, OH.

September 6, 1794 — *West Virginia*

George Tush is attacked by Wyandot Indians while feeding his hogs. Tush's five children are killed and his wife is taken prisoner. Although severely wounded, Tush travels to the home of Martin Wetzel for help. Source: 30

September 12, 1794, Chickamauga Towns Massacre — *Tennessee*

In retaliation for a number of continued raids in middle and eastern Tennessee, militia forces led by Col. Whitely and Maj. Ore with 550 militiamen attack the Chickamauga towns, which include Nickajack and Running Water. They burn the towns and kill a number of natives. Between February 26 and September 6, 1794, Cherokee and Chickamauga raids kill sixty-seven white settlers, wound ten, capture twenty-five, and steal three hundred and seventy-four horses. Source: 35, 76, 97

October 1794—*Georgia*

Forces led by Brig. Gen. John Sevier, acting in violation of orders, attack and burn a number of Cherokee Lower Towns, including Oostanaula. Source: 87

1795

April 1795—*Illinois*

Samuel Chew, five men and several slaves are killed, scalped and mutilated by Potawatomi and Kickapoo Indians. Some of the warriors are captured and taken to Kaskaskia where they are killed. Source: 87

1796

Chouteau's Post is established in Oklahoma.

1800–1899

As the new century begins, white settlers and pioneers push the Indians farther westward as the Louisiana Purchase extends the United States past the Mississippi into the heartland of the American Indian. In the southern woodlands Creek and Seminole Indians continue their struggle against American encroachment and white trappers enter the Rocky Mountains. Santa Fe, New Mexico, becomes the trade goods capital of the southwest. On the Great Plains Cheyenne, Sioux and Arapaho battle U.S. forces, culminating in their greatest victory. As the nineteenth century draws to a close, the slaughter of the buffalo and the failure of the reservation concept threatens the very existence of the American Indian.

1800—*Tennessee*

Tannover Runyan is killed by Indians as he searches for some horses on the Little Pigeon River in Sevier County. Source: 143

> "The Indians can be kept in order only by commerce or war, the former is the cheapest."
> — Thomas Jefferson
> [Source: 33]

1803

Fort Dearborn is established in Illinois. Great Britain begins efforts to try to retake its American colonies by direct warfare, culminating in the War of 1812.

1804

Lewis and Clark establish Fort Mandan.

September 23, 1804, Lewis and Clark's Clash with Sioux—*South Dakota*

Lewis and Clark encounter the Teton Sioux. A deadly confrontation develops when Sioux Chief Black Buffalo and several others refuse to leave the keelboat and warriors grab the towline. Lewis orders the men ready for action as muskets are aimed and swords drawn. Several tense moments follow until Black Buffalo changes the subject. A crisis is avoided. Source: 33

1805

Lewis and Clark establish Fort Clatsop in Oregon.

1805 Massacre Cave—*Arizona*

Spanish forces attack Navajo natives at Canyon de Chelly, killing over 100, mostly women and children who have taken refuge in a nearby cave. Source: 87

1806

JULY 26, 1806, LEWIS AND CLARK'S CLASH WITH BLACKFEET—*Montana*

While exploring the Marias River, Meriwether Lewis and three companions encounter eight Blackfeet Indians and set up camp with them. At dawn the Indians jump Lewis and his party and try to steal their horses. In the clash that follows Lewis narrowly misses being shot, and two of the Blackfeet are killed. Source: 33

1808

Fort Osage in Missouri is established. Fort Madison is established in Iowa.

AUGUST 23, 1808—*Texas*

Anthony Glass, a trader from Natchez, Mississippi, notes in his journal, "the men who were guarding the horses came in this morning and reported a party of Osages had stolen a number and the best we had." Source: 145

SEPTEMBER 28, 1808—*Texas*

From the journal of Anthony Glass: "A party of Osage made their appearance on horseback advancing directly to the village ... the Pallis (Indians) sallied out upon them and killed one of them ... we were persuaded it was the same party who stole our horses on the 22nd of August ... the Osage Indian that was killed was cut into pieces and distributed through the village and the men women and children danced for three days." Source: 145

1809

Fort Carney is established in Alabama.

1810

Fort Henry is established in Idaho.

APRIL 12, 1810, ATTACK ON FUR TRAPPERS—*Montana*

A party of fur trappers led by Andrew Henry, Manuel Lisa and Pierre Menard is attacked by Blackfeet at the Three Forks Trading Post; two of the trappers are killed. A second attack by the Blackfeet kills George Drouillard and two Delaware Indian trappers. Source: 42, 87

SUMMER 1810—*Montana*

Andrew Henry and members of the Fur Brigade are massacred by Blackfeet Indians. Archibald Pelton escapes and spends almost two years with Shoshone Indians. Source: 42

1811

Fort Astoria is established in Oregon.

APRIL 1811—*Illinois*

Winnebago Indians attack a farm on the southeast branch of the Illinois, killing two farmers. Source: 87

NOVEMBER 7, 1811, BATTLE OF TIPPECANOE—*Indiana*

Shawnee leader Tenskwatawa and over 450 Winnebago, Potawatomi and Kickapoo natives attack the U.S. camp at Prophetstown on the Tippecanoe River. Gen. William Henry Harrison's army of 1,000 hold their positions, and the Indians' allied forces withdraw after a heated fight. Sixty-one soldiers are killed, and Indian losses are estimated at forty killed. While burning Prophetstown and all the food supplies, soldiers find weapons supplied to the Indians by the British. Source: 50, 87. Marker: Tippecanoe Battlefield, Battle Ground, IN.

1812

Fort Amanda is established in Ohio. Fort Madison is established in Alabama.

July 17, 1812—*Michigan*

English forces with allied Indians under Gen. Isaac Brock capture Fort Michilimackinac. Source: 87. Marker: Fort Michilimackinac, Mackinaw City, MI.

August 15, 1812, Fort Dearborn Massacre—*Illinois*

After surrendering Fort Dearborn, Potawatomi Indians and British troops attack 148 soldiers, militiamen, women and children two miles from the fort. Only one trader and two women escape, and a number are killed or captured. Fort Dearborn is burned to the ground. Source: 87. Marker: Corner of 18th and Prairie St., Chicago, IL.

August 16, 1812, Fall of Fort Detroit—*Michigan*

Fort Detroit commanded by Gen. William Hull, with a larger force than his attackers, surrenders to English and Indian forces led by Tecumseh and Gen. Isaac Brock. Hull is later court-martialed for cowardice and sentenced to be shot but is given clemency by President James Madison. A number of the American prisoners are threatened with death by the Indians, but an impassioned speech by Tecumseh saves them. Survivor Capt. Leslie Combs wrote: "I was near Tecumseh when he made his speech whereby the lives of hundreds of prisoners were saved.... He was a truly great man and gallant warrior." Source: 87, 88 [Quote 88]

September 3, 1812—*Indiana*

Fort Harrison under the command of Zachary Taylor is attacked by Kickapoo led by Pakoisheecan. Several buildings are set on fire, and two soldiers are killed outside of the fort. A reinforcement force of 1,200 men under William Russell arrives on September 16. Source: 87, 128. Marker: Fort Harrison State Park, 5753 Glenn Rd., Indianapolis, IN.

September 3, 1812—*Indiana*

Kickapoo Indians attack civilians at Pigeon Roost, killing and scalping twenty-one of the settlers. Source: 87. Marker: Pigeon Roost Sate Historic Site, U.S. 31, Underwood, IN.

September 27, 1812—*Florida*

In response to Seminole raids into Georgia (encouraged by Spanish Gov. Kindelan) Georgia and Tennessee militia and settlers attack Seminole towns in Spanish-held Florida. Billy Bowlegs and over 150 Seminoles with runaway slaves, counterattack the militias and drives them into Georgia. Source: 5, 65, 105. Marker: Northeast of Rochelle on the northwest side of CR 234, between SR 20 and SE 16th Ave.

October 18, 1812, Attack at Peoria Lake—*Illinois*

Three hundred and sixty-two militiamen under Illinois Gov. Ninian Edwards march from Edwardsville to Peoria Lake and attack the Kickapoo villages of Chiefs Pawatomo, White Hair and Black Partridge. They burn the villages, over 1,000 bushels of corn and kill over twenty-four Kickapoo natives. Source: 87

November 11, 1812—*Indiana*

A force of over 1,200 militiamen including Kentucky infantrymen attacks and destroys Prophetstown and the Indians' corn crop. Source: 87, 129. Marker: Prophetstown State Park, Battleground, IN.

December 17–18, 1812, Attack on Delaware Village—*Ohio*

On December 17, a 600-man force under Lt. Col. John B. Campbell attacks a Delaware village near Fort Grenville, killing eight, taking forty-two prisoners and burning three native towns. The following day Delaware and Miami Indians attack the soldiers in freezing temperatures, killing ten, wounding forty-eight and killing over 100 horses. A number of soldiers suffering from severe frostbite are abandoned. Source: 66. Marker: The Garst Museum located at 205 N. Broadway, Grenville, OH.

1813

Fort Clark is established in Illinois. Fort Meigs and Fort Ball are established in Ohio.

January 18, 1813—*Michigan*

American forces under Brig. Gen. James Winchester defeat British and Indians at Frenchtown. Thirteen Americans are killed and fifty-four are wounded. Source: 87

January 22, 1813, River Raisin Massacre—*Michigan*

American forces camped on Raisin River are attacked by well-disciplined British and Indian forces which include Chippewa, Delaware, Ottawa and Potawatomi Indians. Without pickets posted and low on ammunition, the American forces are soon overrun. "The savages rushed on the wounded and, in their barbarous manner, shot and tomahawked and scalped them and cruelly mangled their naked bodies while they lay agonizing and weltering in their blood," Elias Darnell wrote. A number of captives and wounded are killed by the Potawatomi, Ottawa, Chippewa and Delaware Indians that night. Source: 28, 35, 87 [Quote 84]. Marker: The River Raisin Battlefield Visitor Center, 1403 E. Elm St., Monroe, MI.

February 1813—*Florida*

Col. John Williams along with the former governor of South Carolina, Maj. Gen. Thomas Pinckney, and the Tennessee militia march into Florida attacking and burning Seminole towns in north-central Florida and destroying over 2,000 bushels of corn. Several hundred cattle and horses are also taken. Continued battles and skirmishes greatly reduce the Seminoles' fighting strength, and many begin taking refuge deep in the Florida swamps. Source: 65

April 25–May 9, 1813, Attack on Fort Meigs—*Ohio*

Indian tribes united under Tecumseh attack Americans at Fort Meigs. The 1,200 Potawatomis and 900 British soldiers are unsuccessful against the fort's 550 defenders. A relief force of 1,100 to 1,200 Kentucky militiamen is caught in an ambush on May 5, and lose over half their number. Source: 1, 43. Marker: Reconstructed Fort Meigs is located on SR 65, Perrysburg, OH.

> "Sell a country! Why not sell the air, the great sea, as well as the earth? Did not the Great Spirit make them all for the use of his children?"
> —Tecumseh
> [Source: 88]

July 8, 1813—*New York*

Indians ambush Lt. Joseph Eldridge and his men near Fort George, killing five. Source: 66

July 22, 1813, The Red Stick Revolt—*Georgia and Alabama*

The Lower Creek Indians of Alabama refuse to join the Upper Creeks in their war on the white settlers, angering the Upper Creeks. Upper Creek Indians raid and kill settlers on the Ohio River and attack settlements in Tennessee and Georgia. To avoid war with the whites, peaceful Lower Creeks led by Menawa and William McIntosh track down and kill eleven of the raiding Red Sticks (Upper Creek warriors) starting a bloody feud among the tribes. Peaceful inhabitants of the Lower Creek towns of Kaliuggee and Hatchechubba flee to the Creek settlement of Tuckabatchee but are attacked there by the Upper Creeks who burn the settlement. Source: 87

July 27, 1813, Burnt Corn Creek—*Alabama*

After trading goods at Pensacola, Florida, Creek Indians set out for home but are ambushed by 180 militiamen of Washington County, Mississippi, at Burnt Corn Creek, Alabama. The Indians are driven into a swamp, but soon counterattack and drive off over 100 of the militiamen. Eighty of the whites hold their ground for a while but are soon forced to withdraw. Source: 87

August 2, 1813—*Ohio*

After an unsuccessful attack on Fort Meigs in May, British Maj. Gen. Henry Proctor advances toward American Fort Stephenson on the Sandusky River commanded by Maj. George Croghan. American Gen. William Henry Harrison sends a message which advises the twenty-one-year-old Croghan to destroy the fort and leave before the arrival of Proctor and his forces. Croghan convinces Harrison that he can successful defend the fort. The British forces attack the fort, and 97 of Proctor's soldiers are cut down by Kentucky sharpshooters. The Indians with Proctor withdraw, and he is forced to abandoned the siege. Source: 87

August 13, 1813—*Alabama*

Part of Daniel Beasley's command is sent from Fort Mims to Mt. Vernon on the Mobile River, weakening his forces there, but Maj. Beasley does nothing to hasten work on Fort Mims' defenses, which leads to disaster on the August 29. Source: 43, 45

August 18, 1813—*Texas*

The Spanish army, commanded by Gen. José Joaquín de Arredondo, defeats the Republican Army of the North, which is made up of Anglos, Mexicans and Indians. The attempts to drive Spain from Texas are abandoned. Source: 148

August 29–30, 1813, Fort Mims Massacre—*Alabama*

Hostile Upper Creek Indians (Red Sticks) prepare to attack Fort Mims. Led by half-breed prophet Paddy Welsh and William Weatherford, also known as Chief Red Eagle, they hide their main forces in the woods six miles from the fort. Two slaves report the massive Indian force, but when scouts cannot locate the well-concealed Indians, the two slaves are whipped for giving false information. At noon a drum roll sounds, and over 700 Red Sticks race across an open field toward Fort Mims and storm the unsuspecting fortress. Buildings are set afire with flaming arrows as the defenders rush to shut the open gate, through which the Creeks are pouring. Several attempts are made to shut the gates but the onslaught of the warriors is too great. Maj. Beasley is killed in the first wave as the militiamen and settlers pour a heavy volley into the attacking Indians. Hand-to-hand fighting commences as the men try to herd the women and children to safety. Several groups of defenders put up a stout defense, but one by one are cut down. Samuel Smith, a survivor, writes: "A large and powerful Negro man wielding an axe killed more Indians than any other man. But he fell at last." The battle rages until three o'clock when the Indians set the last two structures ablaze. Many of the settlers are burned alive, including women and children. The fort's powder magazine finally explodes, driving many of the defenders out of the gates into the attacking Red Sticks, who begin a wholesale slaughter of the whites. Some of the settlers make a run for the Alabama River, but most are shot, tomahawked and stabbed as they try to escape. Many of the victims are scalped before they are killed.

Not all of the attacking Creeks participate in the slaughter; a great many have friends among the whites and help them escape. Over 250 settlers are killed and 100 to 175 slaves are taken captive. Source: 35, 43, 45, 77, 90, 127 [Quote 43]. Marker: Fort Mims State Historic Site off Hwy. 59, Tensaw, AL.

September 1, 1813—*Alabama*

Near Fort Sinquefield the homestead of Ransom Kimbell is attacked by Creek Indians. Fourteen settlers are savagely clubbed, scalped and killed. The house is pillaged and burned. Ransom Kimbell is not home but will die of grief within a year. Source: 43

> "Lift up your hatchets; raise your knives; sight your rifles! Stand up to the foe; he is a weakling and a coward! Fall upon him! Leave him to the wolves and buzzards!"
> — Tenskwatawa, Shawnee
> [Source: 88]

November 4, 1813, Battle of Tallushatchee—*Alabama*

In response to the attack on Fort Mims the Tennessee militia with 3,500 men under Gen. Andrew Jackson and Lower Cherokees attack and kill over 200 Creeks at Tallushatchee. Many of the Creeks flee to Talladaga Town. Source: 43, 87, 90

November 9, 1813, Battle of Talladaga—*Alabama*

After the victory at Tallushatchee Gen. Andrew Jackson and the Tennessee militia follow the Creeks to Talladaga Town and attack, killing over 300 Red Stick Creeks. The Creeks retreat south to Tohopeka on the Tallapoosa River. Source: 43, 87, 90

November 18, 1813, The Hillabee Massacre—*Alabama*

American forces led by Gen. James White attack and destroy a Hillabee native town, which has already surrendered to Gen. Jackson's forces. Undisciplined troops pillage and burn the entire village, killing a number of Hillabee Indians. Gen. White reported, "We lost not a drop of blood and Fort Mims was again avenged." Source: 43, 87, 90 [Quote 43]

November 20, 1813—*Alabama*

A scouting party led by Sam Dale attacks a canoe full of Indians on the Alabama River near Randon's Creek. Some of the Indians are shot, and some are clubbed to death. Source: 87

November 29, 1813—*Alabama*

The Georgia Militia, along with four hundred Indian allies and friendly Tookabatchees commanded by Gen. John Floyd, attack Autosee, killing 200 Indians. Floyd's forces burn over 400 native houses. The Georgians lose eleven killed. Source: 43, 87

December 23, 1813, Battle of Escanachala—*Alabama*

Over 1,000 soldiers of the Mississippi Infantry led by Gen. Ferdinand Claiborne attack the Creek village of Escanachala, killing over thirty-three Creeks. Creek Chief Red Eagle escapes. Source: 43, 87

1814

January 22, 1814, Battle of Emuckfau—*Alabama*

A huge force of Red Sticks falls upon Gen. Jackson's flank and rear in the early morning but are kept at bay by the militiamen and army. Heavy gunfire drives the Indians back, and they are soon pursued for over two miles. A number of the Red Sticks are killed. Gen. John Coffee's troops burn the native village, but a countercharge by the Red Sticks warriors threatens Jackson's right wing. The Indians are soon driven back by a bayonet charge. Source: 35, 43, 90

January 24, 1814, Battle of Enitachopco—*Alabama*

Andrew Jackson's troops begin a general retreat back toward Enitachopco as Red Sticks warriors harass his flanks and soon make an all-out assault on his forces. Firing intensifies, and the Indians are kept at bay by Craven Jackson and Constantine Perkins, whose cannons rake the charging Indians and stop their onslaught. One hundred and eighty-nine Red Stick bodies are counted on the field. Jackson's losses are twenty killed and seventy-five wounded. Maj. A. Donaldson is killed. Source: 35, 43

January 27, 1814—*Alabama*

Red Sticks ambush Jackson's Georgians on Calebee Creek and nearly break the Americans' line but are driven back by the steady fire of the artillery under Capt. Thomas. A charge is made by the militiamen and troops led by Gen. John Floyd and friendly Tuckabatchee and Coweta Indians led by Timpoochy Barnard. Jackson's cavalry drives the Red Sticks back into Calebee swamp with heavy losses. Fifty Red Sticks/Creeks and seventeen militiamen are killed. Although the Red Sticks suffer major losses, they succeed in stopping Jackson's advance into their nation. Source: 43, 87

March 27, 1814, Battle of Horseshoe Bend—*Alabama*

Loyal Creek, Choctaw, Cherokee and Chickasaw natives, under the command of Gen. Andrew Jackson and U.S. military forces, attack Red Sticks (Upper Creeks) led by William Weatherford at Tohopeka (Horseshoe Bend). Two thousand infantry soldiers, 700 cavalry, 600 Cherokees and some Lower Creeks combine to nearly exterminate the Upper Cherokees/Red Sticks. Hand-to-hand fighting lasts for hours as the Red Sticks attempt to fight their way out, but very few escape. The soldiers and their allies pour volley after volley into the fleeing Indians. At least 800 to 1,000 Red Sticks are killed. Jackson's forces lose forty-nine killed and 154 wounded. Many of the defeated Red Sticks flee to Florida to join the Seminoles. Young Sam Houston is wounded three times. Source: 43, 45, 77, 90. Marker: Horseshoe Bend National Military Park on SR 49, Dadeville, AL.

May 30, 1814—*New York*

Battle of Sandy Creek. British troops open fire on American ships at Sackett's Harbor but are attacked by American troops and Oneida Indians who are hidden in a nearby woods. The British troops, caught totally off guard, are routed and lose over seventy killed. Source: 66

July 21, 1814—*Wisconsin*

American troops attempt to recapture the fort at Prairie du Chien but are attacked and driven off by Indians led by Black Hawk. Thirty-four Americans are killed. Source: 87

> "Where today is the Pequot? Where are the Narragansetts, the Mohawks, the Pokanoket, and many other once powerful tribes of our people? They have vanished before the avarice and the oppression of the white man, as snow before a summer sun."
>
> — Tecumseh, Shawnee Chief
> [Source: 153]

1815

January 8, 1815, Battle of New Orleans—*Louisiana*

Fifty-four hundred American soldiers and Choctaw warriors led by Gen. Andrew Jackson are attacked by British soldiers and Hitchitis Indian allies at the Chalmette Plantation east of New Orleans. The Choctaws are commanded by Maj. Pierre Jugeant, who is part Choctaw. The British forces number some 8,900 and attack across open ground. The British advance is halted by Jackson's infantry and artillery fire. The British suffer a staggering 2,306 killed and wounded while the Americans lose only thirteen killed. This battle ends once and for all Britain's attempt to regain possession of America. Source: 16, 87. Marker: Chalmette National Historic Park, 8606 W. St., Bernard Hwy., Chalmette, LA.

MARCH 22, 1815—*Alabama*

Militiamen burn two deserted Red Stick villages at Emuckfau. Source: 43, 90

1816

SPRING 1816—*Kansas*

Auguste P. Chouteau's hunting party is attacked by over 200 Pawnees and retreat to a small island where they hold the Indians off until the natives finally withdraw. Source: 122. Marker: U.S. 50, roadside turnout one mile west of Lakin in Kearney County, KS.

JULY 26, 1816, BATTLE OF NEGRO FORT—*Florida*

As the War of 1812 comes to a close, British forces turn Fort Apalachicola (also known as Blount's Fort) over to Indians and fugitive slaves who have assisted them during the war. The fort is now referred to as Negro Fort. On orders from Andrew Jackson, American and Creek Indian forces move to destroy the fort. A large force under the command of Lt. Col. Duncan L. Clinch attacks at dawn. American warships bombard the fort from the Apalachicola River, setting the powder magazine on fire. The explosion kills over 270 of the fort's 334 defenders. The Creeks are given over $200,000 for their support. A large number of runaway slaves captured at the fort are returned to their owners. Source: 87, 89, 90. Marker: Located in the Appalachicola National Forest, southeast of Panama City, FL.

1817

NOVEMBER 21, 1817, ATTACK ON FOWLTOWN—*Georgia*

Creek Chief Neamathla warns the U.S. Army not to cross the Clinch River into Spanish territory set aside in the Treaty of 1814 for the Creeks. Maj. David Twiggs and a force of over 250 men are ordered to attack the Cherokee town of Fowltown located across the river. Twiggs' force crosses the Clinch River and drives the Indians into a swamp. Fowltown is burned and looted. In retaliation, Creek Indians ambush a boatload of soldiers on the Apalachicola River, killing or capturing forty-six of the fifty-one on board. Source: 50, 77, 87, 90. Marker: Green Shade Rd., Hwy. 309 in Fowltown, GA.

NOVEMBER 1817, THE FIRST SEMINOLE WAR—*Florida*

U.S. forces led by Gen. Andrew Jackson attack Seminole warriors under Billy Bowlegs at Old Town, driving the warriors back into the swamps. Jackson's forces capture over 300 women and children and several thousand cattle and horses. Source: 77, 87, 90

1817—*Oklahoma*

Osage Indians led by Chief Clermont return to their village after a buffalo hunt to find nearly forty people there have been killed in a Cherokee raid led by John McLamore at Claremore Mound. Over 100 Osage Indians are taken captive by the Cherokees; many are children who are sold into slavery. The Osage, natives to the territory, respond with a raid on Cherokee villages. Many southeast tribes slated to be moved to the Indian territory refuse to go until the Osage problem is resolved by the U.S. government. Source: 86

1818

January 4, 1818—*Georgia*
U.S. forces under Gen. Andrew Jackson burn the deserted Creek town of Fowltown. Source: 90

March 20, 1818—*Georgia*
William Butler, a member of the Georgia state legislature, is killed by Indians at Butler Springs. Source: 141

April 7, 1818—*Florida*
Over 3,500 soldiers and 2,000 Lower Creeks under Gen. Jackson attack Red Stick warriors along the Suwannee River, burning villages and driving the inhabitants off. Source: 50, 77, 87, 90

April 13, 1818—*Florida*
Gen. Jackson leads his forces with Creek allies under William McIntosh against the Red Stick and Seminole warriors under Peter McQueen at Ecofina Creek. The Red Sticks lose over thirty-seven killed while Jackson loses only three killed. Source: 77, 87, 90

April 22, 1818—*Georgia*
A force of 270 men led by Capt. Obed Wright attacks the small Creek town of Cheraw, killing seven adults and two young girls. Source: 87

1823

April 2, 1823—*South Dakota*
William H. Ashley and seventy fur trappers arrive at an Arickara village on the Missouri. After friendly negotiations, they are attacked by the Arickara and withdraw down river with a loss of twelve wounded and twelve dead. Source: 42, 78

May 4, 1823—*Montana*
A group of fur traders led by Andrew Henry is attacked by Blackfeet Indians near Great Falls. Four are killed and mutilated. Source: 42, 78, 87

1823—*Texas*
Stephen Austin hires ten men to act as Rangers for the "common defense" of civilians in the Austin colony. The Texas Rangers become a major force in fighting raiding Indians in Texas. Source: 107

May 31, 1823—*Montana*
Members of the Missouri Fur Company are attacked near the mouth of Pryor's Fork by Piegan Blackfeet Indians. Michael Immel, Robert Jones and several others are killed. Source: 42, 78

June 1–2, 1823—*North Dakota*
Jedediah Smith and ninety men under the command of Gen. W. H. Ashley, with two keelboats of supplies, are attacked by Arikara Indians but escape. A number of Smith's men are killed, including Reed Gibson and John Gardiner. Hugh Glass writes Gardiner's parents, "the deth of yr Son wh befell at the hands if the indians 2nd June ... he lived a little while after he was shot and asked me to inform you of his sad fate." The Arickara Indians fear reprisals and head south to Nebraska where they hide out with the Pawnee Indians for two years. Source: 42, 78 [Quote 42]

June 1823—*South Dakota*
William Ashley's trading party is attacked by Arikara Indians near the Missouri River and Cottonwood Creek, killing Aaron Stephens. Source: 42

August 9, 1823, Attack on Arikara Village—*South Dakota*
On April 2, fur trappers led by William Ashley are invited into an Arikara village where they are attacked, and twelve of the trappers are killed. Ashley vows revenge and on August 9, the Missouri Legion under the command of Gen. Henry Leavenworth, along with Sioux allies, attack the Arikara village on the Missouri River.

The Arikaras put up a stout defense: "We had a lively picture of pandimonium, the wailing of squaws and children, the screams and yelling of men the firing of guns ... awful howling of dogs, the neighing and braying of horses and mules." A great number of Arikara natives are killed, including Chief Grey Eyes. Source: 42, 78, 83 [Quote 83]

NOVEMBER 17, 1823—*Arkansas*

Two hundred Osage Indians led by Mad Buffalo attack a party of white hunters and Quapaw natives, killing and decapitating five. Source: 87

1824

U.S. establishes Fort Towson on the Red River and Fort Gibson on the Arkansas River.

FEBRUARY 1824—*California*

Chumash natives destroy a portion of the Santa Ynez Mission and then attack soldiers at Santa Barbara. Seven Indians and four Spaniards are killed. The leaders of the uprising are executed or sentenced to years of hard labor. Source: 87

MARCH 22, 1824—*Indiana*

Friendly Miamis and Seneca are murdered by a band of white men at Falls Creek. The whites are prosecuted, convicted and hanged, a rare event. Source: 87. Marker: Falls Park, Pendleton, IN.

1824 SUMMER—*Texas*

A Mr. Tomlinson and a friend, Newman, are attacked while traveling near present-day Columbus. Tomlinson is killed, but Newman escapes. Capt. John Tomlinson (brother of the slain man) and several men attack a small party of Waco, killing twelve of thirteen. Source: 69

JUNE 1824—*Texas*

Karankawa Indians are caught skinning a calf near the Colorado River settlements and are pursued by Texas militiamen led by Capt. Robert Kuykendall. Five Indians are killed in the skirmish. The Karankawa sign a treaty agreeing not to come east of the San Antonio River. Source: 107

1826

JULY 2, 1826—*Texas*

Indians attack Gonzales, plundering homes and killing one. The survivors flee to Burnham Station in present-day La Grange on the Colorado River. Moore's Fort is later built on the site. Source: 69, 124, 148. Marker: Gonzales, Texas, St. Louis St. between St. John and Water St.

1827

Fort Vancouver is built by the Hudson's Bay Company.

JUNE 26, 1827—*Wisconsin*

Winnebago Indians attack the cabin of Registre Gagnier, killing him, Solomon Lipcap and scalping Gagnier's infant daughter. Source: 87

AUGUST 18, 1827—*Arizona*

While crossing the Colorado River, Jedediah Smith and several trappers watch helplessly from their boat as a number of their men on shore are killed by Mojave Indians and two of their women are carried off. Source: 42

1828

Fort Union is established in North Dakota.

JULY 14, 1828—*Oregon*

Jedediah Smith and John Turner leave their base camp to select the best route to travel. Smith instructs Harrison Rogers not to allow any Indians near the camp. But Rogers permits a large number of Kelawtset Indians to enter camp. Smith and Rogers return later to find fourteen of their men and one boy killed by the Indians. Source: 4, 42

JULY 1828—*Washington*

After Umpqua Indians kill a group of people from the Hudson Bay Company near Vancouver, the company sends a force to attack their camp, which kills eight natives. The natives trade their one white hostage for a wounded Indian. Source: 87

1829

Fort Pulaski is established in Georgia.

1829—*Wyoming*

Blackfeet or Sioux Indians attack Antonio Mateo's trading post and harass the small fort for over forty days. Source: 87

1830

1830—*Mississippi*

Choctaws sign the Treaty of Dancing Rabbit Creek which cedes over 10.4 million acres in Mississippi and Alabama to the federal government. Chief Greenwood signs under the agreement that the Choctaws can stay in their homeland. Once the treaty is signed, they are removed to the Indian Territory. Source: 43

1830 FALL—*Texas*

Indians raid the Cavina farm near Live Oak Bayou, killing Mrs. Cavina and three of her four daughters. Mr. Cavina, working some distance from the house, goes for help. The Indians then proceed to the Flowers residence, kill Mrs. Flowers and wound her daughter. A pursuit party led by Mr. Cavina catches up with the raiding party and attacks the Indians near the Colorado River, killing over forty of the natives. Source: 69

1831

MAY 27, 1831—*Kansas*

While stopping at a water hole, famed mountain man Jedediah Smith is ambushed and killed by Comanche Indians near present-day Wagon Bed Springs. Smith had been leading a wagon train and had gone ahead to look for water. His guns eventually show up in Santa Fe in the possession of a Mexican trader who had acquired them from Comanche Indians. Source: 42, 122. Marker: K 25, 12 miles south of Ulysses, roadside turnout.

JUNE 26, 1831—*Illinois*

Gen. Edmund Gaines and a 1,500-man militia attacks the Sauk village of Saukenuk at Rock Island after a heavy bombardment. The soldiers find the village empty, Black Hawk and his people having fled the night before. Source: 87

NOVEMBER 21, 1831—*Texas*

One hundred and sixty-four Apaches and Caddo Indians attack a small force that includes Jim and Rezin Bowie, Daniel Buchanan, Cephas D. Hamm, Mathew Doyle, Jessie Wallace, Thomas McCaslin, Robert Armstrong, James Coryell and two slaves. The small force reports over eighty Indians killed near present-day Brady. Source: 69

1832

MAY 14, 1832—*Illinois*

Forty warriors under Black Hawk ambush over 272 militiamen at Dixon's Ferry. The soldiers panic and are chased by only twenty-five Indians. It is a humiliating defeat for Maj. Isaiah Stillman. Black Hawk asks the Ottawa, Chippewa and Potawatomi to join his alliance, but only 120 Kickapoo natives join him. The other tribes decline to join. Source: 87. Marker: Battlefield Memorial Park, SR 72, Stillman Valley, IL.

May 18, 1832—*Illinois*

Six Winnebago Indians ambush four privates carrying mail and military information near Buffalo Grove. Pvt. William Durley is killed and scalped. Source: 87

May 20, 1832—*Illinois*

William Davis, a farmer and blacksmith, dams Indian Creek to provide power for his gristmill although he has been warned by local Indians that the dam cuts off their fishing supply. On May 20, over forty angry Potawatomi natives attack the settlement, killing fifteen settlers and taking two women prisoners. Source: 87

June 16, 1832—*Illinois*

Twenty soldiers led by Col. Henry Dodge track and engage eleven Sac Indians on the Pecatonica River. Samuel Wells, F. Montaville Morris and eleven Sac natives are killed in the engagement. Source: 87

June 16, 1832—*Illinois*

Black Hawk and some of his warriors are pursued by Capt. James Stephenson and his men after stealing some horses from the Apple River fort. After hiding in a thicket the Indians ambush their pursuers, killing three of Stephenson's men. Source: 87

June 24, 1832—*Illinois*

The Apple River fort is attacked by twenty-four Sac Indians, and three white settlers are killed. The Indians burn several cabins and steal some livestock. Source: 87

June 25, 1832—*Illinois*

One hundred warriors led by Black Hawk ambush a party of whites, killing twenty-three at Kellogg's Grove. An army of 1,000 militiamen arrive on the scene too late to do anything more than bury the dead. Among the young volunteers is twenty-three-year-old Abraham Lincoln. Source: 87. Marker: Historical Marker, Kent, IL.

July 2, 1832—*Wyoming*

Gros Ventre Indians attack a supply train heading for Pierre's Hole. Ten horses are stolen. Source: 70

July 18, 1832, Pierre's Hole Fight—*Wyoming*

After leaving the annual rendezvous at Pierre's Hole, Milton Sublette and twenty-eight trappers are attacked by a force of 150 to 200 Gros Ventre Indians. Several of the trappers are dispatched immediately to Pierre's Hole for reinforcements. Sublette and his men battle the Gros Ventre until a relief force of 200 trappers and over 500 Nez Perce and Flathead Indians arrive on the scene. The Gros Ventre Indians withdraw to defensive positions in a nearby swampy area and begin building barricades. A number of charges are attempted by the Nez Perce and Flatheads, but the Gros Ventre hold their positions until nightfall when they withdraw. Five trappers, seven friendly Indians, and over thirty horses are killed. Twenty-six Gros Ventre bodies are found. Source: 57, 70

July 21, 1832—*Wisconsin*

Black Hawk and his followers are trailed by Col. Henry Dodge's militia as they prepare to cross the Wisconsin River. Informed of Black Hawk's movement by a Winnebago spy, Dodge attacks the Sauk and Fox warriors near present-day Madison. Black Hawk's warriors fight a rearguard battle, suffering a number of casualties as over 500 of his tribesmen retreat toward the Mississippi River where they are attacked by soldiers and allied Menominee natives. Source: 87, 99

August 1–2, 1832, Battle of Bad Axe River—*Wisconsin*

Black Hawk and his followers cross the Kickapoo River and reach the Mississippi

River where they are fired on by the steamboat *Warrior,* killing twenty-three natives. The militia skirmishes with Black Hawk's rear guard. Trapped between Col. Dodge's militia on one side and the river on the other side, Black Hawk's warriors have but little choice to fight the next day. The Indians fight with desperation but with little effect as they are fired on from two different sides. Over 150 Indians are killed as they are pushed toward the river. Black Hawk and a band of survivors head north to seek refuge with the Winnebago Indians. Source: 15, 50, 99

> "You have taken me prisoner with all my warriors ... Black Hawk is now a prisoner of the white man. But he can stand torture, and is not afraid to die. He is no coward. Black Hawk is an Indian."
> — Black Hawk
> [Source: 88]

1833

Fort Nisqually is established in Washington State.

1833 — *Texas*

Indians attack the Maden settlement in Houston County, killing seven women and children. Mr. Maden and several men flee a nearby house and hide in the cornfield. Source: 69

1833 — *Texas*

Caranchua Indians demand corn from Daniel Gilleland in Wharton County but are driven off. Gilleland and a number of men pursue the Indians and attack them, killing several. Source: 69

1833 — *Texas*

Indians attack a surveying party near the Leon River near the mouth of Coryelle Creek, killing James Coryelle. Source: 69

1834

Fort Laramie is established in Wyoming. Fort Hall is established in Idaho.

June 1834 — *Idaho*

A party of fur trappers is attacked by Blackfeet Indians on the Snake River. Trapper and journalist Osborne Russell, an eyewitness, notes, "I kept a large German pistol loaded by me in case they should make a charge when my gun was empty ... the Indians stood the fight for about 2 hours then retreated through the brush ... one of our comrades was wounded by 3 balls in 3 places ... another had received a slight groin wound ... we lost 3 horses killed." Source: 92

1835

Fort Vasquez is established in Colorado.

Spring 1835 — *Texas*

When a party of thirteen French and Mexican traders camp within sight of John Castleman's homestead, Castleman advises that they camp nearer to his house for protection against Indians. After the traders laugh off the suggestion, Castleman leaves but soon hears heavy firing from the camp. Indian warriors attack the traders and kill all thirteen. Source: 96

Summer 1835 — *Texas*

James Alexander and his sixteen-year-old son are attacked and killed while hauling goods on the road from Columbus to Bastrop. Source: 69

1835 — *Texas*

Comanche Indians attack the DeWitt Lyon homestead, killing Mr. Lyon and taking his young son captive. The young boy is returned after years with the Indians. Source: 69

1835 — *Texas*

Indians attack Kitchen's Station in Fannin County. Kitchen and several other families are prepared for the attack, which begins at night, and several Indians are killed attempting to get into the house. A Negro who has joined the Indians is killed while trying to enter through a window. Source: 69

1835—*Texas*

Indians ambush David Ridgeway and a companion near Fort Marlin, killing young Ridgeway. Source: 69

SEPTEMBER 1835—*Florida*

Orlando Reeves, while standing guard over sleeping soldiers, is shot and killed by Indians, but young Reeves sounds an alarm before he dies. Legend says that "Orlando's Grave" becomes Orlando, Florida. Source: 87. Marker: Lake Eola Park, Orlando, FL.

SEPTEMBER 8, 1835—*Wyoming*

Joe Meeks, Kit Carson and a dozen trappers fight off an attack by some eighty Blackfeet Indians. Source: 42

DECEMBER 18, 1835—*Florida*

The baggage train of Col. John Warren is attacked by eighty warriors led by Osceola at Kanapaha Prairie. A botched charge by Dr. McLemore's company leads to six soldiers being killed. Three to eight Seminoles are killed. (Also known as the Battle of Black Point.) Source: 65

DECEMBER 25, 1835—*Florida*

The Cruger-DePeyster Plantation, one of a number of sugar plantations near Bulowville, is attacked and burned by Philip and Mikasuki warriors. Source: 65

DECEMBER 28, 1835, DADE MASSACRE—*Florida*

One hundred and seven soldiers marching from Fort Brooke are attacked by Chief Alligator and 180 to 400 Seminoles. Half of the soldiers are killed in the first volley, and by 2 P.M. only five are alive. The Seminoles suffer only three killed. The army's slave-guide, Louis Pacheco, may have told the Seminoles of the planned march, but he escapes during the battle and is never seen again. The bodies of the dead soldiers are buried seven weeks later but are re-interred in 1842 in the National Cemetery in St. Augustine. Source: 5, 50, 55, 65, 77. Marker: Dade Battlefield State Historic Site, CR 603 and 605, Bushnell, FL.

DECEMBER 28, 1835—*Florida*

Indian agent Gen. Wiley Thompson, a U.S. representative from Georgia, and Lt. Constantine Smith are ambushed and killed 300 yards from Fort King by Seminoles under Osceola. Osceola had previously been placed in irons by Thompson and had sworn revenge. Source: 5, 50, 77, 141. Marker: Fort King marker at the NW corner of Ft. King St. and 43rd Ave. In Ocala.

DECEMBER 31, 1835—*Florida*

As U.S. regular soldiers are crossing the Withlacoochee River, the volunteers on the bank are attacked by 150 to 250 Seminole natives and thirty Negroes led by Osceola and Alligator. Four whites are killed and fifty-nine are wounded in the attack. Source: 55, 65

> "You have guns, and so do we. You have powder and lead, and so do we. Your men will fight and so will ours, till the last drop of the Seminole's blood has moistened the dust of his hunting ground."
> —Osceola, Seminole, 1836
> [Source: 88]

1836

JANUARY 6, 1836—*Florida*

Seminole Indians attack the lighthouse at Key Biscayne, killing Mrs. William Cooley, her two children and Joseph Flinton, their tutor. Source: 5, 77

January 17, 1836 — *Florida*

Battle of Dunlawton. One hundred and twenty Seminoles led by Coacoochee attack the Florida Volunteers under Maj. Benjamin A. Putnam at the Andersons' Dunlanton Plantation near St. Augustine. Four of Putnam's men are killed and thirteen are wounded. Source: 65, 77

February 21, 1836 — *Texas*

George Hibbins (Hibbons), his wife, two children and brother-in-law George Creath are attacked by Comanche Indians at their home on Rocky Creek near San Antonio. Mr. Hibbins and Creath are killed. Mrs. Hibbins and her children are taken captive, but on the second day her infant is killed by the Indians when it won't stop crying. She finally escapes to Hornsby's Station. Texas Rangers catch up with the raiding party at Walnut Creek, several Comanches are killed and Mrs. Hibbins' other child is recovered. Source: 69, 107

February 27, 1836 — *Florida*

Maj. Gen. Edmund P. Gaines with 980 men is fired on by over 700 Seminoles from the south bank of the Withlacoochee River. The Indians withdraw quickly. Source: 65, 141

February 28, 1836 — *Florida*

Seminoles fire several shots at soldiers preparing to cross the Withlacoochee River. Lt. James F. Izard is mortally wounded. The fighting lasts from 9 A.M. to 4 P.M. when the Indians withdraw. Source: 87, 141

March 4, 1836 — *Texas*

John Douglas, fleeing from the approaching Mexican Army at San Antonio, sends two of his sons to fetch some oxen which have wandered off. The two youngsters ride some distance from the house when they hear gunfire. After hiding in a thicket for a number of hours, they return to a burning home to find Indians have killed their father, mother, sister, little brother and neighbor Mr. Dougherty and his two daughters. Source: 145

March 6, 1836 — *Texas*

The Mexican Army under Santa Anna, which includes 250 Toluca natives, storms the Alamo killing over 250 of its defenders, including David Crockett, James Bonham, William Barrett Travis and James Bowie. A number of women and children survive. Source: 82

March 15, 1836 — *Florida*

South Carolina volunteers commanded by Brevet Brig. Gen. Abraham Eustis are fired on by Seminole Indians at the St. John River near present-day Astor, killing three of the volunteers and wounding six. Source: 87

March 26, 1836 — *Florida*

Forces under Col. William Lindsay are fired on by Seminole Indians as they march toward Chocachatti. Two soldiers are killed in a bayonet charge on the Indians' position. Source: 65, 105

March 29, 1836 — *Florida*

U.S. troops under Gen. Winfield Scott are fired on by Indians as they cross the Withlacoochee River. Source: 65

March 1836 — *Texas*

Texas Rangers rescue Sarah Hibbins who had been taken captive after a February 21 raid on her home by Comanche Indians. Source: 69, 148

1836 Spring — *Texas*

Joseph Reed is attacked by Indians while looking for cattle on Davidson Creek. Reed is pursued for miles and killed as he reaches his house. Reed's brother and a pursuit party catch up with the raiders and kill several Indians. Reed's brother is also killed. Source: 89

April 5, 1836—*Florida*

Two hundred and fifty Seminoles lay siege to the Cooper encampment, a picket post in the cove of the Withlacoochee River. The Seminoles harass the camp until April 17, when they withdraw. Source: 65, 77

April 14, 1836—*Florida*

A burial party from Fort Barnwell is fired on by Seminoles. One man is killed. Source: 65

April 20, 1836—*Florida*

Seminoles launch a rare night attack on Fort Drane but are driven off. Source: 65

April 27, 1836—*Florida*

Six hundred men under Cols. Chisolm and Foster are fired on as they march toward Fort Alabama. They return fire on the Indians with artillery. Five soldiers are killed. Source: 65, 105

May 1836—*Alabama*

Resentful of white encroachment, Lower Creeks along the Chattahoochee River attack settlements, killing a number of whites and burning homes and barns. They also capture two steamboats. A militia force of settlers and Upper Creeks lead an expedition against the hostiles, and by July the Lower Creeks either surrender or flee to Florida. Source: 87

May 19, 1836—*Texas*

Comanche warriors attack Parker's Fort on the Navosota River near Mexia, killing Benjamin Parker and a number of settlers. Nine-year-old Cynthia Ann Parker is carried off. (Years later Cynthia will give birth to a son, Quanah Parker, who will become chief of the Comanche and who will wage war long after other tribes have surrendered.) Source: 32, 89, 124. Marker: Fort Parker Historical Park, off SH 1245 on Park Rd. 35, north of Groesbeck.

May 22, 1836—*Florida*

South Carolina volunteers led by Brevet Brig. Gen. Abraham Eustis are fired on while crossing the St. John River. Three men are killed and six wounded. Source: 141

June 9, 1836—*Florida*

Seminoles under Osceola are driven from the woods surrounding Fort Defiance by an infantry and cavalry charge directed by Lt. Thompson B. Wheeler. Source: 65

July 9, 1836—*Florida*

Sixty-two men and twenty-two wagons of supplies under Capt. William Maitland are fired on by Seminoles while en route to Fort Defiance. A second force drives the Indians off. Source: 65

July 23, 1836—*Florida*

The lighthouse at Cape Florida is attacked by Seminole Indians and set on fire. Keeper John Thompson and his slave Carter climb ninety feet up to avoid burning alive. On the outer planking Carter is killed, and Thompson is shot over six times in both feet. He is rescued the next day by a passing ship. Source: 5, 50, 65. Marker: Cape Florida, Key Biscayne, FL.

July 28, 1836—*Florida*

As Lt. Alfred Herbert's boat nears the Travers Plantation, it is attacked by Seminole Indians. The whites open up with buckshot, killing several Indians. Source: 65

August 21, 1836—*Florida*

Abandoned Fort Drane is taken over by Osceola's Seminoles and fugitive slaves. The fort is attacked by forces led by Maj. B. K. Pierce. Pierce is unable to dislodge the Indians and withdraws. Source: 55, 65

September 18, 1836—*Florida*

In a ninety-minute battle near Gainesville, 100 men of the Florida militia led by

Col. John Warren hold off an attack by Seminoles, who completely surround his force. Source: 65

OCTOBER 8, 1836—*Florida*

The schooner *Mary* is captured and burned by warriors. Source: 65

OCTOBER 13, 1836—*Florida*

Gen. Richard Call's forces attack fifty Indians near Fort Drane, killing fourteen. Source: 65

NOVEMBER 17, 1836—*Florida*

Gen. Thomas S. Jesup commanding the Tennessee Volunteer Brigade, Florida militia and some regulars attacks a camp of Seminoles on the Withlacoochee River. Over twenty Indians are killed. Source: 55, 65

NOVEMBER 18, 1836—*Florida*

A military force under Gen. Richard K. Call charges over 600 Seminoles on the Withlacoochee River. After a thirty-minute battle the Indians withdraw. Three soldiers are killed, and the Indians reportedly lose twenty-five killed. Source: 5, 55, 65. Marker: Located on north side of CR 48 east of Bushnell, FL.

NOVEMBER 21, 1836—*Florida*

Gen. Richard Call's forces attack over 420 Seminoles and 200 fugitive slaves; fifteen soldiers are killed and thirty wounded at Wahoo Swamp five miles from the Dade battleground. Twenty-five Seminoles are killed. Source: 5, 55, 65

1837

Fort Inglish is established in Texas.

JANUARY 17, 1837—*Florida*

The St. Augustine militia catches up with Seminole natives who have been raiding plantations on the peninsula's east coast. Among the Seminole dead is leader John Caesar, probably a fugitive Negro slave. Source: 77

JANUARY 23, 1837—*Florida*

Near Lake Apopka, U.S. Army forces led by Gen. Thomas Sidney Jesup attack Seminoles under Chief Osuchee, killing four including Osuchee. Source: 77, 87

JANUARY 27, 1837—*Florida*

A 1,000-man force under Gen. Thomas Jesup encounter a Seminole force under Alligator, Jumper and Micanopy near Lake Tohopekaliga. A charge by Alabama volunteers overruns the Seminole camp, killing over twenty-eight Indians. Source: 65, 77

FEBRUARY 8, 1837—*Florida*

Seminoles attack Ft. Mellon on Lake Munro, killing Capt. Charles Mellon and wounding fifteen soldiers. Gunfire from the fort drives the Indians off after a three-hour fight. Source: 5, 87. Marker: Located on the NE corner of Mellonville Ave. and 2nd St., Sanford, FL.

FEBRUARY 9, 1837—*Florida*

Capt. George W. Allen leads a force from Company K of the 4th U.S. Infantry against Seminole warriors on Clear River, killing one officer. Source: 87

APRIL 1837—*Montana*

Trapper Joe Meeks' Indian wife, Umentucken, is killed by Blackfeet Indians near Pierre's Hole. Source: 42

1837—*Texas*

James Goacher, his wife, son and son-in-law are killed by Indians in Bastrop County. His daughter and infant son are carried off by the Indians. Source: 69

1837—*Texas*

Manuel Flores, an agent for the Mexican government, meets with the Taovayas Indians and offers them "arms, ammunition and plunder" if they will continue their raids on Texas settlements. The Taovayas agree but are soon devastated by a drought which causes a major crop failure and an epidemic which kills a large number of the natives. Pawnee raids take another toll on the village. Source: 43, 107

SEPTEMBER 9, 1837—*Florida*

Three companies of the 2nd Dragoons and two companies of Florida volunteers capture a Seminole village (the ruined Dunlawton Plantation) near Port Orange. Among the captured are Seminole Chief King Philip, his son Coacoochee and Tomoka John. Lt. John Winfield Scott McNeil is killed. Seminole leaders Yuchi Billy and his brother Jack are also captured. Source: 65, 77. Marker: Sugar Mill Garden is located on Sugar Mill Rd., one mile west of U.S. 1, Port Orange.

DECEMBER 25, 1837 BATTLE OF OKEECHOBEE—*Florida*

One thousand and thirty-two soldiers commanded by Zachary Taylor along with 180 Missouri volunteers, seventy Shawnee and Delaware, and over 480 other Indians led by Sam Jones attack Seminoles near Lake Okeechobee. The battle lasts over two hours, but the Seminoles finally retreat toward the lake, leaving eleven dead on the field. Taylor loses 26 dead and 112 wounded. Source: 50, 65, 77. Marker: Located on Hwy. 441 S., Okeechobee, FL.

1838

Fort Jupiter is built in Florida.

JANUARY 15, 1838—*Florida*

Eighty seaman led by U.S. Navy Lt. Levi Powell attack eighty Seminoles by boat at Jupiter Creek but are driven back. Four officers are wounded. Source: 65

JANUARY 24, 1838, BATTLE OF LOXAHATCHEE—*Florida*

Twelve hundred soldiers commanded by Maj. Gen. Thomas Jesup attack Seminoles in a cypress swamp. Supported by artillery fire, Jesup's men push the warriors out of their village. Seven soldiers are killed and thirty-one wounded. Source: 65, 77

MARCH 22, 1838—*Florida*

Lt. Col. James Bankhead and the 4th Artillery battle Seminoles near Ft. Lauderdale. Source: 65

APRIL 24, 1838—*Florida*

Lt. Col. William Harney leading fifty dragoons and fifty artillerymen attack a Seminole camp south of Ft. Lauderdale. The warriors withdraw, leaving one Seminole dead. Source: 65, 77

SPRING 1838—*Texas*

A group of men led by Robert Sloan and Nathaniel T. Journey attacks an Indian camp at present-day Arlington, killing several Indians and recapturing a number of horses. Source: 69. Marker: Arlington Mosier Valley Rd. & FM 157, Arlington, TX.

MAY 23, 1838, TRAIL OF TEARS BEGINS—*Oklahoma*

The government begins its roundup and removal of all southeastern Cherokees who will be marched to the Indian Territory in present-day Oklahoma. Source: 86, 90

MAY 27, 1838—*Florida*

Capt. Sandelung, commanding forty militiamen, skirmishes with Indians near Okefenokee Swamp close to the Georgia-Florida border. Two soldiers are wounded. Source: 65

SUMMER 1838—*Oklahoma*

Cheyenne and Arapaho Indians attack and kill a Comanche-Kiowa buffalo hunting party between Beaver Creek and Wolf Creek in northwest Oklahoma. The Cheyenne-Arapaho war party then attacks the nearby Comanche-Kiowa camp, killing over fifty-eight natives and losing fourteen of their own war party. A nearby detachment of U.S. Dragoons along with friendly Osage Indians drive the war party off. Source: 124

June 4, 1838—*Florida*

Seminoles battle dragoons and attempt to burn the bridge across the Withlacoochee River. Fort Dade is set on fire. Source: 65

June 17, 1838—*Florida*

Thirty soldiers of the Second Dragoons led by Captain L. J. Beall are fired on by Seminoles, wounding six of the soldiers. Source: 87

July 13, 1838—*Florida*

Mr. and Mrs. Singletary and two of their children are killed by four Indians and one Negro in Jefferson County. Source: 87

August 10, 1838—*Texas*

Twenty-one men under Col. Karnes are attacked by fifty Comanche Indians near Arroyo Seco. Karnes is wounded, and the Comanche withdraw. Source: 87

August 28, 1838—*Idaho*

Fur trapper and journalist Osborne Russell and a companion are attacked by Blackfeet Indians on the Snake River near Lewis' Fork. Russell and his fellow trapper make a run for it through a hail of arrows. Russell is struck by an arrow in the hip: "another arrow struck me in the same place ... the Indian who shot me was within 8 ft ... and sprang forward with uplifted battleaxe ... I made a leap and avoided the blow." Russell and his companion escape through the tangled underbrush, leaving behind all their supplies. Source: 92

1838—*Texas*

A wagon train is attacked by Indians near the San Gabriel River, killing all thirteen men of the group. Mrs. James Webster and her infant child are taken hostage. Source: 69

October 5, 1838—*Texas*

Eighteen people at the Killough family homestead are killed by Indians in Cherokee County. Seven women and children are carried off and never heard from again. Cherokee natives are believed to be responsible for the massacre. Source: 89, 109. Marker: Located at FM 3431 & FM 3411 on Killough Creek, 7 miles northwest of Jacksonville, TX.

October 16, 1838—*Texas*

Two hundred men under Gen. T. J. Rusk attack a force of Mexicans and Comanche near Fort Houston on the Trinity River. Rusk and his men rout the Mexicans and Comanche in a running fight, killing over eleven; the rest flee to Mexico. Source: 87, 109

October 20, 1838—*Texas*

A surveying party is attacked by Comanche as they work some five miles from San Antonio. Nearby residents ride out to see what is going on and are attacked by 100 warriors and lose eight killed. Source: 87

1839

Sutter's Fort is established in California.

February 15, 1839, Rangers and Apaches vs. Comanches—*Texas*

Near the end of January a large Comanche village is discovered by Lipan Apaches about fifty miles northwest of Waterloo. The Lipan Apaches, enemies of the Comanche, ride to nearby white settlements on the Colorado River for reinforcements. At daybreak on February 15,

Col. Moore, sixty-three Rangers and sixteen friendly Lipan Apaches and Tonkawa Indians led by Col. Castro attack the sleeping Comanche camp. The Rangers rush into camp, open the flaps of the teepees and shoot the Indians as they try to climb out of their buffalo robes. The Comanche warriors flee to a nearby ravine where they regroup and countercharge, arching their arrows into the Rangers. Soon the Rangers find themselves outnumbered, but even with their superior firepower, the Comanche once again are forced to retreat to safety. The fight is a draw, and the Comanche pick up their dead and withdraw from the field. Source: 69, 89, 107

February 24, 1839, Battle of Brushy Creek—*Texas*

A force of 100 to 300 Comanche attack the homestead of widow Elizabeth Coleman, killing her and several others. After ransacking the settlement, the warriors ride off with one woman, five children, an old man and several slaves. A force of fifty-two from Well's Fort is soon in pursuit and catches up with the fleeing warriors at Brushy Creek. The Comanche prove too much for the small Ranger force, and the Rangers soon withdraw, leaving several dead on the field. The Rangers attempt a surprise dawn attack the next day on the Comanche camp but find no one there, the warriors having slipped away in the night. Source: 96, 107, 148. Marker: Located on private property off Cir. G Ranch Rd., just to the west of Texas 195, four miles south of Taylor, TX.

March 24, 1839—*Oklahoma*

Trail of Tears. The last group of Cherokees arrives in Oklahoma, but more than 3,000 have died on the trail. (Many other tribes are shipped west through the years. The last known group, Choctaws, was sent to Oklahoma in 1901.) Source: 86, 90

March 29, 1839—*Texas*

At Seguin, over eighty volunteers commanded by General Edward Burleson defeat Vicente Córdova and seventy-five Mexicans, Indians and Negroes, thus ending the "Córdova Rebellion." A letter found on the body of Manuel Flores states that the Mexican government has encouraged Indians to attack white settlements. The Mexican government encourages uprisings among the Native Americans and Mexican population against the new Texas republic. (Texas had declared independence from Mexico in 1836.) Source: 96, 107, 109, 148

May 26, 1839—*Texas*

After a small group of Indians run a buffalo herd through a Ranger camp, they withdraw but are pursued by the Rangers. The Rangers led by Capt. John Bird chase the warriors for several miles until they run into a huge war party that counterattack the Rangers at Bird Creek. The thirty-four-man Texas Rangers force retreats to a nearby ravine where they hold off over 240 Indians and suffer seven killed. The warriors finally withdraw with their dead. Bird, Sgt. William Weaver, Jesse E. Nash, H. M. C. Hall and Thomas Gay are killed. Capt. Nathan Brookshire assumes command. Source: 69, 107, 148

July 15, 1839—*Texas*

Texas forces under Gen. K. H. Douglas attack Cherokees near the Council Grounds; over eighteen Indians and three soldiers are killed. Source: 69, 96, 109

July 15–16, 1839, Battle of the Neches River—*Texas*

Cherokee natives led by Chief Bowles camp along the Neches River in present-day Van Zandt County. Texas forces sent by Texas President Mirabeau Bonaparte attack the Cherokees, killing Chief Bowles. The Cherokee force consists of over 800 warriors while the Texas force is about 500. Source: 69, 107, 109, 148

July 23, 1839—*Florida*

Col. William S. Harney and a party of soldiers and civilians are attacked at the Caloosahatchee trading post on the Seminole reservation. Sixteen soldiers are killed, many while still in their beds. Harney and several others escape by swimming up the Caloosahatchee River. Source: 65, 77

1840

February 5, 1840—*Texas*

Christopher Staley is killed by Indians near Fort Boggy in Leon County. Source: 124. Marker: I-45 south from Centerville, south about five miles to rest area on the south side of the highway.

March 19, 1840, Council House Fight—*Texas*

Over sixty Penateka Comanche arrive in San Antonio to negotiate the release of some fifteen white captives held by the Indians. The Comanche bring only two captives, but it is the disfigurement of sixteen-year-old Matilda Lockhart that sends the Texans into a rage. Seeing her battered, bruised, scarred face with a nose that has almost been burned off, Texas officials order the arrest of some thirty chiefs. A general melee breaks out as the Indians attempt to fight their way out, and the courtyard becomes a battle zone as both sides fire point-blank into each other. One warrior takes shelter in a nearby house, which is set on fire. As the smoke clears, over thirty Indians lie dead, including twelve chiefs. The Texas dead include Sheriff Julian Hood, Judge Thompson and eight others. Word is sent to the tribe to release the captives or else face further reprisals. In retaliation over thirteen captives being held by the Comanche are brutally tortured and killed, several by being burned to death. Comanche Chief Buffalo Hump vows revenge. Source: 69, 89, 107, 109, 124, 148. Marker: Casa Reales Historic Site, Main Plaza off Market St., San Antonio, TX.

March 28, 1840—*Florida*

While scouting near Fort King, sixteen men under the command of Capt. Gabriel J. Rains are ambushed by ninety Seminole warriors, killing two of the soldiers. Rains and his men fight their way back to the fort. Source: 65

May 19, 1840—*Florida*

At Levy's Prairie eight miles from Micanopy over 100 Seminole Indians led by Coacoochee attack soldiers commanded by Lt. James Sanderson, killing him and five soldiers. Source: 65, 77

June 2, 1840—*Florida*

Forces led by Lt. Col. Bennett Riley attack the Seminole village at Chocachatti, killing several and destroying the village. Source: 65

July 4, 1840—*Texas*

Capt. J. R. Cunningham and nineteen volunteers attack Indians near the Frio and Leona Rivers, killing several Indians and burning their property. Source: 107

August 5, 1840—*Texas*

On their way to Gonzales, Tucker Foley and Dr. Joel Ponton are attacked west of Ponton's Creek. Ponton escapes into a thicket and watches as Foley is tortured and killed. The Indians are later pursued by an armed group of settlers who kill several of the warriors. Source: 69, 107

August 6–7, 1840, Battle of Victoria—*Texas*

After an unsuccessful attack in Victoria on the day before, Comanche under Buffalo Hump attack Victoria again, but the small town delivers a blistering defense.

After looting several stores but unable to burn the town, the Comanche pull off. They now begin a widespread attack on south Texas settlements, looting, killing and burning anything and everything in their path. They next attack settlers at nearby Peach Creek. Source: 32, 124, 148. Marker: DeLeon Plaza in downtown Victoria, TX.

AUGUST 7, 1840—*Florida*

Seminoles led by Chakaika attack Lower Key Island in the middle of the Florida Keys, killing over seventy residents and burning their homes. Among the dead is Dr. Henry Perrine, a botanist who has come to the Keys to research native plants. Perrine's wife and children escape by hiding under their burning house. Source: 77, 105, 148

AUGUST 8, 1840, ATTACK ON LINNVILLE, TEXAS—*Texas*

After their unsuccessful attack on Victoria the day before, the Comanche attack Linnville. Hugh Oran Watts is killed while returning to his house for a watch. The Indians slaughter large numbers of cattle and hogs and destroy over $300,000 worth of trade goods. The Comanche under Buffalo Hump raid the stores of Linnville, taking hats, cloth and umbrellas. A Mrs. Crosby, said to be Daniel Boone's granddaughter, is carried off by the Comanche and her baby is killed along with two whites and two Negroes. Buffalo Hump, now arrogant and bold, turns north and heads home toward the Colorado River straight through the more densely populated white settlement areas. Linnville never recovers and is soon abandoned as a town. Source: 32, 69, 89, 107, 148. Marker: Three and a half miles from Port Lavaca, TX.

AUGUST 12, 1840, BATTLE OF PLUM CREEK—*Texas*

A large force that includes "Bigfoot" Wallace, Mathew Caldwell, John Moore and Edward Burleson and other seasoned Comanche fighters heads toward Plum Creek to cut off Buffalo Hump and his Comanche raiding party. A force of U.S. Cavalry under the command of Lt. Owens harasses the retreating Indians' rear. Brig. Gen. Felix Huston takes command of the growing army, which now includes the Bastrop militia and Chief Placido of the Tonkawa. At Plum Creek they attack the Comanche war party. The Texans plunge into the Comanche Indians who are dressed in top hats, women's clothes and other goods taken in the Linnville raid. The panic-stricken Comanche now endeavor to escape, and many are shot out of the saddle by the heavily armed Texans. The Texans and Tonkawa pursue and crowd the fleeing Comanche, and in a running fight over fifteen miles the Comanche begin killing their captives, including the granddaughter of Daniel Boone whose body is found tied to a tree and shot full of arrows. In the evening fires the Tonkawa butcher and roast the arms and legs of the dead Comanche. Source: 32, 69, 89, 96, 107, 109, 124, 148. Marker: Near intersection of U.S. 183 and Texas 142 in Lion's Park, Lockhart, TX.

1840—*California*

Ute Indians led by Walkara and a mountain man named Pegleg Smith raid San Luis Obispo, stealing over 1,200 horses. Source: 87

1840 FALL—*Texas*

A Comanche raiding party steals a number of horses near San Antonio. A pursuit party led by Capt. Jack Hays catches up with the raiders, killing several warriors including the chief. Source: 148

OCTOBER 23, 1840—*Texas*

A mounted force of over ninety men led by Col. John H. Moore and friendly Lipan Apaches attack a large camp of Comanche near the Concho River. Men, women and children flee toward the river, but Lt. Owen and fifteen men fire from the other side, killing indiscriminately. Forty-eight Indians are killed in the village, and eighty more are shot or drowned at the river. Thirty-four Indians are taken prisoner by Moore's men, but seven escape during the night. Source: 32, 69, 87

DECEMBER 1840—*Florida*

Ninety men under the command of Lt. Col. William S. Harney attack Chekika's Seminole camp at sunrise, killing four warriors including Chekika and capturing thirty-six warriors. Four of the natives are hanged. Source: 32, 65, 148

DECEMBER 28, 1840—*Florida*

A party of thirteen including Lt. Walter Sherwood and Lt. Montgomery's wife are attacked by thirty Miccosukee Indians four miles from Fort Wacahoota. Sherwood, Mrs. Montgomery and four soldiers are killed. Source: 65, 77

1841

JANUARY 1841—*Florida*

At Fort Walker slaves are attacked by Seminoles while working in a nearby field; six are killed. Source: 87

JANUARY 9, 1841—*Texas*

Judge James Smith and his son are out riding when they are attacked by Indians. Smith is caught and killed, and his son is taken hostage. Source: 69, 109

SPRING 1841, BATTLE OF BANDERA PASS—*Texas*

Texas Rangers under John Coffee Hays are ambushed by a large force of Comanche warriors near present-day Bandera. The Indians hide their horses in the hills north of the pass and conceal themselves as the Rangers approach from the south. Caught totally off guard, the Rangers suffer several killed and wounded, but Hayes, cool and collected, regroups his men and begins pouring a deadly volley into the oncoming warriors. Hand-to-hand fighting ensues, and the Comanche begin to suffer heavy casualties and withdraw from the field. The Rangers lose five killed and six wounded. The Comanche war party losses are estimated at sixty killed and wounded. Source: 32, 69, 70, 96, 107. Marker: Ten miles from the town of Bandera on FM 689 and intersection with Hwy. 16.

MARCH 2, 1841—*Florida*

Near Fort Brooks in Putnam County, U.S. soldiers under Lt. William Alburtis fight two skirmishes with Seminoles, losing three soldiers. Source: 87

AUGUST 30, 1841—*Texas*

Kiowa and Arapaho warriors attack and kill all members of a Pawnee party at White Bluff on the upper Canadian River but are soon attacked themselves by U.S. troops who lose five men in the battle. Source: 87

NOVEMBER 1841—*Florida*

Troops led by Capt. R. D. A. Wade attack two Seminole camps, killing eight Indians and capturing forty-eight at Lake Worth. Source: 87

DECEMBER 20, 1841—*Florida*

Seminoles led by Billy Bowlegs (Boleck) skirmish with soldiers under Maj. William Belknap in the Great Cypress Swamp in the Everglades. A few casualties and several prisoners taken are reported. Source: 65

1842

Fort Bridger is founded in Wyoming. Fort Scott is founded in Kansas.

JANUARY 25, 1842—*Florida*

Miccosukee warriors led by Halleck Tustenuggee attack the settlement at Mandarin, killing four settlers and burning several buildings. Source: 65

APRIL 19, 1842—*Florida*

Four hundred men led by Col. William Jenkins Worth attack a redoubt at Lake Ahapopka defended by over forty Seminoles, who retreat under heavy fire. Three Seminoles and one soldier are killed. Source: 55, 65

MAY 17, 1842—*Florida*

Creeks and Seminoles raid along the Suwannee River at Blue Peter Springs, killing several settlers and burning a home. They then ambush a patrol, killing two soldiers. Source: 87

SUMMER 1842—*Wyoming*

Fur trappers led by Henry Fraeb, along with friendly Shoshones are attacked by Sioux or Cheyenne Indians near the Snake River. Fraeb and several trappers are killed. Source: 29, 42

1842 FALL—*Texas*

A group of Indians approach Judge Jaynes' house near Austin and begin talking with him. The Indians then attempt to pull Jaynes' young son from his arms. Jaynes is killed while attempting to get into his house. A hired hand is also killed by the Indians. Source: 69, 109

1842 WINTER—*Texas*

A war party raids the farm of Michael Young, but he and fourteen men attack and pursue the warriors, killing five Indians. Source: 69

1843

DECEMBER 1843—*Texas*

Chief Narshatowey and forty Wacos raid a number of ranches along the Little River in Milam County, killing one slave and stealing twelve horses. Source: 148

1844

APRIL 1844—*California*

The Hernandez family is attacked at a place called the Archilette, or Resting Springs, and four of the six are killed. Andres Fuentes and eleven-year-old Pablo Hernandez survive the attack and are later found by an expedition led by Kit Carson. Carson and Alexis Godey track the raiding party, kill several Indians and recover a number of horses. Source: 29

1844—*Washington*

Salish Indians fire on Fort Nisqually but are driven off. Source: 87

JUNE 9, 1844—*Texas*

Near the Pedernales River fifty miles north of Seguin fifteen Texas Rangers led by Capt. John Coffee Hays are attacked by eighty to over 100 Comanche and Waco Indians led by Yellow Wolf. The Rangers are armed with the new five-shot Colt pistols. Hays' men charge in among the Indians and fight hand-to-hand. The Rangers kill twenty-three Indians and badly wound over thirty. Source: 22, 69, 96, 148

1844—*Oregon*

After their fight with Indians in California in April, the Fremont-Carson expedition arrives at Klamath Lake in Oregon. The party is attacked by Klamath Indians. Basil Lajeunesse, a man named Crane and a Delaware Indian known as Denny are killed. A Klamath chief is killed in the fight. The expedition leaves the area but is followed by Klamath warriors who are ambushed by Delaware Indians with the expedition. Source: 29

AUGUST 1844—*Texas*

Four Texas Rangers are attacked in Nueces Canyon while looking for Indians. Rangers Kit Ackland and Rufus Perry are shot and wounded while swimming but survive by hiding in the brush. Rangers

James Dunn and John Carlin make it to San Antonio where they get help and return to the canyon, rescuing Ackland and Perry. Source: 96

1846

Fort Benton is established in Montana by the American Fur Company. Fort Polk is founded in Texas. Fort Wingate is established in New Mexico.

APRIL 1846—*California*

A party of men led by John C. Fremont and Kit Carson attack a large party of Indians several miles from the Peter Lassen ranch. Fremont and Carson report that their force of thirty-six men attacked over 3,000 Indians killing 175. Source: 29

MAY 8–9, 1846—*Oregon*

A surveying party led by John Fremont is attacked by Klamath Indians who want the party's horses. Three of Fremont's men are killed, and the survivors led by Kit Carson track the Klamaths. On May 13, Carson and his men attack and burn a Klamath village. Source: 4, 87

1846—*Texas*

Comanche Indians attack and kill M. F. H. Golled, Joe Jonnes, Vincent Jonnes and twelve-year-old Joe Bassiel while they sleep in their camp above Castroville. Nichalus Haby discovers the snow covered bodies while hunting. Source: 96

1847

JANUARY 19, 1847—*New Mexico*

Bent Massacre. Several people including Gov. Bent are killed by Pueblo Indians under Chief Tomasito. Bent's wife, Kit Carson's wife and several others escape. Source: 42, 87

FEBRUARY 3, 1847—*New Mexico*

U.S. troops attack Taos Pueblo with several six-pounder cannons to avenge the death of Gov. Bent. Source: 42

SUMMER 1847—*Oregon*

During the summer of 1847 Modoc Indians attack a number of wagon trains, killing twenty-four settlers. Source: 87

NOVEMBER 29, 1847, WHITMAN MISSION MASSACRE—*Washington*

The Whitman Mission at Waiilatpu (Place of Rye Grass) is attacked by Cayuse Indians. Dr. Marcus Whitman, his wife, Narcissa, and twelve others are brutally murdered by the Indians who believe Whitman is responsible for a measles outbreak which has taken a bad toll on their village. The Indians also take fifty captives of whom forty-seven will later be released. (Cayuse Chief Tiloukaikt will later be hanged for his part in the massacre.) Source: 42, 57, 150. Marker: Whitman Mission National Historic Site, 7 miles west of Walla Walla, WA.

1847—*Texas*

Indian raiders steal stock from German immigrants near Castroville. A tracking party sent to recover the stock finds the Indians in camp at Quihi Lake, kills several of the raiders and recovers their stock. In retaliation for the attack the Indians begin a number of raids on Castroville, killing several settlers. Source: 96

DECEMBER 1847—*Texas*

Four settlers from Castroville go up the Medina River to start a homestead but are killed in their camp while they sleep by Indians. The dead men are reported as F. H. Gullett, Vincient Chan, Joe Chan and a young man named Bassalle. Source: 96

DECEMBER 24, 1847—*Washington*

Fur trapper Peter Skene Ogden and several men travel to the scene of the Whitman Massacre to try to obtain the release of the white missionaries taken prisoner in the assault. He arranges a meeting with the chiefs of Walla Walla, Nez Perce and Cayuse Indians who are impressed with his bravery, and forty-seven captives are released to him. Source: 42

1848

Fort McIntosh and Fort Leaton are established in Texas.

January 8, 1848 — *Oregon*

Cayuse and Tenino Indians are pursued by seventeen militiamen after stealing a herd of cattle at the Dalles. In a three hour fight three natives are killed, but the Indians withdraw with the cattle. The Cayuse begin a series of raids, killing a number of settlers. Source: 87

January 29, 1848 — *Oregon*

Scouts led by Maj. Henry A. G. Lee skirmish with Cayuse Indians on the Deschutes River. Source: 87

January 1848 — *Texas*

Indians raid the homestead of Rudolph Charobiny, carry his wife off and kill her brother. Mrs. Charobiny later escapes but is shot with several arrows in the process. Source: 96

February 24, 1848 — *Oregon*

Three commissioners attempt to negotiate with a force of Cayuses, Coeur d'Alenes and Pend d'Oreilles near Wells Springs. Shamans Grey Eagle and Five Crows attack the commissioners and the 300 militiamen under the command of Col. Cornelius Gilliam. Capt. Thomas McKay shoots Grey Eagle and Baptiste Dorion bludgeons him to death. The Indians attempt several charges on the militiamen but are driven off by a nine-pounder cannon. Source: 87

June 18, 1848 — *Kansas*

Two hundred Comanche and Osage Indians clash with 140 U.S. troops under the command of Lt. Phillip Stremmel at Coon Creek in southwest Kansas. Howitzers and the army's new breech loading carbines drive the Indians from the field. Troops under the command of Lt. William B. Royal pursue the fleeing Indians but are surrounded several miles away. The Indians' weapons are no match for the army's new carbines, and they withdraw. Only four troopers are wounded; Indian casualties are unknown. Source: 131. Marker: Two miles east of Kinsley at Oak River Bridge on U.S. 50 in Edwards County.

October 8, 1848 — *Texas*

Dr. George Washington Barnett, a member of the Texas Republic Senate, is killed by Lipan Apaches while deer hunting near Gonzales. The war party also kills a young man named Vivian on the San Antonio road near Ecleto Creek. Source: 69, 124, 141. Marker: Old City Cemetery, N. College St., Gonzales, TX.

1849

Fort Yuma, Arizona, is established. Forts Worth, Graham and Bliss are established in Texas.

July 13, 1849 — *Florida*

Renegade Seminoles kill James Barker and wound William Russell at Little Trout Eating Creek four miles north of Fort Pierce. Seminole chiefs, fearful of military reprisals, send out search parties to apprehend the murderers. Source: 77, 87

July 17, 1849 — *Florida*

Renegade Seminoles attack and burn the trading post at Little Trout Eating Creek, killing Capt. George S. Payne and Dempsey Whidden. William McCulloch escapes with his wife and child. Source: 87

October 1849 — *New Mexico*

Jicarilla Apache kill a Mrs. White, Mr. Lawberger and several other members of a wagon train near Rock Creek. Source: 87

1850

Fort Atkinson is founded in Kansas.

April 7, 1850—*Texas*

The 1st Infantry under the command of Lt. Walter W. Hudson tracks and attacks Indians who have stolen about 30 horses. Four Indians are wounded in the fight, but Hudson is mortally wounded and dies on April 19. Source: 73

April 21, 1850—*California*

A party of settlers refuse to pay John Glanton's ferry fees and build their own boat to cross the Colorado River. After crossing the river the emigrants give the boat to Quechan Indians who begin their own ferry business. Glanton and several men attack the Indians' ferry dock, killing one native and burning the boat. The Indians later attack Glanton and his men while they are sleeping, killing all of them. Several of Glanton's men downriver escape the massacre and flee to a Mexican settlement. Source: 73

May 15, 1850, Battle of Bloody Island—*California*

U.S. troops under the command of Brevet Capt. Nathaniel Lyon attack Pomo Indians encamped on an island at Clear Lake. Many of the villagers drown while trying to escape while others are shot down. The attack is retaliation for the murder of two whites. Over sixty Indians are believed to have been killed. Source: 87

May 1850—*New Mexico*

Jicarilla Apache and Ute Indians attack a train of U.S. mail wagons near Santa Fe, killing ten whites and all of the animals. Source: 73

June 12, 1850—*Texas*

A U.S. mail detachment escorted by U.S. Cavalry under Lt. Charles N. Underwood is attacked near Laredo by Comanche. Underwood and three of the soldiers are wounded, and four are killed. Source: 73

1851

Fort Belknap, Fort Phantom Hill and Fort Mason are established in Texas. Fort Union is established in New Mexico.

January 1851—*California*

Over 300 Tulare Indians attack and kill thirteen vaqueros herding cattle near present-day Bakersfield. The Tulares then attack the nearby French Ranch but are driven off by the ranch hands. Source: 73

March 19, 1851, Oatman Massacre—*Arizona*

After leaving a wagon train the Royse Oatman family is attacked by Yavapai Indians near Gila Bend. Mr. and Mrs. Oatman and four of their children are killed. Olive, fourteen, and Mary Ann, seven, are taken captive. Mary Ann dies the following year, but Olive is held captive for over five years before being rescued. Source: 73

June 1851—*Oregon*

Rogue Indians ambush twenty-six whites south of the Rogue River Ford. Source: 4

June 2, 1851—*Oregon*

Miners are attacked by Rogue Indians near Bear Creek, and the fight lasts for hours. Seven Indians are killed. Mules and horses packed with gold are taken by the Indians. Source: 4

June 10, 1851—*Oregon*

Rogue Indians attack Capt. William Tichenor and his men near Port Orford after they put ashore from the *Sea Gull*. A cannon blast from the boat drives the Indians off and kills seventeen natives. Source: 4

JUNE 17, 1851—*Oregon*

Shasta Indians attack a pack train between Indian Creek and Scott River, killing three of the packers. Rogue Indians also attack twenty-eight soldiers under the command of Maj. Philip Kearny on the Rogue River. Capt. James Stuart is killed. Source: 4

JUNE 23-26, 1851—*Oregon*

Volunteers led by Maj. Philip Kearny fight a number of skirmishes with Rogue Indians in the Rogue Valley. Joseph Lane, second in command, reports fifty Indians killed. Source: 4

SEPTEMBER 14, 1851—*Oregon*

A party of whites scouting a route from Port Orford to Fort Umpqua is attacked by Coquille Indians near the Coquille River. Several of the whites are reported wounded. Source: 4

FALL 1851—*California*

Twenty settlers led by Ben Wright raid the Rogue Valley to recover mules and horses stolen during the summer by Indians. They attack the villages of the Tolowa and Shasta Indians, killing several natives. Source: 87

1852

Forts Chadbourne and McKavett are established in Texas.

1852—*Idaho*

Shoshone Indians attack fifteen members of the Ward party along the Boise River, killing thirteen. Source: 87

SEPTEMBER 1852—*California*

A number of settlers are massacred along the shores of Tule Lake. Modoc natives are believed to be responsible. The bodies of twenty-two to thirty-six settlers are found. Source: 70, 80

NOVEMBER 1852—*California*

After numerous attacks on wagon trains, settlers led by Ben Wright call for a meeting with the Modoc Indians but then attack their village, killing some forty-one warriors. Source: 80, 87

1853

Fort Ridgely is established in Minnesota and Fort Riley in Kansas.

AUGUST 17, 1853—*Oregon*

Rogue Indians attack homesteaders in the Rogue River Valley, killing John Gibbs, William Hudgins and three others. Source: 4

AUGUST 24, 1853—*Oregon*

Soldiers under the command of Col. John Ross surprise a Rogue camp and in a four-hour fight Lt. Alden and Capt. Pleasant Armstrong are killed. Eight Rogues are killed, and four die of their wounds later. Source: 4

SEPTEMBER 22, 1853—*Oregon*

Troops led by Capt. Smith attack Indians in their camp in the Siskiyous, killing fifteen. Source: 4

OCTOBER 26, 1853—*Utah*

A thirty-seven-man U.S. Corp of Engineers expedition led by Capt. John W. Gunnison is attacked by a party of Paiute or Ute Indians near present-day Delta. Seven surveyors are killed. Source: 73

1854

Fort Davis is established in Texas.

JANUARY 29, 1854—*Oregon*

Miners angry over repeated Indian attacks surprise a Nasomah native camp at dawn on the Coquille River, killing fifteen men and one woman. Source: 4

February 15, 1854 — *Oregon*

A. F. Miller angers local Coquille Indians when he announces he will be starting a ferry boat service near theirs on the Chetco River. He promises peace if the natives will give up their guns, which they do. Miller and his friends open fire, killing twelve Indians; the women and children are allowed to escape. Source: 4

March 5, 1854 — *New Mexico*

U.S. Dragoons under Lt. David Bell clash with Jicarilla Apaches led by Lobo Blanco. Five Apaches are killed, including Lobo Blanco. Source: 29

March 30, 1854 — *New Mexico*

Jicarilla Apaches ambush a stagecoach guarded by sixty soldiers. The fight lasts over three hours, and some twenty-three soldiers are killed. A force under Lt. Col. Philip St. George Cooke and Kit Carson track the Apaches to a canyon where they are routed and lose four or five killed. Source: 29, 78, 87

August 1854, Ward Wagon Train Massacre — *Idaho*

The Ward wagon train is attacked by Shoshone Indians, and eighteen of twenty people are killed. A number of the women are raped, tortured and killed, and several of the travelers are burned to death. Thirty-nine volunteers led by Nathan Olney along with Nez Perce and Umatilla Indians track the raiding war party, killing a number of Shoshone natives. Four are hanged later. Source: 73, 87, 150. Marker: West Boise, on old U.S. 20–30 at Middleton Rd. and Lincoln Rd.

August 19, 1854, Grattan Massacre — *Wyoming*

When a Mormon's cow is shot and killed by a Sioux near Ft. Laramie, trouble ensues. Sioux tribal elders offer to pay for the animal, but Lt. John Grattan is sent by Fort Commander Lt. Hugh Fleming to arrest High Forehead. Grattan commands only nineteen men and one twelve-pound howitzer, and after continuing insults from both sides, the howitzer goes off. Indian and soldier alike open fire. The warriors swarm over the troopers, killing them all including Lt. Grattan whose mutilated body is found with twelve arrows in it. Source: 20, 47, 78, 102. Marker: Grattan Battlefield is located 5 miles east of Fort Laramie on Wyoming 157.

October 6, 1854 — *Washington*

Soldiers under Maj. Granville O. Haller attempt to round up Yakima Indians who are willing to live peaceably with white settlers near the Yakima River. The soldiers and Indians battle for three days, and the troops pull out. Source: 78, 87, 150

1855

Fort Stanton is established in south-central New Mexico.

January 1855 — *Oregon*

Miners from Sailor's Diggings attack a native camp on the Illinois River, killing several women and children. Source: 4

January 19, 1855 — *New Mexico*

Mescalero Apaches ambush Company B, 1st Dragoons on the Penasco River, killing Capt. Henry Whiting Stanton and two privates. Source: 78

June 30, 1855 — *Texas*

Indians attack the home of Ed Westfall, killing a Frenchman named Louie and Westfall's dog. Source: 69, 96, 109

July 21, 1855 — *Texas*

Cattle overseer Jesse Lawhorn and a young Negro boy are attacked by Indians at Curry's Creek in Comal County. The young boy is chased for some distance by

Indians but escapes. The body of Lawhorn is found later and buried. Source: 69, 96, 109

SEPTEMBER, 3 1855, BATTLE OF BLUE WATER—*Nebraska*

Col. William S. Harney of the 2nd Dragoons leads a 600-man force of infantry, artillery and dragoons against a Sioux village encamped about three miles from Blue Water Creek. Eighty-six Indians are killed in the attack. (This battle is also known as the Battle of Ash Hollow or The Harney Massacre.) Source: 78, 137. Marker: On U.S. 26, one and a half miles west of Lewellen in Garden County, NE.

SEPTEMBER 25, 1855— *Oregon*

Rogue River Indians attack a wagon train, killing two. Source: 4

OCTOBER 3–6, 1855— *Washington*

Agent Andrew J. Bolton is sent to the Yakima camp to investigate the murders of some local miners, but he is reportedly killed by Chief Showaway's son. One hundred and four men under Maj. Granville O. Haller are sent in to punish the Yakimas but are met by 1,500 Indians and driven off. Five soldiers and two natives are killed. (September 23, 1855, is also given as the date for the death of Bolton.) Source: 57, 150 Source: 5 miles northeast of Goldendale, WA.

OCTOBER 8, 1855— *Oregon*

After raiding several settlements along Bear Creek and the Rogue River, a tracking party led by James Lupton locates the Rogue Indian raiders in camp on Little Butte Creek. Lupton and his men open fire on the Indians while they sleep, killing a number. A number of the survivors seek refuge at Fort Lane. Source: 73

OCTOBER 9, 1855—*Oregon*

Rogue Indians sweep through the Rogue Valley, attacking six homesteads and killing over sixteen settlers. Source: 4

OCTOBER 17, 1855—*Oregon*

Miners working on the Rogue River are attacked by Indians; four miners are killed in the eight-hour fight. Source: 4

OCTOBER 28, 1855— *Washington*

The homesteads at Brannon's Prairie along the White River are attacked by Indians. A number of settlers are killed. Source: 150. Marker: North of downtown Auburn along the old Kent-Auburn Hwy. At the junction of 30th St. NE and Auburn Way N.

NOVEMBER 1855—*Washington*

At Union Gap near Yakima seven hundred U.S. troops along with citizen forces under Maj. Gabriel Rains plus mounted volunteers attack Cayuse, Yakima and Walla Walla Indians, driving them across the Columbia River. Maj. Rains and his forces have come to punish the natives for the killings of local miners and two agents. Source: 57, 150

NOVEMBER 25, 1855—*Oregon*

Rogue Indians attack Maj. James Bruce and 286 soldiers as they prepare to attack the Rogue encampment. In a day-long skirmish one soldier is killed and four wounded. Source: 30

DECEMBER 4, 1855—*Oregon*

Cayuse Indians attack Fort Henrietta, killing and scalping one soldier, Pvt. William Andrews. Source: 87

DECEMBER 7–10, 1855— *Washington*

Oregon volunteers led by Lt. Col. James Kelly attempt to negotiate with Walla

Walla Indians but suspect treachery and hold over forty Cayuse warriors under Chief Peopeomoxmox hostage. Kelly withdraws toward the Whitman Mission site, but as the volunteers reach the Touchet River, they are attacked by 300 Cayuse warriors and fight an all-day battle. The Walla Wallas and Cayuse Indians lose over 100 casualties. The troops lose 8 killed and 18 wounded. Chief Peopeomoxmox is killed and scalped along with nineteen others natives. Source: 57, 73

DECEMBER 20, 1855—*Florida*

Seminole Chief Billy Bowlegs is told to leave his home in the Everglades after years of living in peace. When he refuses, soldiers attack and burn his farm and cut down several banana trees. Gathering together thirty warriors Bowlegs attacks a military camp, killing two soldiers, and flees back into the Everglades. The army finally gives up its search for him and his followers. The U.S. government reconsiders its removal policies and begins buying Seminole land. Source: 5, 77. Marker: Located at the site of Fort Hartsuff, FL.

1856

Fort Bellingham, Fort Walla Walla and Fort Townsend are established in Washington State.

JANUARY 6, 1856—*Florida*

Six miles south of Fort Dallas (Miami) the home of Peter Johnson is attacked by Seminoles, killing Johnson and Edward Farrell. Source: 77, 87

JANUARY 18, 1856—*Florida*

Outside of Fort Denaud on the Caloosahatchee River a party of soldiers is attacked by Seminole Indians led by Oscen Tustenuggee while gathering wood. Five of the six men are stripped of weapons and ammunition by the Seminoles and then killed. Source: 77, 87

JANUARY 26, 1856—*California*

Twenty volunteers attack Shasta Indians who take refuge in a cave. The troops fire a few howitzer charges into the cave. Both sides agree to a cease-fire, and over fifty Shasta natives leave the cave. Source: 87

JANUARY 26, 1856—*Washington*

Nisqually Indians led by Chief Leschi, plus some allies, attack Seattle but are driven off by shelling from the ships in Puget Sound. Source: 87, 150 Source: Located in small park at the corner of First and Cherry, Seattle, WA.

FEBRUARY 22, 1856—*Oregon*

Totutni Indians attack a number of settlements near Gold Beach, killing twenty-three. Source: 4

MARCH 2, 1856—*Florida*

A Seminole war party attacks the homestead of Florida State Senate President Col. Hamlin Snell. They take with them a number of Snell's slaves. Near Sarasota Bayou they brutally torture and kill Owen Cunningham. They then attack and burn the home of Joseph Woodruff as area settlers flee toward Fort Hamer (Bradenton). Source: 77, 87

MARCH 1856—*Florida*

Seminoles fire on soldiers in boats on the Fake-Hatchee River (Turner's River), killing two and wounding one. Source: 87

MARCH 10, 1856—*Washington*

Washington volunteers defeat Nisqually Indians led by Chief Leschi at Connell's Prairie. Source: 150. Marker: Ten miles east of Sumner, north of State Hwy. 410 & off Sumner-Buckley Hwy. on Connell's Prairie Road.

MARCH 19–22, 1856—*Oregon*

U.S. troops led by Capt. Christopher Augur attack and burn a Rogue village on the Illinois and Rogue Rivers fork on March 19. Troops arrive from Fort Lane on the twenty-second and exchange gunfire with the natives. Capt. Robert C. Buchanan orders an attack on the Rogue village, and it is assaulted by 112 men under the command of Capts. E. O. C. Ord and DeLancey Floyd Jones. Source: 87

March 26, 1856—
Washington

Col. George H. Wright leads a 350-man force into the Columbia Valley to have peace talks with the Yakima, Klickitat and Chinookan natives. Wright's men are attacked in the cascades of the Columbia River Valley, and fifteen of his men are killed. Source: 57, 78, 150

March 31, 1856—*Florida*

Seminoles led by Billy Bowlegs attack the Braden Plantation and attempt to burn it down but are driven off by gunfire. Seven slaves and several mules are taken. Source: 87

April 3, 1856—*Florida*

Militiamen track a Seminole raiding party and attack them at Apopka Creek, killing several natives and driving the rest into the swamp. Source: 87

April 7, 1856—*Florida*

Maj. Lewis Arnold leads the 1st and 2nd Artillery into Big Cypress Swamp in southern Florida where they erect a blockhouse. Arnold then leads his men toward the Seminole village of Billy Bowlegs, but his forces are ambushed by over fifty Seminole warriors; four soldiers are killed. Source: 77, 87

April 12, 1856—*Florida*

Asa Goodard's home, two miles from Addison's Fort on the upper Manatee River, is burned by Seminole natives. Source: 87

April 16, 1856—*Florida*

John Carney is killed by Seminole Indians while plowing his field near Bloomington. Source: 87. Marker: Carney's grave is located on Stearns Rd., Bloomington, FL.

April 20–22, 1856—*Oregon*

On April 20, sixty Rogue Indians fire on Fort Henrietta and then kill and scalp Pvt. Lot Hollinger. As they paddle down the Rogue River on April 22, twelve Indian men and three women are ambushed near Lobster Creek by a militia company, killing twelve. Source: 4, 87

April 28, 1856—*California*

One hundred miners and settlers under the command of Walter Harvey attack a Yokut village located near Tulare Lake on what is now known as Battle Mountain. Eleven Yokuts are killed in the engagement. Source: 135

April 29, 1856—*Oregon*

As they cross the Chetco River, troops under Capt. E. O. C. Ord are fired on by Rogue Indians. Several natives are killed, and one sergeant is killed. Source: 4, 73

May 1, 1856—*Texas*

In central Texas Company C of the 2nd Cavalry under the command of Capt. Oakes track and attack a Comanche war party, killing several Indians. Source: 32

May 2, 1856—*Florida*

Two men of Capt. Abner D. Johnston's Mounted Volunteers are shot and wounded at Big Cypress Swamp. The Seminole Indians are pursued into the woods, and the soldiers burn their village. Source: 87

May 13, 1856—*California*

Military forces led by Lt. Benjamin Allston attack a Yokut village on the Tule River in retaliation for Indian attacks. In the pre-dawn attack over twenty Yokut are killed and the village burned. Capt. John Gardiner writes, "Our Indian war is over for the present, and I do not think it will be revived unless whites commit more murders." Source: 135

May 14, 1856—*Florida*

At Big Cypress Swamp in southern Florida Indians fire on the cabin of Capt. Robert Bradley, killing two of his children playing near the cabin. Source: 5. Marker: Pioneer Florida Museum Association marker is located on SR 578 and 581, Darby.

May 17, 1856—*Florida*

Near Moore's Lake, Seminoles ambush three grain wagons which have stopped for water, killing James Starling, his son and Albert Hinson. Source: 5. Marker: Located on U.S. 92 west of McIntosh Rd. in Plant City.

May 28, 1856—*Oregon*

After agreeing to peace terms Rogue Indians on their way to the surrender point near Big Bend are fired on by a company of volunteers. Believing they are going to be exterminated, the Indians attack U.S. troops under Col. Robert Buchanan at the surrender point. After a two-day fight fresh troops led by Capt. Christopher C. Auger arrive and drive the Indians toward the river where they finally surrender. Source: 4, 87

June 5, 1856—*Oregon*

After a number of Rogue River Indians surrender, U.S. troops enter Copper Canyon to push several hostile bands out. They attack and burn a Shasta Costa village and kill four Indians. Source: 118

June 14, 1856—*Florida*

Near Fort Meade Mrs. Willoughby Tillis sees Seminole Indians hiding near her farm, gathers her children and runs toward the house followed by firing warriors. Two boys nearby go to Fort Meade for help. The Indians kill ten horses and retreat toward the swamp pursued by soldiers. The soldiers are soon outnumbered and driven back. Lt. Alderman Carlton, Lott Whidden and William Parker are killed. Source: 5, 77. Marker: Fort Meade Park contains the graves of the killed militiamen, Ft. Meade, FL.

June 16, 1856—*Florida*

Battle of Peace River Swamp. Soldiers led by Lt. Streaty Parker attack Seminoles, killing several. Seminole Chief Oscen Tustenuggee and soldiers Robert Prine and George Howell are killed. A cavalry company led by Capt. William B. Hooker drives the Seminoles off. Source: 5, 87. Marker: Same as above

June 1856—*Florida*

Seminoles burn the Hooker Plantation. Source: 87

July 17, 1856—*Oregon*

U.S. troops attempt to remove Cayuse and Walla Walla natives from the Grande Ronde River area. After a heated exchange troops charge and kill over forty men, women and children. Source: 57, 150. Marker: At the intersection of Couch Lane and Mount Glen Road, Riverside Park, near La Grande, OR.

August 2, 1856—*Florida*

Lt. H. Benson and two soldiers are fired on by Seminoles near the blockhouse at Punta Rassa. Source: 87

September 1856—*Texas*

Raiding Comanche attack the home of John Babb in Wise County while Babb and his oldest son are away. When the Indians attempt to carry off Mrs. Babb's two young children, she puts up a fight; the Indians stab her to death. The two children and a neighbor, Mrs. Luster, are carried off. Mrs. Luster manages to escape after several days, but the children remain captive for over two years. Source: 69, 118

NOVEMBER 1856—*Texas*

U.S. Cavalry forces under Capt. Bradfute clash with Comanche on the Concho River; four Indians are killed. Source: 32

DECEMBER 17, 1856—*Florida*

Eight miles south of New Smyrna Beach, Seminoles attack the homestead of Peter Shives, killing him and three others. Several houses are burned. Source: 87

1857

Fort Abercrombie is established in North Dakota.

FEBRUARY 12, 1857—*Texas*

The Second Cavalry led by Lt. Wood rides upon a Comanche war party on the North Concho River. In the engagement Lt. Wood is wounded, but three Indians are killed. Source: 32

FEBRUARY 16, 1857—*Arizona*

While on a hunting trip in the fall of 1856, Navajo Indian Agent Henry L. Dodge disappears, and he is later found murdered. Dodge is believed to have been killed by Apaches. He is buried with ceremony at Fort Defiance. His wooden headboard reads: "To the memory of H. L. Dodge aged 45 years, agent for Navajos, killed by Apache Indians on the 15th of Nov. 1856. A portion of his remains rest underneath this spot." Source: 29

MARCH 8, 1857, SPIRIT LAKE MASSACRE—*Iowa*

A band of Sioux led by Inkpaduta attack a number of settlements near Spirit Lake, killing thirty-four settlers and burning homes and barns. Source: 73, 87, 130. Marker: Pilsbury's Point on West Okoboji Lake, Arnold's Park, Iowa.

MARCH 27, 1857—*Texas*

Over 250 Comanche attack Johnson's Station, defended by six men and one woman. A dust cloud thrown up by an incoming stage drives the Indians off. Source: 69, 73

MARCH 27, 1857—*Florida*

Indians ambush soldiers near Palm Hammock, killing two. Source: 87

MAY 1857—*Florida*

Company G of the 5th Infantry is fired on by a band of Miccosukee as they enter Bowlegs' town near Fort Myers, killing one and wounding three. Source: 87

1857—*Washington*

On present-day Whidbey Island Haida natives attack the homestead of Issac Ebey, beheading him. Source: 150. Marker: Hwy. 525 from the Mukilteo ferry crossing, Whidbey Island, WA.

JULY 7, 1857—*Texas*

Indians kill Robert Adams while he is hunting hogs in Burnet County. His body is found badly mutilated and filled with arrows. Source: 69, 118

JULY 20, 1857—*Texas*

A twenty-man detachment of the 2nd Cavalry under Lt. J. B. Hood is ambushed near Devil's River by Comanche Indians after they call for a truce. Hood takes an arrow in the left hand. Source: 32, 78

JULY 29, 1857—*Kansas*

Col. Edwin Sumner and 300 troopers catch up to a large band of Cheyenne warriors led by Ice and Dark on the Solomon River in northwest Kansas. Sumner's three squadrons draw their sabers and charge some 300 warriors, who retreat and are pursued for seven miles. The Cheyenne lose nine warriors killed; the soldiers lose two killed and several wounded, including Lt. J. E. B. Stuart. Source: 87

September 7–11, 1857, Mountain Meadows Massacre—*Utah*

Pahvan Indians, prompted by local Mormon leaders and led by War Chief Moshoquop, attack a wagon train of Arkansans led by Capt. Alex Fancher and John T. Baker. Several of Fancher's party are killed in the first day's fighting. On the third day John D. Lee, a spokesman for the Mormons, tries to persuade the members of the wagon train to surrender their weapons in return for safe passage. By the fourth day fifteen of the party have been killed and are buried within the wagon train circle. With the wagon train's provisions and morale running low, Mormon spokesman John D. Lee finally persuades the Fancher Party to surrender their weapons in exchange for safe passage through the Paiute Indians. After loading all their firearms in a Mormon wagon, the party starts on its way. Mormons and Indians follow the defenseless wagon train into an open meadow where the signal to attack is given. The Paiutes and Mormons fall on the unsuspecting party and massacre fourteen men, twelve women and thirty-five youngsters. Of the entire attacking force of 300 Indians and fifty-eight Mormons, only John D. Lee will be tried and executed for the killings. Lee maintains his orders came from Brigham Young and the Mormon hierarchy. No one else will be brought to justice. Source: 15, 73. Marker: Mountain Meadow Valley, off Utah 18 between St. George and Enterprise.

November 21, 1857—*Florida*

Capt. William Cone leads a force of Florida militia against a Bowlegs village south of Fort Doane, near Lake Istokpoga, burning houses and a field of corn, rice and pumpkins. Source: 87

November 26, 1857—*Florida*

A force under Capt. John Parkhill burn Seminole crops near Royal Palm Hammock. Parker and five soldiers are ambushed and killed the next day. Source: 87

December 1857—*Florida*

The 5th Infantry led by Capt. C. L. Stephens is ambushed in Big Cypress Swamp, killing one soldier. Stephens' men follow the warriors and later ambush them, killing six. Source: 87

1858

Fort Lemhi is established in Idaho. Fort Stockton is established in Texas. Fort Abercrombie is established in North Dakota.

January 1858—*Florida*

Soldiers led by Col. S. St. George Rogers burn several villages and crops in Big Cypress Swamp. The soldiers continue their search in the swamp and find many of the Seminole hiding places and burn them. In a negotiated peace the Seminoles agree to be moved to reservations, ending the third and last Seminole War in Florida. Source: 87

May 6, 1858—*Washington*

Maj. William J. Steptoe with three companies of the 1st Dragoons and a twenty-five man mounted detachment from Company E, 9th Infantry, leave Ft. Walla Walla for Colville. Steptoe's objective is to take corrective action against the Palouse Indians for cattle stealing and to develop an understanding between the settlers and the Indians. Source: 70, 150

May 12, 1858—*Texas/Oklahoma*

Over 200 men, including friendly Tonkawa allies under the command of Texas Ranger Rip Ford, attack a Comanche camp on the Canadian River on the Texas-Oklahoma border. Ford orders a direct charge on the village, and the out-gunned 300 Comanche natives are no match. The Comanche warriors withdraw and, in a running battle, are pursued for seven hours and lose over seventy-six killed, including their leader Iron Jacket. Source: 17, 86, 107

May 15–17, 1858, Battle of To-Hoto-Nim-Me—*Washington*

Nine days out of Ft. Walla Walla Maj. William J. Steptoe's forces encounter a large force of Palouse, Spokane and Coeur d'Alene Indians who at first advise him to turn back and then began harassing him. Steptoe's expedition, outnumbered eight to one, begins a running battle with the Indians back toward Ft. Walla Walla. The troopers, who are only issued forty rounds per man, fight valiantly but begin taking heavy casualties. On the third night, in a desperate situation and running low on ammunition, Steptoe and his men creep through the warriors' line and begin an all-night run for the Snake River and the friendly Nez Perce camp located there. Steptoe's losses are two officers, ten men, and three friendly Indians killed, plus ten wounded and twenty-nine horses killed or lost to wounds. Source: 57, 70, 78. Marker: Hwy. 195, Rosalia, WA.

August 1858—*Arizona*

A California-bound wagon train is attacked by Mojave natives. The settlers retreat back to New Mexico. Source: 87

September 1–5, 1858, Battle of Four Lakes & Spokane Plains—*Washington*

Col. George Wright, commanding a force which includes over 600 soldiers, two companies of the First Dragoons, Third Artillery, 9th Infantry and thirty Nez Perce Indians, encounters a hostile force of Palouse, Spokane and Coeur d'Alene Indians at Four Lakes. In a retaliatory strike for To-Hoto-Nim-Me, Col. Wright's forces with Nez Perce allies inflict heavy casualties on the hostile Indians. Wright's forces then strike the Indians at Spokane Plains. The tribes surrender, and some of the warriors are hanged. Source: 57, 70, 78

October 1858—*Arizona*

Fort Defiance. Maj. William T. H. Brooks orders the Navajos to keep their livestock at least twelve miles from the fort. When the Navajos refuse, Brooks has some of their livestock shot. The Navajos begin raiding the fort's livestock and supply trains, and the soldiers begin attacking bands of Navajos. Source: 87, 133. Marker: At the mouth of Canyon Bonito, 7 miles north of Window Rock, AZ.

October 1, 1858—*Texas*

The 2nd U.S. Cavalry under Capt. Earl Van Dorn along with 135 friendly Waco, Caddo and Tonkawa attack a camp of 500 Comanche and Kiowa, killing fifty-six and burning their lodges. Several soldiers are killed, and most of the Comanche escape to the Arkansas River where they join up with the Kiowa. Source: 17, 67, 69, 107

1859

Fort Stockton is established in Texas. Fort Larned is established in Kansas.

March 15, 1859—*Texas*

Comanche kill four settlers in Bell County, including John and Jane Riggs. Source: 69, 109

May 13, 1859—*Kansas*

Soldiers searching for a Comanche camp find it on Crooked Creek, south of the Arkansas River. The 500 soldiers, commanded by Capt. Earl Van Dorn, attack the native camp but are held at bay by the warriors' gunfire. Capt. Kirby Smith is wounded in the thigh, and Lt.

Fitzhugh Lee is shot by an arrow in the chest. Over forty-nine Comanche are killed, and over thirty-two women are taken hostage. Two soldiers are reportedly killed and fifteen wounded. Source: 73

JUNE 17, 1859—*Kansas*

A Kansa (Kansas) raiding party steals two horses near Council Grove but are pursued by citizens who confront the thieves. Gunfire breaks out, killing two whites, and the Indians flee but later return and turn over the two warriors responsible for the killings. They are hanged. Source: 87

1859—*Texas*

Comanche raid the Hondo area killing a Mexican herder and two cowboys, Huffman and Sebastian Wolfe. A tracking party which includes Jack Davenport catches up with the raiders and recaptures a number of stolen horses. Source: 96

1859—*Texas*

A party of settlers shoot and kill an Indian near the Nueces River. A closer inspection of the body proves it to be a longhaired white boy dressed as Indian. The captive white boy was living as an Indian at the time of his death. Source: 96

AUGUST 1859—*New Mexico*

Kit Carson reports the killing of five miners and two Indians by Tabeguache Ute. Source: 29

AUGUST 31, 1859, MILTMORE MASSACRE—*Idaho*

Near present-day American Falls an immigrant train of nineteen people is attacked by Shoshone led by Pageah and Sowwich. The Indians kill and mutilate five men, one woman and two children. One of the chiefs is reportedly killed, and the Indians withdraw. The survivors are found by a squad of the 2nd Dragoons under Lt. Henry B. Livingston. Source: 73

OCTOBER 28, 1859—*Texas*

John Bowles is killed by Indians while hunting stock. Bowles' body is found at a place called Guide Hill six miles from the Sabinal Station. Jim Davenport is also killed by Indians near Sabinal Station. Source: 69, 96

FALL 1859—*Texas*

John F. Bottorff is killed by Indians ten miles west of Graham. Source: 118

1860

Fort Belmont is established in Kansas.

FEBRUARY 25, 1860, HUMBOLDT BAY MASSACRE—*California*

Twenty men led by Capt. Thomas Wright take boats and row across Humboldt Bay to Gunther's Island where they kill nine Indian men and forty-seven women and children. When the editor of the *Northern California* newspaper criticizes Wright and his men for their actions, the editor is told to leave town. Source: 73, 152

FEBRUARY 1860—*Texas*

Comanche and Kiowa warriors raid Young County. Chief Pine-O-Chumney and two other Indians are killed by a single shotgun blast fired by Rev. J. Pleasant Tackett, a Methodist minister. Source: 87, 124

MARCH 3, 1860—*Texas*

Gid Foreman is killed by Indians in Comanche County. Foreman is usually well-armed but had sold his pistols several days before the attack. The Indians then ride to the homestead of John Baggett where they attack his daughter, stabbing her several times and killing and scalping little Jowell Baggett. Source: 69

APRIL 1860—*Texas*

A Comanche party kills fifteen-year-old James Hamby, an employee on the

Thomas Lambshead farm near the Comanche reservation. Source: 17

April 30, 1860—*Arizona*

One thousand Navajos led by Manuelito and Barboncito attack Fort Defiance nearly over-running it. They are finally driven off after killing one soldier. Source: 87

May 9, 1860—*Nevada*

Paiute warriors rescue a number of their women who have been captured by miners and return to their camp on Pyramid Lake. A force of 105 miners led by former Texas Ranger Jack Hays follow the Indians but are ambushed, and forty-six of their men are killed, including Capt. Edward Storey. Source: 73, 87, 96. Marker: SR 447, seven miles south of Nixon, NV.

June 1860—*Texas*

While searching for cattle Josephus and Frank Browning are attacked by Indians. Josephus, mounted on a slower horse, is overtaken and killed. Frank outruns his attackers and escapes with an arrow in him. Source: 17, 69, 89, 109

July 1860—*Colorado*

Twenty soldiers led by Lt. J. E. B. Stuart track a party of Kiowa several miles from Bent's Fort. They attack the Indians, killing two warriors and capturing sixteen women and children. Source: 87

August 1860—*Texas*

While on their way to take the oath of allegiance to the Confederate government, B. F. Watkins and J. B. Richardson are attacked and killed by Indians about eight miles from Uvalde. Source: 96

September 13, 1860, Attack on Otter Wagon Train—*Idaho*

Bannock and Shoshone Indians attack the Otter wagon train. After a two-day fight only thirteen of the forty-four members of the wagon train survive. Source: 78

October 1860—*Arizona*

In retaliation for the April 30, attack on Ft. Defiance Col. Canby attacks several Navajo villages, killing thirty-four and capturing hundreds of sheep and horses. Source: 87

November 26, 1860, Nocona's Raid—*Texas*

After a series of defeats by Texas Rangers, ranchers and settlers, Comanche Indians led by Nocona begin raiding and committing depredations south from Jacksboro toward Mineral Wells. The Indians first attack the home of James Landman while Mr. Landman is away. They kill Mrs. Landman and her seven-year-old son and take daughters Jane and Katherine captive. Katherine is put on a horse, but young Jane is roped and dragged behind. Nocona's band then attack the Calvin Gage home, killing Jane Masterson and Katy Sanders and wounding several members of the Gage family. Source: 69, 124

November 27–28, 1860—*Texas*

Nocona's Raid. A Comanche raiding party led by Nocona attacks the home of John Brown, killing Mr. Brown with a lance and scalping him. The raiders then attack the home of Ezra Sherman. Mrs. Sherman is raped by a number of warriors, scalped and fatally wounded. She dies in three days. After leaving the Sherman ranch the Comanche chase Tom Mullins and Billy Conatser but cannot overtake them. In all, the Comanche take over 600 horses before heading back toward their village. Source: 69, 124

December 15, 1860—*Texas*

When Steve Brannon's wife becomes sick, he travels to the home of a Grandma

Cohen who is a midwife/doctor. While riding back on his horse with Mrs. Cohen riding behind him, they are attacked by Indians. As they race for Brannon's home with the Indians in full pursuit, Mrs. Cohen is struck in the back by an arrow. They finally make it to Brannon's home, and his two sons drive off the Indians. Mrs. Cohen recovers. Source: 69, 124

1861

FEBRUARY 4, 1861—*Arizona*

Chiricahua Chief Cochise is invited to Lt. George Bascom's tent at Apache Pass. Once inside the tent he is surrounded by soldiers and is accused of abducting Felix Ward, a twelve-year-old boy. After claiming to know nothing about the youth, he rushes from the tent in a hail of gunfire but returns later demanding to see his brother. Once again he is fired on and flees. This incident sparks twelve years of fighting. Source: 12, 68, 87

FEBRUARY 5, 1861—*Arizona*

After the previous day's fight Lt. Bascom moves his forces to a nearby stage station, but Apaches attack and kill one stage employee and take driver James Wallace prisoner. Source: 68, 87

FEBRUARY 6, 1861—*Arizona*

Stage driver James Wallace is held for ransom by Cochise who wishes to exchange prisoners with Lt. Bascom. When Bascom refuses, the Apaches attack a Mexican wagon train, tying the occupants to the wagons and setting them on fire. The mutilated bodies of Wallace and three other Americans are found a week later. Source: 12, 87, 109

FEBRUARY 8, 1861—*Arizona*

In response to the killing of several whites, including stage driver Wallace, Lt. Bascom hangs three of Cochise's relatives, including his brother Coyuntara. Bascom frees Cochise's wife and his two children. Source: 68

FEBRUARY 13, 1861—*Arizona*

Apache Indians fire on members of the 7th Infantry under Lt. Bascom at Apache Pass. A rescue party marches over 100 miles to rescue the entrapped soldiers. A Medal of Honor is awarded to Asst. Surgeon Bernard Irwin who takes command of troops and leads a rescue force to Lt. Bascom and his men. Three Coyotero Indians and three Chiricahua are taken prisoner and hanged on February 19. Source: 68, 73, 115

APRIL 1861—*Arizona*

In retaliation for the murder of his brother and several other relatives, Cochise and his men attack a Butterfield Stage at Doubtful Canyon and burn two captives to death. Seven others are also killed. Cochise, determined to drive all of the settlers out of Arizona, kills a number of them through the summer. Source: 12, 68

APRIL 12, 1861

Confederate forces fire on Union Fort Sumter, South Carolina, beginning the Civil War. Western Indian tribes again realign themselves, either for the North or the South, blurring the lines of conflict.

JUNE 20, 1861—*Wyoming*

Oglala and Sioux warriors led by Hump attack a Snake village near the Sweetwater River, killing and scalping several of the inhabitants. Source: 87

JULY 1861—*New Mexico*

Apaches led by Cochise and Mangas Coloradas ambush and kill a dozen men at a stage stop near Cooke's Spring. Source: 68

1861—*Texas*

John Schreiber is killed by Indians while hunting some oxen near the settlement of D'Hanis. Source: 96

July 1861—*Texas*

In a running battle with Indians near the Red Fork of Brazos, Capt. Barry and his men kill several Indians. "We lost three killed in this fight, to wit, Thomas J. Weathersby, Lip Conley and Bud Lane. Two men were wounded. We may have killed seven Indians we know of." Source: 69

August 11, 1861—*Texas*

Fourteen troopers under Lt. Reuben Mays are ambushed while pursuing Mescalaro Apache. A Mexican guide, Juan Fernandez, is sent for help, but when the rescue party arrives, they find all the troopers dead. Source: 73

September 27, 1861—*Arizona*

Mangas Coloradas and Apache forces attack the town of Pinos Altos. Source: 68

November 19, 1861—*Oklahoma*

Chief Opotheyohola leads a force of Unionist Creeks and Seminoles toward the safety of Kansas but is attacked by a combined force of Confederates and Indians at Round Mountain (Round Mounds). The Confederate force under Col. Douglas H. Cooper includes Creeks, Choctaws, Seminoles, Cherokees and Chickasaws loyal to the Confederacy. The battle is indecisive, and the Creeks withdraw in the night. Cooper claims a Confederate victory. Source: 21, 36

December 9, 1861—*Oklahoma*

Confederate forces under the command of Col. Douglas H. Cooper and 500 Cherokees under the command of Col. Drew skirmish with Creeks on December 9, at Bird Creek north of present-day Tulsa. The pro-Union Creeks and their allies withdraw with twenty-seven of their force dead. Source: 21, 46

December 26, 1861—*Oklahoma*

Union-loyal Creeks led by Opotheyohola are routed by Confederates under Col. Douglas H. Cooper at Patriot Hills or Chustenahlah. Many of the Creeks freeze to death in the frigid weather. Confederate Cherokees led by Stand Watie follow the loyal Unionists Creeks, kill another twenty and capture seventy-five. Source: 21, 36, 46

1862

Fort Douglas is established in Utah. Fort Bowie is established in Arizona.

March 6–8, 1862, Battle of Pea Ridge—*Arkansas*

Cherokee Chief and Confederate General Stand Watie and Albert Pike lead over 1,000 Cherokees against Union troops at the Battle of Pea Ridge (Elk Horn Tavern). Union artillery drives the Confederates and Indians from the field. Source: 21, 46. Marker: Pea Ridge National Military Park, U.S. 62E, Pea Ridge, AR.

March 28, 1862—*New Mexico*

Confederate troops led by Gen. Henry H. Sibley are defeated near Glorieta Pass by U.S. forces and Apache allies under Col. John Chivington. Source: 68. Marker: Pecos National Historic Park, 2 miles south of Pecos, NM, on SR 63.

April 1862—*Wyoming*

Bannock Indians attack several stage stations, including Split Rock Station, killing several men and stealing sixty horses and mules. Source: 87

April 18, 1862—*Arkansas*

The 1st Regiment of Confederate Choctaw and Chickasaw Mounted Rifles under Col. Tandy Walker defeat Union forces at the Battle of Poison Springs, Arkansas, near present-day Camden. Source: 21, 87. Marker: Arkansas 76, ten miles west of Camden, AR.

1862—Idaho

Over 200 warriors attack several wagon trains on the Oregon Trail near present-day American Falls, killing nine whites and stealing clothes and livestock. Source: 87. Marker: Massacre Rocks State Park at I-86/U.S. 30, American Falls, ID.

July 3, 1862, Battle of Locust Grove—Oklahoma

Delaware Indians allied with the Union and under the command of Col. Benjamin Weer surprise Confederate forces at Locust Grove. Confederate Col. James J. Clarkson is captured along with 110 of his men. Weer's forces kill over 100 Confederates and capture sixty ammunition wagons. Many Indians allied with the Confederacy desert and join Union Col. Ritchie's 2nd Kansas Indian Home Guard. Source: 21, 46. Marker: Located in roadside park on Oklahoma 33, Pipe Springs, OK.

July 14, 1862—Arizona

Apaches led by Mangas Coloradas ambush 120 infantrymen as they approach Apache Pass, killing fourteen. Pvt. John Teal shoots and wounds Mangas, but he later recovers. Source: 68, 119

July 15, 1862, Battle of Apache Pass/Fort Bowie—Arizona

A supply train with sixty-eight soldiers and 242 head of cattle is attacked by over 200 Apaches led by Cochise, Geronimo and Mangas Coloradas at Apache Pass. Exploding shells from two twelve-pounders finally drive off the Indians. Two soldiers are killed. Source: 12, 68. Marker: Fort Bowie National Historic Site is located on Apache Pass Rd. off SR 186, Bowie, AZ.

July 17, 1862—Arizona

U.S. troops fight an engagement with hostile Indians near Big Dry Wash, Arizona. First Sgt. Charles Taylor is awarded the Medal of Honor for Gallantry in Action. Source: 68, 115

Summer 1862—Oklahoma

Angered that some Cherokees have switched to pro-Union allegiance, Cherokee Confederate Gen. Stand Watie leads a force to punish them. At Bayou Menard Gen. Watie's force is attacked by the pro-Union 1st Kansas Indian Home Guard Regiment under the command of Maj. William A. Phillips. Phillips' command kills thirty-two Confederates and captures twenty-five. Killed with the Confederate forces is Lt. Col. Thomas Fox Taylor, Capt. Hicks and two Choctaw captains. Source: 87. Marker: Bayou Menard, 7 miles northeast of Fort Gibson on U.S. 62.

August 9, 1862, Massacre Rocks—Idaho

Shoshone and Bannock Indians attack several wagon trains on the Oregon Trail. The Adams and Smart trains are attacked, and five people killed. A tracking party from the Kennedy wagon train follows the Indians and attacks them, killing several. The leader of the tracking party, John K. Kennedy, is killed in the fight. Source: 73

August 17–18, 1862, The Great Sioux War—Minnesota

What starts out as an excursion to steal eggs by four Sioux boys ends with the murder of five settlers. Brown Wing, Killing Ghost, Breaking Up and Runs Against Something While Crawling, of the Mdewakanton village of Rice Creek try to steal eggs from the farm of Robinson Jones. Jones, Howard Baker, a Mr. Webster, Mrs. Jones and a fourteen-year-old girl are killed by the Sioux boys. Chief Little Crow, knowing the white settlers will strike back, declares war. Several Sioux are against war, including Big Eagle. "Wabasha, Wacouta, myself and others still talked for peace, but nobody would listen."

> "Count your fingers all day long and white men with guns in their hands will come faster than you can count. You will die like the rabbits when the hungry wolves hunt them. But Little Crow is not a coward. He will die with you."
> — Little Crow, Santee Sioux
> [Source: 88]

Little Crow and his warriors attack the Lower Agency in the early morning, killing twenty men and capturing twenty women and children. They then move on toward the Episcopal Mission and attack some forty-seven residents fleeing across the Minnesota River, killing several including the ferry boat operator Hubert Millier. The Sioux now splinter off and begin a sweep of the local farms, killing all inhabitants. Milford Township, downstream from the Lower Agency, is attacked. Some fifty Germans are killed. Source: 2, 8, 12, 15, 20, 50, 70, 88, 101, 108 [Quote 2]

AUGUST 19–23, 1862, BATTLE OF NEW ULM—*Minnesota*

Sioux Indians, against the advice of Little Crow, fall on the German settlement of New Ulm. The 900 residents are well dug in. In a driving rainstorm the Sioux warriors attack with a vengeance but are repulsed by gunfire from the 900 residents. Unable to take New Ulm, Little Crow and his Santee Sioux attack again on the twenty-second. New Ulm casualties are reported to be thirty-four settlers killed, sixty wounded and 190 buildings burned. Indian losses are unknown. Source: 2, 12, 15, 50, 70, 101, 108. Marker: At New Ulm on Minnesota 15.

AUGUST 20–22, 1862, ATTACK ON FORT RIDGLEY—*Minnesota*

On Wednesday morning Fort Ridgley is attacked by Little Crow and 400 Lakota Sioux warriors. The defenders are well prepared and open fire on the warriors with heavy artillery. The Sioux continue their onslaught and drive the defenders back several times, but the exploding shells prove to be too much for the battered Indians, and by evening they withdraw. After failing to take Fort Ridgley Sioux warriors assault New Ulm again on the August 22, but are forced to withdraw after a stout defense from the settlement. Source: 1, 12, 15, 70, 50, 101, 108, 119. Marker: Fort Ridgley State Park, located on Minnesota 4, about 7 miles south of Fairfax.

AUGUST 25, 1862— *South Dakota*

William Amidon and his father are killed by Santee Sioux that they find hiding in their cornfield on the bluffs of Sioux Falls. The Sioux are possibly refugees fleeing the uprising in Minnesota. Source: 151

SEPTEMBER 2, 1862— *Minnesota*

After attacking Fort Ridgley and New Ulm, Santee Sioux led by Chief Little Crow surround and attack a 170-man volunteer force led by Capt. Hiram P. Grant at Birch Coulee. Besieged for over thirty-one hours, Grant's command is finally rescued by reinforcements under Col. Sibley. Twenty-two soldiers are reportedly killed and sixty wounded. The Indians suffer only light casualties. Source: 2, 70, 101, 108, 119. Marker: Birch Coulee Battlefield, off U.S. 71, about one mile north of Morton, MN.

SEPTEMBER 23, 1862, BATTLE OF WOOD LAKE—*Minnesota*

U.S. troops under the command of Col. H. H. Sibley pursue Little Crow and 800 Sioux warriors to Wood Lake. The Santee Sioux attempt an ambush but are driven back by the troops' fire. Chief Manato is killed, and the Indians withdraw with their wounded and captives. Fifteen Santee are killed. Sibley marches into the Sioux camp two days later and demands the hostages, who are handed over to him. Some 2,000 warriors are taken prisoner and tried by a military court. Over 300 are sentenced to die but are pardoned by President Abraham Lincoln. Thirty-eight are hanged in Mankato in December. Source: 2, 70, 73, 88, 101, 108. Marker: Monument at the corner of Front and Main St., Mankato, MN.

OCTOBER 23, 1862—*Kansas*

Union cavalry with Kickapoo, Delaware and Shawnee allies attack Confederate forces and their Indian allies at the Wichita Agency, killing four whites and one Indian. They take over 100 horses and burn the agency building. Source: 21, 87

NOVEMBER 1862—*New Mexico*

Chief Cadette is escorted to Santa Fe by Kit Carson for peace talks but is given an ultimatum by Gen. Carleton: "Surrender and go to the reservation on the Pecos, or be killed!" Source: 12, 29 [Quote 12]

DECEMBER 24, 1862— *North Dakota*

A Sioux war party of 600 warriors attack Fort Berthold and set some of the homes of Arikara, Mandan and Hidatsa Indians on fire but are driven off. Source: 87. Marker: Little Missouri State Park, Fort Berthold Reservation, Hwy. 22, New Town, ND.

DECEMBER 26, 1862— *Minnesota*

For their part in the Minnesota uprising, 392 Sioux men have been sentenced to be hanged, but most have been pardoned by Pres. Abraham Lincoln. On the day after Christmas thirty-eight Sioux Indians, convicted in the Sioux uprising, are hanged at Manakato, Minnesota. It is America's largest mass execution. The Minnesota Historical Society's figures on the Sioux uprising: homesteaders and settlers killed, 644, soldiers killed, 757. Indian casualties are unknown. Source: 2, 12, 101, 108

1862—*Texas*

Indians attack the homestead of Mr. Barnes, who puts up a stout defense along with his Mexican employee until their ammunition runs out. The Indians rush him and kill him. His Mexican hired hand flees but is pursued and killed. Source: 69, 118

1863

Fort Lincoln is established in New Mexico.

JANUARY 29, 1863, BATTLE OF BEAR RIVERS—*Utah/Idaho*

Col. Patrick Connor and the 3rd California Infantry attack Shoshones under Chief Bear Hunter at Bear River and Beaver Creek on the Utah-Idaho border. Over 400 Indians dig in as Connor's force attacks the village. After several hours of heavy fighting the Indians' ammunition begins to run out, and a general slaughter begins. Over 350 Indians are killed by the troops; a great number are women and children. Source: 73, 87. Marker: Fort Douglas, Potter St., Salt Lake City, UT.

FEBRUARY 28, 1863—*Texas*

Benjamin Baker is attacked by Indians en route to the homestead of Dr. G. P. Barber. The Indians chase Baker for several miles until he nears the Barber homestead where the Indians are driven off. With two arrows in his back, Baker collapses and dies at Barber's gate. Source: 69, 89, 109

MAY 1863—*Utah*

Goshute Indians attack a stagecoach near the Utah-Nevada border, killing the stage driver. Maj. Egan, a passenger, brings the stage in. After learning the army has pulled out of the area, possibly because of the Civil War, the peaceful Goshute natives go on a killing rampage, raiding a number of nearby homesteads. Source: 87

May 1863 — Kansas

Osage Indians attack a force of twenty-two Confederate soldiers on the Verdigis River, killing all of them. Source: 87

June 16, 1863 — New Mexico

A detachment of Company H, 1st New Mexico Cavalry, led by Lt. L. A. Bargie, is ambushed by about seventy Mimbres Apache while traveling from Franklin to Fort McRae. Three troopers, including Lt. Bargie, are killed, but the soldiers drive the Indians off after three hours. Source: 68, 74

June 23, 1863 — Nevada

After his wife and child are killed by troops at Government Springs on June 20, Chief Peahcamp and about seventeen Goshute warriors attack the Egan Canyon Stage Station. Station keeper William Riley is shot by Indians and his body burned. Cpl. Hervey is ambushed and killed 500 yards from the station. Pvts. Burgher and Elliott are killed while hunting nearby. Source: 73

July 3, 1863 — Minnesota

Sioux Chief Little Crow goes on a horse-stealing expedition and is shot and killed while picking berries near Hutchinson. A $500 reward is paid to farmer Nathan Lamson for the killing of Little Crow. Source: 2, 101, 108

July 5, 1863 — Wyoming

After raiding a relay station and running off some stock Ute Indians are pursued by the 1st Colorado Volunteer Cavalry led by Maj. Edward W. Wynkoop. The soldiers catch up with the natives about thirty miles from Fort Halleck and kill over twenty. Source: 87

1863 — Texas

Henry Arhelger and a companion are attacked while riding near Fredericksburg in Gillespie County. Arhelger's companion is mounted on a fast horse and escapes, but Arhelger, mounted on a mule, is killed, scalped and shot full of arrows. Source: 69, 124

July 8, 1863 — Utah

The once peaceful Goshute Indians have been on the warpath ever since troops have left, possibly for Civil War duty. They attack men working at Canyon Station while eating breakfast and kill and scalp all five. Source: 87

July 11, 1863 — New Mexico

Sgt. E. W. Hoyt with three men of Company B and three of Company D are attacked in Cooke's Canyon by Apaches. The troopers kill four of the Indians and drive the rest off. Source: 74

July 17, 1863 — Oklahoma

Union troops attack the Confederate 1st and 2nd Creek Regiments under the command of Col. D. M. McIntosh and Col. Chilly McIntosh near Honey Springs, killing several and driving them off. The routed Creeks retreat to the Choctaw and Chickasaw territories along the Red River. Source: 21, 87. Marker: Honey Springs Battlefield Park, 4 miles north of Checotah near Rt. 69.

July 24, 1863 — North Dakota

U.S. troops led by Brig. Gen. Henry Sibley clash with Santee and Sioux Warriors under Chief Inkpaduta at Big Mound. Several warriors are killed by howitzer shells, and the natives are driven south two miles. The Indians are pursued to Dead Buffalo Lake, but night ends the chase. About forty Sioux are reported killed, and Sibley reports three troopers killed. Source: 73

1863—*Texas*

A detachment led by Capt. R. M. Whiteside from Camp Cooper discovers a deserted Indian camp, the warriors away on a raid. The soldiers hide their horses and wait for the Indians who presently return leading a horse herd. The whites rise up from concealment and open up on the unsuspecting warriors. A Mr. Seymour empties his six-shooter and charges in on the Indians. In a hand-to-hand fight with one warrior, Seymour beats the Indian to death with his six-shooter. Trooper Lewis Collins is killed. Source: 124

AUGUST 10, 1863—*Texas*

William and Stewart Hamilton are attacked and killed by Indians while collecting wood near Patrick's Creek in Parker County. Source: 69, 109

SEPTEMBER 1863, BATTLE OF WHITESTONE HILL— *North Dakota*

U.S. troops under the command of Gen. Alfred H. Sully and Gen. Henry H. Sibley miss a planned rendezvous with each other, but Sully finds a recent Sioux trail and pursues it. The 6th Iowa and 2nd Nebraska Cavalry engage the Sioux warriors at Whitestone Hill. Darkness halts the battle. "I could have annihilated the enemy," Sully wrote. "I gave them one of the most severe punishments that the Indians have ever received." About 100 to 150 warriors are reported killed. Twenty-two soldiers are killed. Source: 73, 87, 137 [Quote 73]. Marker: Whitestone Battlefield Historic Site located at intersection of CR 2 and 3, southeast of Kulm, ND.

OCTOBER 29, 1863—*Oklahoma*

Confederate forces led by Cherokee Gen. Stand Watie attack the pro–Union Cherokee capital at Tahlequa, burning the council house, capturing pro–Union Cherokees and killing four Union soldiers. Source: 46

DECEMBER 13, 1863—*Arizona*

A 736-man command led by Kit Carson is ambushed by Apaches in Canyon de Chelly. The Apache warriors led by Barboncito run a number of mules off. A U.S. pursuit party captures thirteen Apache women and children. Source: 87

1864

Fort Mitchell is established in Nebraska. Fort Sisseton is established in South Dakota.

JANUARY 6, 1864, BATTLE OF CANYON DE CHELLY—*Arizona*

Over 1,000 soldiers under Kit Carson enter the western end of Canyon de Chelly while Capt. Albert Pfeiffer's force enters from the east. The 8,000 Navajos caught between fight the soldiers with stones and wood but are no match for them and finally surrender. Over 8,000 Navajos are forced to walk from Arizona to Fort Sumner, New Mexico. Source: 12, 87, 88

JANUARY 24, 1864—*Arizona*

Rancher King Woolsey and twenty-eight volunteers open fire on an Apache camp, killing twenty-four. Source: 87

> "The Blackfeet appeared in every respect superior to the tribe I had left. The chief, Tall Soldier, displayed at all times the manners and bearing of a natural gentleman."
> — Fanny Kelly, Indian captive, 1864 [Source: 58]

FEBRUARY 2, 1864— *North Carolina*

The 14th Illinois Cavalry attack Confederate Col. William Thomas and his Cherokee soldiers near Deep Creek, close to the Cherokee town of Quallatown.

Union Maj. Francis Davidson claims that over 200 Confederates are killed, including twenty-two Cherokees, but Confederates claim to only losing one killed. Source: 87

FEBRUARY 25, 1864— *New Mexico*

Apaches attack the mining town of Pinos Altos in southwest New Mexico, killing several miners. The 5th California Infantry under the command of Capt. James H. Whitlock march to Pinos Altos where they ambush the Apaches at night as they enter the town. Thirteen of the nineteen Apaches are killed, including Chief Luis. Source: 73

MAY 16, 1864— *Colorado*

Battle of Ash Creek. As Colorado volunteers led by Col. John Chivington approach the Cheyenne camp of Lean Bear, he rides out to talk with them, but at twenty or thirty yards they fire on him and his escort. The force withdraws after killing Lean Bear and several others. Source: 87

JUNE 10, 1864— *Oklahoma*

Confederate Cherokees, Creeks and Seminoles led by Cherokee Commander Stand Watie attack the Union ferry steamboat *J. R. Williams* on the Arkansas River at Pleasant Bluff. Watie's men drive the Union soldiers from the boat, and its contents are plundered by the natives. Source: 21, 46

JUNE 11, 1864— *Colorado*

The mutilated bodies of rancher Nathan Hungate, his wife and two children are brought into Denver. The Hungate family's bodies are found at their homestead on Box Elder Creek, thirty miles southeast of Denver. Cheyenne and Arapaho Indians are believed to be responsible. (This incident may have lead to the Sand Creek Massacre the following November.) Source: 9, 73

JUNE 24, 1864— *Nebraska*

A dozen hay cutters working for farmer Patrick Murray on Looking Glass Creek are approached by a party of Lakota who demand food. When they begin taking the hay cutters' mules, a shot is fired. The Indians attack and kill seven of the workers and mortally wound three. Two escape, including a young boy who makes his way to the Pawnee Agency for help. Source: 73

JULY 12, 1864— *Wyoming*

Near Little Box Elder Creek in Wyoming a wagon train is attacked by a band of Oglala Sioux, killing three men, wounding two others and carrying away two women. One of the women is Fannie Kelly. (Kelly later writes of her account in *Narrative of My Captivity among the Sioux Indians,* published in 1871.) Source: 20, 58

JULY 1864— *Colorado*

In northeastern Colorado Indians kill two hired hands at the Bijou Ranch and steal seventeen horses. They then go to Murray's Ranch and steal sixty horses. Source: 87

1864— *Texas*

A Negro boy of about fifteen is attacked and killed while herding a Mr. Arnold's sheep two miles west of Lampasas. A pursuit party tracks and overtakes the raiding party. One Indian is killed and another captured. Source: 69, 124

Texas

Mark Boren is chased by Indians south of the Red River Station. Boren's horse gives out, and he is killed and scalped. Source: 69

JULY 17, 1864— *Wyoming*

A detachment of soldiers from Deer Creek Station find the body of young

Mary Larimer, kidnapped with Fanny Kelly on July 12, in a raid on their wagon train. The young girl's lifeless body is shot full of arrows, tomahawked and scalped. Source: 58

JULY 28, 1864, BATTLE OF KILLDEER MOUNTAIN— *North Dakota*

Brig. Gen. Alfred Sully continues his campaign against the Sioux and advances up the Missouri River. On July 28, the expedition finds the Indians dug in at Killdeer Mountain and begins shelling them with howitzers. Sully's force numbers 2,200 men while the Indian warriors are estimated at over 5,000. The huge 1,600 lodge camp is comprised of over 8,000 Hunkpapa, Santee, Blackfeet, Yanktonais, Sans Arcs and Minneconjou, including women and children. Warriors dug in along the mountain's rim battle the troops until afternoon when they begin withdrawing over the mountains. Long-range artillery firing causes most of the Indian casualties. The empty village is burned, and 150 Indians and over 3,000 dogs are reported killed. Source: 73

AUGUST 7–17, 1864— *Nebraska*

A war party of Cheyenne raid a number of stage stations and ranches along the Oregon Trail for 400 miles from Julesburg to Big Sandy. The upper Little Blue River is hit the hardest, and about 100 settlers are killed. On August 17, troops and militia attack and drive the Indians off. Source: 87, 137. Marker: Nebraska 14, north of Nelson, NE.

FALL 1864, FORT MURRAH MASSACRE— *Texas*

Clashes between Texas settlers and Comanche Indians led by Little Buffalo boil over in 1864 when over 500 Comanche and Kiowa combined strike settlements along Elm Creek near the Brazos River. From Ft. Murrah, settlers watch as helpless farmers, caught out in the open fields, are killed and scalped by the raiding Comanche. Franz Peveler watches from the fort as his neighbor Issac McCoy and son are brutally killed. "I never had a more horrible and helpless moment," Peveler said. The smoke from their burning cabins is visible for miles. At a nearby home, warriors force a Mrs. Fitzpatrick to watch them scalp and split open the head of her daughter. At the nearby Bragg home men are able to keep the Indians at bay by accurate firing. Rangers and settlers battle the Indians for hours before retreating into the safety of Fort Murrah. The warriors withdraw toward the Red River with loot and captives. The loss in cattle is estimated at between five and ten thousand, and over a dozen women and children are abducted. The wrath of the Indians doesn't end here though; the bodies of many of these unfortunates are found on the path of the Indian withdrawal, horribly mutilated. The Comanche-Kiowa raiding party suffers high casualties during this raid although exact numbers are never known. Source: 17

SEPTEMBER 19, 1864, BATTLE OF CABIN CREEK— *Oklahoma*

Confederate and Indian forces led by Cherokee Confederate Gen. Stand Watie attack a Union supply train en route to Fort Gibson. The 500-man Union force, which also includes a 300-man Indian Home Guard, is driven from the field and suffers over 200 casualties. Watie's Confederate and Indian forces capture over one million dollars in supplies, including much needed clothing, food, medicine and blankets. Cherokee Confederates are accused of massacring pro–Union Cherokees. Source: 21, 46, 86. Marker: Battle of Cabin Creek site is located in Mayes County in northeast Oklahoma.

October 10, 1864—*Colorado*

Forces led by Capt. David H. Nichols attack the Cheyenne camp of Big Wolf at White Butte Creek, killing the entire camp of six warriors, three women and a teenage boy. Source: 73

October 13, 1864—*Texas*

Over 1,000 Comanche and Kiowa led by Little Buffalo attack the settlements on Elm Creek, killing a number of settlers and burning homes. Fourteen militiamen led by Lt. N. Carson track and attack over 300 warriors but are driven off after losing five men. Six women and children are kidnapped, and over 10,000 head of cattle stolen. Source: 84, 87

November 25, 1864, The First Battle of Adobe Walls—*Texas*

On the morning of November 7, a military strike force made up of California and New Mexico volunteers under the command of Col. Kit Carson attack a Comanche and Kiowa camp in the valley of the Canadian River. Carson's command consists of 14 officers and 321 men. The expedition also includes seventy-two Ute and Apaches and two twelve-pound howitzers. The Kiowa camp puts up a stiff resistance but is driven four miles to an old adobe building called Adobe Walls where they are reinforced. Carson quickly puts his two howitzers to work on a small hill, and the Indians start a rapid retreat toward the next village but once again regroup and counterattack. During the course of the day the Indian forces grow to an estimated 1,000 to 3,000. Carson's forces, greatly outnumbered, begin a difficult but orderly retreat as the warriors set fire to the tall, dry grass and harass the columns. Army losses are two killed and twenty-one wounded while the Indian losses are reported to be sixty killed and wounded. Source: 32, 67, 70, 78, 102. Marker: Historical markers on Texas 15/FM 278 five miles north of Stinnet. Private land.

> "The Indian idea was to have the Government feed the old people, women and children, while the bucks would ravage the country."
> — Captain Eugene F. Ware
> [Source: 106]

November 29, 1864, Sand Creek Massacre—*Colorado*

Col. John M. Chivington, commanding 750 men of the 3rd Colorado Volunteers, attacks a sleeping village of Cheyenne under Chief Black Kettle camped along the banks of Sand Creek (Big Sandy Creek) in southeast Colorado. The Colorado volunteers open up with four twelve-pound howitzers as the cavalry charges into the snow covered village. The initial charge is repulsed by some 100 warriors streaming from the village. Chief White Antelope is killed in the first volley as women and children retreat toward Sand Creek. A second charge, frontal and both flanks, drives the warriors back toward the creek. The howitzers, loaded with canister, rake the fleeing Indians as the carnage continues. The fighting continues until four o' clock when Chivington reassembles his troops, now on the alert for a counter-charge from the second camp down river. Col. Chivington reports, "between 500 and 600 Indians were left dead on the field." Rage sweeps through other Cheyenne and Kiowa camps, and raids begin on wagon trains on the Platte. Source: 12, 20, 78, 88, 101, 102, 108. Marker: Marker is on dirt road leading from SR 96 about 8 miles north of Chivington, CO. Note: the exact site of the massacre is in dispute. Some place the location less than half a mile from the present recognized site.

November 30, 1864—*Colorado*

Sporadic fighting continues near Sand Creek with two soldiers and twelve Indians killed. Source: 20, 88, 101, 102

1864—*Texas*

Fifteen miles from Weatherford, Andrew Barry and his two sons are attacked on their way home. Barry and his five-year-old are killed and scalped. His ten-year-old is also scalped, but a detachment of Capt. Newt White's Company G drives them off before they can kill the young boy. Source: 69, 124

1865

Fort Dodge, Fort Hays, Fort Harker, Fort Wallace, Fort Aubrey and Fort Downer are established in Kansas. Fort Bidwell is established in California. Fort Verde in Arizona and Fort Selden in New Mexico are established.

January 7, 1865—*Colorado*

The 7th Iowa Cavalry under the command of Capt. Nicholas O'Brien observes a large Indian force approaching Julesburg and retreats to the town. The inhabitants of the town escape to nearby Fort Rankin. A thousand Cheyenne and Sioux Indians attack and burn the town, killing fourteen soldiers and four civilians. Source: 73. Marker: Fort Sedgewick Depot Museum, 200 W. 1st St., Julesburg, CO.

January 8, 1865—*Texas*

Kickapoo Indians leave their reservation in Kansas and head for Mexico. They are attacked by Texas militia and Confederate cavalry near Dove Creek in Tom Green County. The Kickapoo suffer great losses and are driven a short distance but finally rally and charge the Texans, killing over eleven and wounding a great deal. The Kickapoo make it to Mexico and, from their camp in the Santa Rosa Mountains, raid the Texas border for a number of years. Source: 87, 96

January 1865—*Idaho*

At Battle Creek U.S. troops track and attack raiding Bannocks, killing 224. Source: 87

February 2, 1865—*Wyoming*

Cheyenne and Sioux warriors attack Fort Laramie, burning the stagecoach station house, several stores and two houses before being driven off. Source: 87

February 2, 1865—*Colorado*

Cheyenne and Sioux Indians attack the town of Julesburg for the second time. Troops led by Capt. Nicholas J. O'Brien, returning from an expedition, arrive as the Indians are attacking nearby Fort Rankin. O'Brien and his men fight their way through the Indian force estimated at over 1,000 warriors. The warriors withdraw after sacking the town. Source: 73

February 8, 1865—*Nebraska*

Troopers of the 11th Ohio Volunteer Cavalry led by Col. W. O. Collins clash with Sioux and Cheyenne forces near the present-day town of Bridgeport. Source: 87

April 9, 1865—*Virginia*

Gens. Robert E. Lee and Ulysses S. Grant sign articles of surrender, ending the Civil War.

May 12, 1865—*Nebraska*

The 1st Nebraska Veteran Cavalry skirmish with Indians at the Gilmans' or Smiths' Ranch. Pvt. Francis W. Lohnes is awarded the Medal of Honor for "Defending Government property against Indians." Source: 73, 115

1865—*Texas*

A Mrs. Joy and her infant daughter are attacked by Indians while traveling in Kerr

County. They are both killed, and Mrs. Joy's infant daughter's head is severed. Mr. Joy later tracks and kills three Indians near his ranch. Source: 69, 109, 124

JUNE 8, 1865—*Wyoming*

Five troopers led by Lt. James A. Brown are attacked by about 100 Sioux and Cheyenne warriors on the Overland Road west of Fort Halleck. The troopers are chased for over eight miles toward Pine Grove Station. Pvts. George Bodine and Perry Stewart are killed in the chase, and Pvt. Orlando Ducket is wounded and falls into the Indians' hands. Ducket's body is never found. Source: 73

JUNE 14, 1865—*Nebraska*

Soldiers relocating some Indians near the Red Cloud Agency are fired on, and an officer Fouts is killed. Source: 87

JUNE 23, 1865—*Oklahoma*

Confederate General and Cherokee Chief Stand Watie surrenders his forces at Doaksville, the Choctaw capital. Marker: NE corner of Fort Towson Cemetery, Ft. Towson, OK. Source: 21

JULY 4, 1865—*Texas*

Indians attack a Fourth of July celebration near the mouth of the Leona River in Frio County. Eleven of the men from the settlement give chase for a number of miles and in the process use up most of their ammunition. The Indians turn and charge the settlers, killing Bud English, Dan Williams and Dean Oden. Source: 96

JULY 25–26, 1865—*Wyoming*

Fort Caspar. After the massacre at Sand Creek a number of Southern Cheyenne chiefs decide to attack the army outpost along the Bozeman Trail. The Indians try to draw the soldiers out of their fortifications the next day. Cannon fire from the fort drives the Indians off. Source: 15, 73. Marker: Fort Caspar Museum, 4001 Fort Caspar Rd., Caspar, WY.

JULY 26, 1865—*Wyoming*

Fort Caspar. A party of army wagons led by Sgt. Amos T. Custard is attacked by Indians at Willow Spring. Greatly outnumbered, a force under Lt. Caspar W. Collins is sent out as a rescue party but is attacked by some 600 Cheyenne and 1,800 Sioux warriors. Four troopers manage to escape, but Custard, Collins and the rest of their men are all killed. Source: 73, 108

AUGUST 29, 1865, BATTLE OF TONGUE RIVER—*Wyoming*

U.S. Cavalry under Gen. Patrick Connor attacks an Arapaho and Cheyenne village under Chief Black Bear and Little David on the Tongue River near present-day Ranchester. One thousand horses are captured and sixty-five Indians are killed. Although Connor loses only eight men, the main force of Indians escape. Source: 12, 78, 87, 154. Marker: Connor Battlefield located in the Ranchester City Park five miles from Dayton, WY.

AUGUST 31, 1865—*Wyoming*

An expedition led by Col. James Sawyer surveying the Bozeman Trail is attacked by an Arapaho and Cheyenne war party in retaliation for the attack on Black Bear's village four days before. The expedition is besieged for thirteen days and is finally rescued by Gen. Connor's Powder River Expedition. Source: 17. Marker: On U.S. 14 three miles from Dayton where the Bozeman Trail crosses the highway.

SEPTEMBER 1865—*Texas*

Comanche Indians attack the Babb homestead, capturing thirteen-year-old Dot and nine-year-old Bianca Babb. Mrs. Babb is killed, and her two smaller children are held captive for over two years and then ransomed. Mrs. Luster is also taken captive but later escapes. Source: 69, 124. Maker: Two miles from Chico on FM 1810.

SEPTEMBER 17, 1865—
South Dakota

Sgt. Charles L. Thomas is awarded the Medal of Honor for carrying a dispatch through hostile Indian country in Dakota Territory. Source: 115

DECEMBER 1865—*Texas*

Tom Norris is killed by Indians on the old Dumas Ranch south of Henrietta. Source: 69

1866

Fort Buford is established in North Dakota. Fort Phil Kearney is established in Wyoming.

JANUARY 17, 1866—
New Mexico

Six privates of Company G, First Battalion of California Veteran Infantry are attacked by forty Apaches while cutting wood four and a half miles from Fort Cummings. Four privates are killed: Thomas Daley, Charles Devine, Louis Hunter and Thomas Ronan. Prvt. John Mathews drives the Indians off and carries Pvt. Nathaniel B. Goldsberry to safety. Source: 74. Marker: Fort Cummings ruins, Luna City, NM.

MARCH 31, 1866—*Arizona*

Arizona Volunteers led by Lt. John D. Walker along with Pima Indians attack Apache Indians in the Pinal Mountains. The Apaches are caught by surprise, and over twenty-five are killed while Walker loses only one man. Source: 73

JULY 1866—*Idaho*

Paiutes attack and kill all members of a wagon train near Warm Springs. The women and children are tortured before they are killed. Source: 87

JULY 17, 1866—*Wyoming*

Oglala Sioux under Red Cloud run off 175 mules from Fort Laramie and wound several soldiers. Near Fort Phil Kearney Sioux Indians attack the Cazeau wagon train, killing five men. Source: 56, 73

JULY 24, 1866—*Wyoming*

Five men from a wagon train are attacked by Indians at Clear Creek. William Dillion is fatally wounded and dies that night. Troops arrive from Fort Phil Kearney and escort the wagon train to the fort. Source: 54, 73

1866 SUMMER—*Texas*

Pleas Boyd is killed and scalped while herding cattle two miles south of Lipan. Source: 69, 124

1866—*Texas*

Isaac Briscoe and his wife are killed and scalped by Indians five miles north of Jacksboro. Briscoe's daughters and sons are carried off by the Indians. Source: 69, 124

AUGUST 6, 1866—*Texas*

A Kiowa war party led by Satanta raid the settlement of James Box, killing him and taking his wife and four children captive. Mrs. Box's seven-day-old baby is thrown into a ravine by the Indians and dies. Mrs. Box and her daughters are held for three months and ransomed by officers at Fort Dodge in October. Source: 20, 69, 75, 78, 102. Marker: Fort Dodge site on Hwy. 400 east of Dodge City, KS.

SEPTEMBER 8, 1866—
Montana

Two thousand soldiers commanded by Cols. Samuel Walker and Nelson Cole are attacked by Sioux along the Powder River. The 400-man Sioux force harass the soldiers as they march along the Powder River until a sleet storm drives them off. The starving soldiers leave a trail of dead horses and mules behind them. Source: 87

September 13, 1866— Wyoming

Sioux Indians attack hay cutters near Ft. Phil Kearney, killing one man and setting fire to some of the hay cutting machinery. John Bratt, a bullwhacker, wrote, "One afternoon the Indians made several attacks on us. They killed three of our men and wounded some others, captured nearly all our mowing and rake teams and had us all corralled on a high hill." A pursuit team led by Capt. Tenedor Ten Eyck is unsuccessful in retaking a number of stolen cattle. Pvt. John Donovan is wounded with an arrow in his thigh. Source: 13, 70 [Quote 13]

Fall 1866— Texas

Six miles from town on the Medina River Thomas B. Click is killed by Indians as he travels from Bandera to visit a man named Huffman. Click is unarmed and is killed by a lance thrust. The following year Click's brother Rufus is attacked by Indians, shot with a poison arrow but recovers. Source: 96

September 14, 1866— Wyoming

Pvt. Allando Gilchrist is presumed killed by Indians near Ft. Phil Kearney after his bloody clothes are found. Source: 13, 70

September 16, 1866— Wyoming

Peter Johnson, a hay cutter at Ft. Phil Kearny, is cut off by Indians while riding near the fort and taken captive. Johnson's remains are never found. Photographer Ridgway Glover, warned numerous times not to wander alone from the fort, disappears some distance from the fort. His scalped, naked body is found less than two miles from the fort. Source: 13, 70

September 16, 1866— Texas

Ernest Jones, his son and two Negroes are killed by Indians while cutting hay twelve miles from Jacksboro. The Indians raid Wise County where they kill a woman and carry off two children. Source: 44

September 1866— Montana

Cpl. Abraham Staples and Pvt. Thomas Fitzpatrick are killed near Fort C. F. Smith while cutting hay. Source: 70

December 6, 1866— Wyoming

Lt. Horatio Bingham and Sgt. G. R. Bowers are killed during an engagement near Fort Phil Kearney. Lt. George Grummond escapes. Between July 26, and December 21, Sioux Indians kill five officers, ninety-one enlisted men, fifty-eight civilians and wound twenty soldiers. The Indians steal 306 oxen and cows, 304 mules, and 161 horses. (These figures include the casualties of December 21.) Source: 7, 13, 102

December 21, 1866, Fetterman Massacre— Wyoming

On the morning of December 21, with the thermometer well below zero, a party of woodcutters and teamsters leaves Fort Phil Kearney crossing south of Sullivant's Hill heading for Pilot Hill. At approximately 11:00 a picket reports to Post Commander Col. Henry B. Carrington that the wood party is under attack by Indians. Carrington details a relief party under the command of Capt. William J. Fetterman of forty-eight men of the 18th Infantry and twenty-seven troopers of the 2nd Cavalry to go at once to the aid of the wood party. Fetterman is given explicit orders by Carrington not to cross Lodge Trail Ridge for any reason. The seventy-six-man force crosses Big Piney River, moves up over the southern slopes of Lodge Trail Ridge and soon is lost to sight. Soon after Surgeon C. M. Hines and several men are dispatched to go with Fetterman but return with news that the valley below the ridge is swarming with Indians. Although the wood train arrives back safely, heavy gunfire can be heard from the direction of Peno Creek. Capt. Tenedor Ten Eyck and a party of forty-eight men are sent to find Fetterman, but soon return to report Indians swarming in the valley below. Late in the day, another search party finds the dead, frozen and mutilated bodies of Fetterman and his men strung out along Peno Creek. Carrington reports, "eyes torn out ... brains taken out ... hands and feet cut off ... skulls severed in every form." Indian casualties are unknown. Source: 7, 12, 20, 54, 70, 78, 102, 108, 119 [Quote 70]. Marker: Fort Phil Kearney State Historic Site, located just off I-90 between Buffalo and Sheridan, WY.

DECEMBER 23, 1866—*Texas*

William Bailey and D. B. Green, both about eighteen years of age, are killed by eleven Indians near Sandy Creek in Montague County. Source: 69, 124

1866—*Texas*

James Ball, age nine, and William Ball, age eight, are taken captive by Indians in Wise County while on their way to borrow a handsaw. They are released one year later. Source: 69, 124

1867

Fort Lyon is established in Colorado. Fort Griffin, Fort Richardson and Fort Concho are established in Texas. Fort D. A. Russell and Fort Fetterman are established in Wyoming. Fort Shaw is established in Montana and Fort Totten in North Dakota.

JANUARY 30, 1867—*Texas*

Jack and George Miller and two other young men, August Rothe and Herbert Wenand, are attacked by Indians while searching for cows near Fort Lincoln. George Miller is killed and Wenand carried off. Source: 96

MARCH 14, 1867—*Texas*

Indians kill Hiram Gerdes about two and a half miles southeast of Quihi. Source: 96

APRIL 1867—*Montana*

John Bozeman, the man who gave his name to the Bozeman Trail, is killed by Blackfeet on his way to Ft. C. F. Smith. Source: 108, 117

APRIL 1867—*Arizona*

Eighty-five U.S. cavalrymen from Fort Whipple led by Capt. J. M. Williams attack and kill fifty Apache Indians on the Verde River. Source: 102

APRIL 1867—*Texas*

Sixty Kiowa Indians led by Satank and Satanta raid the William Hamelton homestead on Walnut Creek while Mr. Hamelton is away. The Indians kill Hamelton's wife Sally and take his two daughters, Lavina and Mary. Lavina is soon released, but Mary grows up as a Kiowa. Source: 69, 124. Marker: Intersection of FM 730 and SH 199 at Azle, TX.

JUNE 1867—*Texas*

Indians raid the Rabb farm while Mr. Rabb is away. They kill Mrs. Rabb and a family friend and carry the Rabb children off. Source: 69, 109

JUNE 22, 1867—*Kansas*

A wagon train consisting of eight wagons led by Capt. Francisco Baca is attacked by Cheyenne Chief Lame Bear and seventy-five warriors near present-day Cimarron. Baca's men are successful in holding the Cheyenne off, but the Indians steal over fifty of the wagon train's mules. Source: 73

JUNE 24, 1867—*Kansas*

Sioux Indians led by Pawnee Killer attack the camp of Gen. George Armstrong Custer. After a brief engagement a council is held, and then the Indians withdraw. Custer pursues the Indians but loses them. Source: 73, 131

JUNE 26, 1867—*Kansas*

Gen. George Crook's wagon train is attacked by several hundred Indians halfway between Fort Wallace and Beaver Creek. After a three-hour engagement, the Indians withdraw. Sgt. Frederick Wylyams is killed in the skirmish, and his mutilated body is photographed by Dr. William Abraham Bell. Source: 34, 44

JUNE 1867—*Arizona*

Troops from Fort Mojave engage over 250 Havasupai Indians for over nine hours along the Grand Canyon's walls. The Havasupai surrender two years later and are sent to a compound at Camp Beale Springs north of Kingman. Source: 87

JULY 2, 1867, KIDDER MASSACRE—*Kansas*

Second Lt. Lyman S. Kidder, ten enlisted men and Sioux scout-guide Red Beard are detailed to deliver orders to Gen. George Armstrong Custer. Kidder's small command arrives at Custer's deserted camp on July 1. Kidder then pushes on in search of Custer but is spotted by Sioux and Cheyenne warriors near Beaver Creek. Kidder and his men are pursued for several miles and finally dig in near a small ravine. The Sioux scout Red Beard calls out to his people to let him go, but the warriors refuse. The Indians pour a heavy fire on the small force as they work their way closer to the doomed patrol. Kidder and his men, along with Red Beard, are finally overwhelmed and all killed. Source: 8, 55, 73, 78. Marker: A stone marker stands exactly 1 mile from CR 28 and 74. A roadside marker at the junction gives additional information. This is a designated Kansas Historical Site.

JULY 9, 1867—*New Mexico*

Lt. Henry M. Bragg attempts to confiscate horses from Navajos near Fort Sumner. Bragg believes the horses are stolen but has no proof, and when the Navajo natives refuse to give the animals up, Bragg returns to Fort Sumner. Lt. Charles Porter, angry at Bragg's failure then leads a force to recover the horses. Porter, who is drunk at the time, attempts, to take the horses by force and gunfire breaks out. The troopers are chased back to Fort Sumner, and five are killed, including Lt. Porter. Source: 73. Marker: Crossroads of U.S. 60 & 84 and New Mexico 20, Ft. Sumner, NM.

JULY 11, 1867, SCHOOL HOUSE MASSACRE—*Texas*

Comanche Indians attack a schoolhouse on the Leon River in Hamilton County, killing schoolteacher Ann Whitney, a Mr. Strangeline and one of the children. John Kuykendall is carried off but returns years later after being sold to an Indian agent. Source: 73, 89, 109

JULY 12, 1867—*Kansas*

A force under Gen. George Armstrong Custer finds the bodies of Lt. Lyman Kidder and his small command killed July 2. "Mangled bodies of poor Kidder and his party," Custer wrote, "yet so brutally hacked and disfigured as to be beyond recognition save as human beings." There is evidence that some of Kidder's men have been burned alive. Source: 55, 78 [Quote 55]

JULY 17, 1867—*Texas*

Reuben Johnson, Ewell Proffitt and Rias Carrollton are attacked by Indians while branding cattle on the Fitzpatrick Ranch. The young cowhands are chased over three quarters of a mile and killed. Source: 69, 124. Marker: On U.S. 380 west of Newcastle, TX.

July 19–21, 1867 — *Texas*

A wood cutting detail of soldiers prepare for their supper at their camp on the West Fork of the Trinity River, eighteen miles from Jacksboro, when Indians stampede the army's mule herd through the camp. The Indians kill one teamster and take a number of mules. The next day the warriors return but are held at bay by the soldiers' rifle fire. Source: 44

July 24, 1867 — *Nebraska*

The Peter Campbell homestead is attacked by Sioux and Cheyenne Indians. Campbell's two daughters and twin sons are carried off. The Indians then attack the home of Mrs. Thurston Warren a half a mile away, killing her. The Campbell children are exchanged for Cheyenne Chief Turkey Leg's nephew in September at North Platte. Source: 137. Marker: West of Doniphan along Hwy. 34 & 281 in Hall County, NE.

August 1, 1867, The Hayfield Fight — *Montana*

Soldiers at Fort C. F. Smith have been warned by friendly Indians that a large Sioux force is headed for the fort. A hay-cutting party of nineteen soldiers under the command of Sec. Lt. Sigmund Sternberg and six civilians leave the fort early on the morning of August 1, 1867, for their hayfield camp some two miles away. After arriving at camp the hay-cutting party begins its work in a nearby field while the soldiers relax near the camp's corral. At 9:30 shots are heard from the hayfield as the mule teams gallop back to camp under fire. Soldiers and civilians take cover inside the corral as some 2,500 Sioux warriors led by Red Cloud attack the small band of defenders. Sec. Lt. Sternberg is killed in the first wave of attack as the Sioux try to ride over the small force of men. One of the civilian haymakers Al Colvin, who was a captain during the Civil War, assumes command. The soldiers are armed with newly issued fifty-caliber Springfield rifles and plenty of ammunition. The civilians are armed with Spencer and Henry repeating rifles. Almost all have pistols. The Indians' second charge is met with a fusillade of bullets, and they withdraw to nearby sniping positions. A third charge by the Indians is stopped by the heavy gunfire of the defenders from behind the corral. The Indians make a final charge on the south side of the corral, but the foot attack is staggered by volley after volley from the small party of defenders. The warriors finally withdraw. The party of defenders lose five killed. The Indian losses are estimated at 50 to 100. Source: 70, 102, 108, 119. Marker: South of Hardin near Yellowtail, Fort C. F. Smith, MT.

August 1, 1867 — *Kansas*

A war party of about thirty Cheyenne attack several railroad workers a few miles east of Fort Harker, killing and scalping them. The warriors then attack the Big Creek Station, killing one worker. Two Indians are reported killed. The 10th Cavalry led by Maj. George A. Armes pursues the war party but is soon surrounded and has to fight its way back to Fort Hays. Source: 73

August 2, 1867, The Wagon Box Fight — *Wyoming*

Company C of the 27th Infantry under the command of Capt. James W. Powell is assigned escort duty for wood contractors on August 1. The wood party, six miles from Fort Phil Kearney, is cutting timber near Piney Island. Two camps are set up, one on an open, leveled plain with corrals nearby, the second near the woods. The soldiers are well armed with the new breech-loading Springfield rifles and seven thousand rounds of ammunition recently brought to the fort. At 7:00 A.M. on August 2, a force of over 200 Sioux warriors attacks the first camp who fight their way to the corral and dig in. At the same time another force of 500 Indians attacks the wood train at the camp in the woods. The soldiers and civilians there make an orderly retreat eastward toward the fort, bypassing the corral. This party makes it to Fort Kearney, losing four men. Capt. Powell and his men dig in for an assault on the corral. Over 500 mounted warriors make a mad dash toward the corral where they are met by a heavy volley from the small party of defenders. Some of the men fire while others reload. Dead and wounded Indians and ponies pile up outside the corral. The second assault by an estimated 700 warriors on foot is repelled by the soldiers and civilians. The Indians withdraw a distance and late in the afternoon make a third foot attack on the corral defenders. The massed foot assault is staggered by the troopers' first volley from the corral, but the wave of warriors continues on toward the small group of defenders. Volley after volley soon drives the warriors back. After some random sniping the Indians pick up what dead and wounded they can and withdraw. Post records differ on the number killed, but it is believed that the whites lose ten while the Indian casualties are believed to be 50 to 100. Source: 7, 47, 54, 70, 102, 108, 119. Marker: Fort Phil Kearney State Historic Site, located off I-90 midway between Buffalo and Sheridan, WY.

AUGUST 6, 1867, TRAIN ATTACKED BY CHEYENNE—*Nebraska*

Cheyenne led by Turkey Leg attack a train near present-day Lexington, Nebraska. The Cheyenne hiding nearby attack and kill several workers and scalp William Thompson as he works on a broken telegraph line. After being shot by Cheyenne braves, Thompson is knocked to the ground where a warrior "commenced sawing and hacking away at my scalp." Another train arrives on the scene and Cheyenne warriors attack it and kill an engineer and brakeman. Seven civilians are reported killed, and the bodies are burned by the Indians. Thompson survives, minus hair. Dr. R. C. Moore attempts to stitch the scalp back on but is unsuccessful. Source: 20, 73, 116 [Quote 20]

AUGUST 17, 1867—*Nebraska*

Southern Cheyenne led by Turkey Leg pry up rails and cause the wreck of a train near Lexington. Engineer "Bully Brooks" Bower and fireman Hendershott are killed. Lt. Issac Davis and twenty men repairing telegraph lines are attacked by Turkey Leg's raiding party. Pawnee Indians with Capt. James Murie's force attack the Cheyenne and drive them off. The Pawnees kill and scalp fifteen Cheyenne and capture a woman, a boy and a girl. Source: 73, 87

AUGUST 20–21, 1867—*Kansas*

U.S. Cavalry led by Maj. George A. Armes is attacked by over 200 Cheyenne at Prairie Dog Creek. The attack begins at 9:00 A.M. and lasts until sundown when the troops withdraw. Eleven soldiers are badly wounded. Another company of soldiers with the supply wagons under Capt. George B. Jenness is attacked several miles away. One Buffalo Soldier is killed and fourteen are wounded. (The Indians call black soldiers "Buffalo Soldiers" because of the texture of their hair.) Source: 73

AUGUST 1867—*Kansas*

Indians attack Union Pacific Railroad workers near Fort Arbuckle, killing seven. Company F, Buffalo Soldiers (a company of black troopers), pursue and engage the Indians in a running battle for over two hours. They report killing a number of Indians. Sgt. Christie and Capt. Armes are reported killed. Source: 118

SEPTEMBER 19, 1867 — Kansas

Forty-five miles west of Fort Hayes Buffalo Soldiers of the 9th or 10th Cavalry are attacked by Indians. Sgt. Davis and his men drive the Indians off, but the Indians return later to finish the troopers off and are met with a more prepared defense. The soldiers kill or wound thirteen warriors. Source: 73, 118

OCTOBER 1, 1867 — Texas

Two Buffalo Soldiers of the 9th Cavalry are killed by Indians while escorting the military mail stage from Camp Hudson to Howard's Well. The driver and several passengers are wounded. Source: 113, 118

OCTOBER 16, 1867 — Arizona

Apaches ambush cavalrymen led by Col. Reuben Bernard in the Chiricahua Mountains. Sgt. Stephen S. Fuller and Pvt. Thomas Collins are killed. Source: 68

DECEMBER 26, 1867 — Texas

The 9th Cavalry commanded by Capt. William Thompson Frohock is attacked while camped near the ruins of Fort Lancaster. The large raiding party, made up of Kickapoo, Apache and renegades, kills three troopers, thirty-one horses and six mules. The Indians' loss is estimated at twenty killed. Source: 113, 118

> "No white person or persons shall be permitted to settle upon or occupy any portion of the territory, or without the consent of the Indians to pass through the same."
>
> — Treaty of 1868
> [Source: 153]

1868

Fort Omaha is established in Nebraska and Fort Washakie in Wyoming.

JANUARY 14, 1868 — Arizona

The 8th U.S. Cavalry under the command of Capt. Samuel Young attacks a Walapai native camp in Red Wing Canyon, also called Difficult Canyon. Seven Indians are hit in the attack, including Chief Scherum. Young and his men battle the Indians for over an hour and a half but are forced to retreat when their ammunition runs low. Source: 73

FEBRUARY 2, 1868 — Texas

Indians attack the homestead of John J. Alexander on the south prong of the Guadalupe River while he is away. Indians kill his wife, but a neighbor, Mrs. W. C. Wachter, escapes. The Alexander home is burned. Source: 69

MARCH 2–3, 1868 — Texas

After a skirmish with Comanche at Battle Creek stockmen find the body of George Hazelwood and a dead Indian nearby. The retreating Comanche head northwest and attack the Ledbetter Salt Works where they besiege several men, women and children. Source: 17, 69, 109

MARCH 6, 1868 — Texas

After an aborted raid on the Clear Fork area in northwest Texas, Comanche warriors slowed by their wounded are caught near present-day Haskell by a force of U.S. Cavalry and friendly Tonkawa Indians. The Tonkawa, victims of Comanche raids for years, carry a heartfelt hatred for their enemy. After battling with the troops for hours, the Comanche warriors are finally overcome and turned over to the Tonkawa, who take revenge for years of abuse at the hands of their enemy. None of the Comanche prisoners survive. Source: 17

March 6, 1868 — *Texas*

A sixty-two-man military force under the command of Capt. A. R. Chaffee, along with Tonkawa, trail Indians responsible for the Ledbetter Salt Works attack. In a morning attack on the Indians' camp at the two forks of Paint Creek, seven Comanche are killed. Source: 69

March 7, 1868 — *Texas*

The eighteen-year-old daughter of Dr. Bowman, Sallie Bowman, is attacked while riding her horse. Her horse outdistances the Indians for quite a ways but eventually begins to fatigue. The Indians kill her as she nears the home of Mr. and Mrs. Jones. Source: 69, 124. Marker: On old Decatur-Aurora Rd., north of Aurora, TX.

1868 — *Texas*

George R. Bevers fires on an Indian attempting to steal one of his horses on his Palto Pinto County farm; the Indian escapes. Source: 69

April 16, 1868 — *Nebraska*

Sioux Indians attack railroad workers near Elm Creek, killing five section men and stealing some cattle. The Indians then attack the post at Sidney, scalping conductor Tom Cahoon and shooting four arrows into William Edmundson, but both men survive. Source: 87

April 29, 1868 — *Nebraska*

Indians attack and kill section foreman Timothy Tobin and section hands Schulz and McCarthy. A Mrs. Costin sets out to warn the other section crews of the danger and is eventually picked up by a passing train. Mrs. Timothy Tobin is also rescued. Source: 73, 137. Marker: Hwy. 30 approx. one and half miles east of Overton, NE, in Dawes County.

May 30, 1868 — *Arizona*

The 8th U.S. Cavalry clash with Apaches at San Carlos. Pvt. William G. Cubberly and Pvt. Edgar R. Aston find a way out of a canyon while under fire from Indians. Cubberly and Aston are awarded the Medal of Honor. Source: 115

July 3, 1868 — *Texas*

Two boys, Martin Cathey and Johnnie Hale, are killed by Indians north of the Old Newberry place. Source: 69

July 8, 1868 — *Arizona*

Pima Indians, enemies of the Apaches, attack and drive some Apaches into a cave in Big Rump Canyon. The Pima send a runner to Camp Reno for reinforcements. The troops arrive and fire from the canyon's rim, but soon Apache reinforcements arrive and the fight escalates. The Apaches finally withdraw but are pursued by troops from Camp Reno led by Lt. Camillo Carr. Source: 73

August 1868 — *Texas*

A stagecoach escorted by former Texas Ranger "Big Foot" Wallace and eight companions is attacked by Indians near Van Horn's Well. Wallace and his men shoot some of the horses for a barricade and hold off the warriors until the next day when a thunderstorm develops and the Indians withdraw. Source: 73

August 21–22, 1868 — *Kansas*

Near Prairie Dog Creek, several hundred Cheyenne and Lakota warriors attack the supply train of the 10th Cavalry led by Capt. George Jenness. A nearby force under Capt. George A. Armes is also attacked at the Prairie Dog Creek. At daybreak the following morning Armes fights his way south and links up with Jenness. The fight continues until nightfall when the Indians withdraw. Source: 73

August 13, 1868 — *Kansas*

Cheyennes raid the White homestead, killing Mr. White and capturing his eighteen-year-old daughter Sarah C. White. Source: 58

> "If I were an Indian, I often think I would greatly prefer to cast my lot among those of my people adhered to the free open plains rather than submit to the confined limits of a reservation."
> —Lt. Col. George Armstrong Custer [Source: 20]

AUGUST 13, 1868—*Texas*

At Spanish Fort four people are killed, eight people scalped and one woman "outraged by 13 warriors," who scalp and kill her and her four children. Source: 84

SEPTEMBER 2, 1868— *Kansas*

Four soldiers under the command of Sgt. George J. Dittoe transporting a wagon along Coon Creek are attacked by thirty-six Indians. Three Indians are killed. Cpl. Leander Herron goes to the assistance of four men under attack by over fifty warriors. Herron is awarded the Medal of Honor. Source: 115

SEPTEMBER 10, 1868— *Colorado*

Maj. "Sandy" Forsyth receives a report at Fort Wallace, Kansas, that Cheyenne raiders have attacked a wagon train at Sheridan City, few miles east of the fort. Source: 70

SEPTEMBER 12, 1868— *Texas*

Sixty troopers of the 9th Cavalry under Lt. Cusack pursue and catch up with an Indian raiding party at Horsehead Hill. The troopers kill over twenty-five Indians and capture two Mexican boys, an Indian girl, 198 horses and mules and then burn a number of tepees and supplies. Source: 113

SEPTEMBER 1868—*Nebraska*

Sioux Indians pry up rails and wreck a train near Elm Creek. Pawnee scouts led by Frank North catch up with the Sioux and kill two of them. Source: 87

SEPTEMBER 17, 1868, BEECHER ISLAND—*Colorado*

After Cheyenne warriors attack a wagon train near Sheridan City, a force is organized to go after the marauding Indians. The fifty-man party, made up mostly of Indian scouts, is led by Maj. Sandy Forsyth, and it follows the Indian trail toward the Republican River. The small force is well armed with Spencer seven-shot carbines and 170 rounds per man. Another 4,000 rounds are carried on pack mules. On the morning of the 18th, Forsyth and his men are surprised by over 500 Cheyenne warriors who charge down on the small force. The men dig in on a small island located on the Republican River as the long, wide front of warriors bears down toward them. The Indians, intending to ride over the small force, are staggered by the gunfire from the island, and the charge splits. A second attempt by the Indians to dislodge the whites fails as heavy gunfire from the island checks the Indians charge. A third charge headed by Cheyenne leader Roman Nose grinds to a halt when the famous warrior is shot and killed. The Indians now begin sniping from the banks as a shower of arrows rain down on the whites, and soon all horses and mules lie dead or dying from the Indians' fire. The night is filled with the moans and groans of over nineteen wounded men lying in a cold drizzling rain. Several men lie dead, including Lt. Fredrick H. Beecher. Dr. Mooers, the party's surgeon, lies nearby slowly dying from a bullet in the head. Jack Stilwell and Pierre Trudeau answer the major's call for volunteers and slip off in the night on foot for Fort Wallace, 125 miles away. The Indians pull out on the third day. On September 25, a relief force of the 10th Cavalry under Capt. Louis Carpenter arrives. Source: 7, 12, 70, 102, 108, 119. Marker: Roadside pull off, north side of U.S. 34, east of Yuma, CO.

October 15, 1868 — *Kansas*

The 10th Cavalry under Capt. Louis Carpenter engages hostile Indians. For this action and for his part in the rescue of Forsyth's men at Beecher Island, Carpenter is awarded the Medal of Honor. Source: 7, 70, 115

October 21, 1868 — *Arizona*

The U.S. Cavalry skirmishes with hostile Indians. Pvt. John Kay is awarded the Medal of Honor for saving a wounded comrade. Source: 115

November 11, 1868 — *Utah*

Near Cienaga Springs, U.S. troops clash with hostile Indians. Saddler Julius H. Stickoffer is awarded the Medal of Honor for Gallantry in Action. Source: 115

November 27, 1868, Battle of the Washita — *Oklahoma*

On a frigidly cold morning in sub-freezing temperatures, forces under Lt. Col. George Armstrong Custer attack Black Kettle's village on the Washita River in present western Oklahoma. The slumbering village puts up some resistance, but most inhabitants flee toward the river where they are shot down. Black Kettle and his wife are killed by a fusillade of bullets. The village is captured in about fifteen minutes, but it takes hours to burn all of the lodges. Custer's losses include several killed, among them the grandson of Alexander Hamilton, Capt. Lewis Hamilton. Maj. Joel Elliott is reported missing. Soldiers find the bodies of Clara Blinn (Blynn) and her small son Willie who had been taken hostage earlier by the Indians and killed as the troops charged the village. Over 400 Indian ponies are shot, and Custer withdraws from the field under pressure from Indians warriors down river. Infantryman Delos G. Sanderson is scalped but survives. A number of items from farmhouses and homesteads in the Saline and Solomon raid are found. Custer reports 19 troopers killed, 14 wounded and 103 Indians killed. On December 10, a party of soldiers returns to the battlefield in search of the body of Maj. Elliott and his men. Source: 7, 11, 12, 20, 36, 67, 102, 108. Marker: Washita National Battlefield, SR 47A near Cheyenne, OK.

November 1868 — *Oklahoma*

Troops under Maj. A. W. Evans from Fort Bascom attack a Comanche camp near a Wichita village, driving the Indians off and burning the village. One soldier is killed. Source: 67

November 1868 — *Texas*

A tracking party consisting of the Allen brothers, Baker Ballew, Andrew Carter and others catch up with an Indian raiding party near Mansker Lake in present Eastland County. After a short skirmish they manage to kill several Indians. Source: 100

December 7, 1868 — *Kansas*

Ralph Morrison, a hunter, is killed and scalped by Cheyenne warriors near Ft. Dodge. His lifeless body is photographed by William S. Soule. Source: 34

1869

Fort Sill is established in Oklahoma.

April 24, 1869 — *Texas*

Nine cowhands track a war party and attack them near present Mineral Wells, killing several warriors. Elbert Doss is killed in the fight. Source: 69. Marker: Ten miles west from Weatherford, TX, on U.S. 180, Porter Cemetery.

May 1869 — *Texas*

A party of whites going to or from El Paso is attacked by Apaches. Charles Keerl, his wife and four others are killed and their bodies mutilated. Source: 69, 124

May 13, 1869—*Kansas*

Maj. Eugene Carr and several companies of the 5th Cavalry surprise Cheyenne warriors under Tall Bull at Elephant Rock, along Beaver Creek in northwest Kansas. At least twenty-five warriors are killed along with four cavalrymen. Source: 18, 147

May 16, 1869—*Nebraska*

A troop of U.S. Cavalry under the command of Maj. Carr tracks an Indian trail and soon runs into a large force of Lakota at Spring Creek. Carr and his troopers hold off an attack by a vastly superior force of Indians. First Lt. John B. Babcock leads his men to high ground where they are able to hold the Indians until relief comes. Babcock is awarded the Medal of Honor. Source: 73, 115

May 28, 1869—*Kansas*

Cheyenne Dog Soldiers led by Tall Bull attack a railroad crew near Fossil Creek near present-day Russell, killing two workers and wounding four. Source: 147

May 30, 1869—*Kansas*

Cheyenne Dog Soldiers led by Tall Bull raid into Lincoln County thirty miles west of Saline and north of Fort Harker. Maria Weichel, a recent arrival from Germany, is taken captive and her husband George is killed. Also captured is Susanna Alderdice who is forced to watch the murders of her small boys, ages from two to five. Erskild and Stine Lauritzen are killed and scalped while on their way to a nearby neighbor's house. Source: 11, 18, 147

June 4, 1869—*Arizona*

At the Picacho Mountains the 8th U.S. Cavalry clash with Apache warriors. Bugler Thomas Gay and Pvt. Joseph Watson are awarded the Medal of Honor. Gay's citation: "Bravery in scouts and actions against Indians." Watson's citation: "Killed an Indian and captured his arms." Source: 115

June 1869—*North Dakota*

Friendly Arikara, Mandan and Hidatsa Indians at Fort Berthold are attacked by over 500 Sioux warriors. Although the Sioux are driven off, the attack demoralizes the Indians at the fort. Source: 87

June 19, 1869—*Kansas*

Cheyenne Dog Soldiers attack a surveying party guarded by Company E, 7th Cavalry. Surveyor Howard Schuyler is shot at point-blank range but survives. Four Indians are killed and twelve wounded. The soldiers report two wounded. Source: 73

June 29, 1869—*Arizona*

The U.S. Cavalry skirmishes with Apache Indians at the Santa Maria River. Pvt. Albert Sale is awarded the Medal of Honor. Citation: "Gallantry in killing an Indian warrior and capturing his effects." Source: 115

July 3, 1869—*Arizona*

At Hell's Canyon the U.S. Cavalry skirmishes with Apache Indians. First Sgt. Sanford Bradbury, Cpl. Paul Haupt and Cpl. John J. Mitchell of the 8th U.S. Cavalry are awarded the Medal of Honor for Gallantry in Action. Source: 115

July 8, 1869—*Colorado*

Cpl. John Kyle and three men of Company M are sent to a previous camp to recover some horses but run into hostile Cheyenne. Kyle and his men seek shelter in nearby rocks and hold off the Indians until they finally withdraw. Source: 73

July 8, 1869—*Kansas*

U.S. Cavalry forces clash with hostile Indians near the Republican River. Cpl. John Kyle (Kile), and Pawnee scout Co-rux-te-chod-ish (Mad Bear) are awarded the Medal of Honor. Source: 115, 147

July 11, 1869, Battle of Summit Springs—*Colorado*

U.S. soldiers under Gen. Eugene Carr with Buffalo Bill Cody as guide and 150 Pawnee scouts under Maj. Frank North surprise and attack the Cheyenne village at Summit Springs. The troops attack from two directions, driving the Cheyenne into a ravine. Over fifty-two Cheyenne are killed, including Chief Tall Bull. Among the slain in the Indian village is Susanna Alderdice and her young son who are believed to have been killed by Indians as the troops attacked the village. After the burial of Mrs. Alderdice and her son the troops return to Fort Sedgewick. Source: 7, 10, 78, 87, 102, 108, 124. Marker: U.S. 34, town roadside park, intersection of 1st and Custer, Akron, CO.

July 12, 1869—*Texas*

One hundred Kiowa warriors led by Kicking Bird are pursued by troops after robbing a train at Rock Station. The outnumbered troops under Capt. Curwen B. McClellan are forced to withdraw after a short skirmish. Source: 87

July 1869—*Texas*

Indians raid settlements at Mary's Creek near Weatherford, killing and scalping four people and running off a number of cattle. Source: 44

August 25, 1869—*Arizona*

Indian warriors fight an engagement with the U.S. Cavalry at the Agua Fria River. Cpl. Michael Corcoran, Sgt. Cornelius Donavan, Pvt. Frank Hamilton, Pvt. Herbert Mahers, Pvt. John Moran, Cpl. Philip Murphy and Cpl. Thomas Murphy are awarded the Medal of Honor for Gallantry in Action. Source: 115

August 26, 1869—*Arizona*

U.S. troops and Apache Indians clash near the Seneca Mountains. Cpl. Edward Stanley is awarded the Medal of Honor. Citation: "Gallantry in Action." Source: 115

September 23, 1869—*Arizona*

At Red Creek, U.S. Cavalry forces clash with Apache Indians. Cpl. George Ferrari, Sgt. John Harris and Pvt. John Walker are awarded the Medal of Honor for Gallantry in Action. Source: 115

September 26, 1869—*Kansas*

Cheyenne warriors attack Buffalo Bill Cody, Frank North and two Pawnee scouts while they hunt buffalo at Prairie Dog Creek. Troops camped nearby come to Cody's rescue, but they are soon attacked from the rear by another force of Cheyenne. The Indians withdraw at dusk. Source: 73

October 5–6, 1869—*Arizona*

Apaches attack a stagecoach near Dragoon Springs in southern Arizona, killing John Finkel Stone, owner of the Apache Pass Mining Company, the stage driver and four privates, W. H. Bates, M. Blake, D. B. Shallaberger and J. W. Slocum. The Apaches then attack a herd following close behind, killing one of the six drovers and stealing 120 of the cattle. The next day a pursuit party of the 3rd Cavalry led by Col. Rueben Bernard catches up with the raiders seven hours later and drives the cattle back toward Fort Bowie. Twelve warriors are reported killed. Source: 68, 73, 87

October 14, 1869—*Arizona*

At Lyry Creek, the U.S. Cavalry skirmishes with Apache Indians. Pvt. David Goodman, Pvt. John F. Rowalt and Pvt. John Raerick are awarded the Medal of Honor for Gallantry in Action. Source: 115

October 20, 1869—*Arizona*

Chiricahua Apaches led by Cochise attempt to ambush Company G, 1st Cavalry led by Col. Reuben Bernard near the

Chiricahua Mountains. The ambush fails, and the troopers drive the Apaches from the nearby hills. The Medal of Honor is awarded for Gallantry in Action to Cpl. Charles Dickens, Pvt. John Donahue, Pvt. Edwin Elwood, Blacksmith Mosher Harding, Sgt. Frederick Jarvis, Trumpeter Bartholomew Keenan, Pvt. Charles Kelly, Cpl. Nicholas Meaher, Pvt. Edward Murphy, First Sgt. Francis Oliver, Pvt. Edward Pengally, Cpl. Thomas Powers, Pvt. James Russell, Pvt. Charles Schroeter, Pvt. Robert B. Scott, Sgt. Andrew J. Smith, Pvt. Theodore F. Smith, Pvt. Thomas Smith, Pvt. Thomas J. Smith, Pvt. William Smith, Pvt. William H. Smith, Pvt. Orizoba Spence, Pvt. George Springer, Saddler Christian Steiner, Pvt. Thomas Sullivan, Pvt. James Sumner, Sgt. John Thompson, Pvt. John Tracy, Pvt. Charles H. Ward and Pvt. Enoch Weiss. (The Southwest Indian wars of the 1870s was a period in which an excessive number of Medals of Honor were awarded, some merely for "Good Campaigning." In 1916 a general review of all Medals of Honor deemed 900 unwarranted. Civilians awarded the Medal of Honor also had theirs revoked. Cpl. Charles Dixon's medal listed above was among those stricken from the list. In June 1989, the U.S. Army Board restored Dixon's Medal of Honor citation.) Source: 68, 87, 115

October 28, 1869—*Texas*

First Lt. George E. Albee with two men attack and drive eleven Indians from their position on the Brazos River. Lt. Albee is awarded the Medal of Honor for his actions. Source: 115

October 29, 1869—*Arizona*

The U.S. Cavalry engages hostile Indians near the Chiricahua Mountains. Pvt. John Carr, Company G, 8th Cavalry is awarded the Medal of Honor for Gallantry in Action. Source: 115

November 1869—*Texas*

Mrs. J. Brown, the mother of twin babies, is killed and scalped near her home. Source: 124

November 26, 1869—*Arizona*

Sgt. John Crist, Company L, 8th U.S. Cavalry is awarded the Medal of Honor for "action against Apache Indians on this date." Source: 115

December 1, 1869—*Wyoming*

At Horseshoe Creek Sioux attack a mail stage heading from Fort Fetterman to Fort Laramie. Ten soldiers under Sgt. Conrad Bahr drive the Lakota off. Three soldiers are wounded. Source: 73

1870

Fort Apache is established in Arizona.

January 2, 1870—*North Dakota*

Two hundred Sioux warriors attack the villages of the Arikara, Mandan and Hidatsa Indians near Fort Berthold but are driven off by artillery fire from the fort. Source: 87

January 1870—*Oklahoma*

Kiowa Indians led by Chief Satanta stampede over 300 head of cattle on a cattle drive and steal cash and food from the cowboys. Source: 118

January 23, 1870—*Montana*

Six companies of U.S. Cavalry under Maj. Eugene Baker attack a Piegan Blackfeet village on the Piegan River in twenty-degree weather, killing over thirty-three men, ninety women and fifty children. The U.S. Army tries to cover this up, but the news eventually gets out, inciting a number of uprisings at Indian agencies. Source: 87

January 27, 1870—*Arizona*

Troops under Col. Reuben Bernard attack Apaches led by Cochise in the Dragoon Mountains killing thirteen Indians. Source: 78

1870—*Texas*

Fourteen year-old George Bishop is killed by Indians on the C. J. Johnson Ranch on Little Cedar River. Source: 69

MAY 5, 1870—*Arizona*

Apaches led by Cochise ambush the 3rd Cavalry, killing First Lt. Howard B. Cushing and three others at Bear Springs in the Whetstone Mountains. Source: 23, 78

MAY 17, 1870—*Nebraska*

The 2nd U.S. Cavalry engages hostile Indians at Spring Creek. While looking for horses five soldiers are attacked by over fifty Indians but drive them off after a two-hour skirmish near Camp Bingham. Pvt. Heth Canfield, First Sgt. James Hill, Pvt. Michael Himmelsback, Pvt. Thomas Hubbard, Sgt. Patrick Leonard and Pvt. George W. Thompson are awarded the Medal of Honor for Gallantry in Action. (Leonard wins a second Medal of Honor April 28, 1876.) Source: 115, 137. Marker: On Hwy. 136 west of Ruskin in Nuckolls County, NE.

MAY 20, 1870—*Texas*

The 9th U.S. Cavalry skirmishes with Indians at Kickapoo Springs. Two captured white children are taken from the Indians. Sgt. Emanuel Stance, Troop F, is awarded the Medal of Honor for Gallantry on scouting after Indians. (Stance is the first Buffalo Soldier to win the Medal of Honor.) Source: 113, 115, 118

MAY 1870—*Texas*

Apache Indians raid the farm of Philip Buchmier near Fredericksburg and carry off his two stepsons, Willie and Herman Lehman. Willie escapes and returns to his parents' home, but his brother Herman is held captive for years. Herman Lehman will later write of his experiences in his autobiography, *Nine Years Among the Indians*. Source: 60, 69, 115, 124

JULY 10, 1870—*Texas*

Gottlieb (Goodleck) Koozer, a Quaker from Illinois, has been warned by others that he will be killed if he stays settled where he is, but he believes he can live in peace with the Indians. Kiowa Indians approach his cabin near Henrietta, and as he offers his hand in friendship, he is shot through the heart and killed. The Indians take Mrs. Koozer, her five children and fourteen-year-old Martin Kilgore captive. The captives are later ransomed by authorities. Source: 69, 84, 124

JULY 1870—*Oklahoma*

Kiowa led by Satanta raid near Ft. Sill but are pursued by Capt. Walsh with D and F Troops. Two Indians are killed, and two soldiers are wounded. Source: 118

JULY 12, 1870, BATTLE OF LITTLE WICHITA—*Texas*

The 6th Cavalry under Capt. Curwen B. McClellan encounters over 250 Kiowa led by Kicking Bird north of the Little Wichita River. Fighting against overwhelming odds McClellan orders a retreat and is pursued by the Kiowa warriors for several miles. Two troopers are reported killed and twelve wounded. McClellan's report stated, "I regard the expedition as a perfect success. I ... fought them with my small command ... and taught them a lesson they will not soon forget." The Medal of Honor is awarded for Gallantry in Action to Cpl. John Given (KIA), Pvt. George Blume (KIA), Cpl. John Connor, Sgt. George H. Eldridge, Cpl. John Given, Sgt. Thomas Kerrigan, First Sgt. John Kirk, Blacksmith Albert Glavinski, Sgt. John May, Farrier Samuel Porter, Cpl. Charles E. Smith, First Sgt. Alonzo Stokes, Cpl. James C. Watson, Bugler Claron Windus and Sgt. William Winterbottom.

(KIA is "killed in action.") Source: 44, 73, 115 [Quote 44]. Marker: FM 25, 2 miles north of Archer City, TX.

SEPTEMBER 28, 1870—*Texas*

The Thomas W. Stringfield family is ambushed and killed by Indians and Mexicans in McMullen County. Thomas and his wife, Sarah, are stabbed to death along with their six-year-old son Adolphus. Four-year-old Thomas is taken by the Indians and never seen again. Source: 69, 124

OCTOBER 5, 1870—*Texas*

Wichita River. In action on this date Cpl. Samuel Bowden, Cpl. Daniel Keating, Pvt. James Anderson, Post Guide James B. Doshier, Sgt. Michael Welch and Pvt. Benjamin Wilson, 6th U.S. Cavalry, are awarded the Medal of Honor for Gallantry during pursuit of Indians. Source: 115

NOVEMBER 18, 1870—*Texas*

Marcus Dalton, James Redfield and James McAster are killed by Indians on the Weatherford-Belnap Road. Source: 69, 109, 124

1871

JANUARY 1, 1871—*Arizona*

The U.S. Cavalry under the command of Col. Reuben Bernard catch up with Apache raiders in the Pinal Mountains. Nine Indians are killed, and a number are wounded. Source: 23, 68

JANUARY 24, 1871—*Texas*

A Kiowa-Comanche war party led by Mamanti attacks a wagon train at Turtle Hole Creek, killing three Negro teamsters including Britton Johnson. Johnson is a well-known scout and recognizes the Indians that attack and kill him. Source: 32, 44, 67, 69, 118

FEBRUARY 7, 1871—*Texas*

Nine Texas Rangers led by Sgt. E. H. Cobb are attacked by about forty Kiowas in present-day Wise County. The better-armed rangers kill two Indians and drive the rest off. Source: 73

APRIL 19, 1871—*Texas*

John W. Welburn is killed and scalped by Indians on Salt Creek Prairie. Source: 44, 84

APRIL 28, 1871, CAMP GRANT MASSACRE—*Arizona*

After numerous raids and murders by the Apaches a committee of citizens from Camp Grant decides to take matters into their own hands. A force consisting of six Americans, forty-eight Mexicans and ninety-two Papago under the command of William Oury attack the unarmed Apache village near Camp Grant. From 85 to 144 Indians are killed and twenty-seven children are captured and sold into slavery in Mexico. Oury and several others are later tried by a jury for their actions but are found not guilty. Source: 12, 23, 78, 87

MAY 5, 1871—*Arizona*

A patrol led by Lt. Howard Cushing is ambushed by Juh's band of Southern Apaches near Bear Springs. Cushing and a number of soldiers are killed, and the survivors are pursued for over four miles. Pvt. John Kilmartin, Pvt. Daniel Miller, Sgt. John Mott and Pvt. John P. Yount are awarded the Medal of Honor for Gallantry in Action. Source: 68, 87, 115

MAY 18, 1871, WARREN WAGON TRAIN MASSACRE—*Texas*

A Kiowa war party led by Chiefs Satanta, Satank and Big Tree attacks a wagon train belonging to Henry Warren near Salt Creek Prairie, killing four. Those who survive the onslaught are tortured by hot coals applied to their abdomens. One victim is found tied between two wagon wheels and burned to a crisp. All are stripped, scalped and mutilated. Thomas Brazeal escapes to Fort Richardson with a bullet wound. A military group which includes Gen. William T. Sherman had passed the same way some hours before but was not attacked. (Gen. Sherman visits the scene of the atrocity and realizes the seriousness of the Indian problem in Texas.) Source: 32, 44, 67, 69, 84, 89, 109. Marker: Texas 16 northeast of Graham, TX.

May 1871— *Texas*

Rivers Ranch employees Henry Eberson and John O. Allen leave the ranch in Young County looking for a lost herd. Riding some distance from each other, Indians attack the cowhands. Allen makes a run for it: "The Indians were shooting at me with bullets and arrows ... an arrow struck my right middle finger and one bullet struck my left leg." Eberbson is not so lucky. Cowhands find him still alive but wounded in fourteen places and scalped. He is taken back to the ranch but dies four days later. Source: 69, 124 [Quote 69]

May 28, 1871— *Texas*

Kiowa Chief Satank is killed trying to escape near Fort Richardson while being transported for trial. Satank tells George Washington, a Caddo chief who stands nearby, "Take this message to my people: tell them I died beside the road. My bones will be found there." Satank's body lies in a ditch for several days but is finally buried at Fort Sill, Oklahoma. Source: 20, 44, 84, 108 [Quote 84]

1871— *Texas*

Indians raid near the McCoy Ranch in present-day Cotulla. J. W. Gardiner runs into the war party and is shot with an arrow through the side and suffers a gunshot through the mouth. Nearby Nearny Ranch hands hear Gardiner's cries for help and drive the Indians off. Source: 96

July 18, 1871— *Arizona*

Apaches led by Cochise ambush troops under Gen. George Crook near Fort Bowie. A counterattack by the troops kill twenty-five Apaches and wound over thirty. Source: 68

Fall 1871— *Arizona*

A stagecoach carrying Lt. Wheeler is attacked on the road to Wickenburg by Yuma Apaches, killing several. On September 8, Gen. George Crook attempts to arrest those Indians involved near Date Creek but is met with resistance. Several Apaches are killed in the skirmish. Source: 87

August 1871— *Kansas*

A Kiowa raiding party is captured by soldiers after a fight at the Wichita Agency on the Red River and is sent to prison at Fort Marion, Florida. Source: 87

September 4, 1871— *Arizona*

Fort Crittenden is attacked by Apaches led by Cochise. Fifty-four horses and seven mules are driven off. Source: 87

September 19, 1871— *Oklahoma*

A detachment of Troop B of the Seminole-Negro scouts from Fort Sill is attacked by a large war party. One soldier, one horse and two Indians are killed. Source: 118

October 1871— *Texas*

Troop B of the Seminole-Negro Indian Scouts is ambushed on the Red River by Kiowa Indians, killing Trooper Larkin Foster. Source: 84, 118

October 10, 1871— *Texas*

The 4th Cavalry fights an engagement with Comanche Indians near the Brazos River. When the 4th's right line breaks and runs, First Lt. Robert G. Carter holds the left line and keeps the Indians at bay. Friendly Tonkawa Indians from nearby

Camp McKenzie attack and drive the Comanche off. Carter is awarded the Medal of Honor. Source: 73, 44, 115

November 5, 1871—*Arizona*

Indians from the Date Creek reservation attack a stagecoach eight miles west of Wickenburg, killing six men. Two badly wounded passengers, a woman named Shephard and a man named Kruger, escape to town. Source: 73

1872

Fort Abraham Lincoln is established in North Dakota and Fort Grant in Arizona.

January 20, 1872—*Texas*

In Jack County, Scott Cooley and his two brothers track down a Comanche raiding party and kill two of the four, one of whom they scalp. Source: 53

February 26, 1872—*Arizona*

Chiricahua Apaches attempt to run off a beef herd grazing near Bear Springs, a short distance from Fort Bowie. Herder John Williams is killed. Source: 68

April 20, 1872—*Texas*

The Gonzales wagon train is attacked by Comanche and Kiowa Indians near Howard's Well. All sixteen of the wagon trains' men are killed. The wounded mule herders are tied to the wagon wheels, soaked with kerosene and set on fire. Mrs. Marcela Sera and her infant child are captured, but her child is soon killed by having its head dashed against a wagon wheel. The war party is attacked by a small company of cavalry but holds them off and soon withdraws. Source: 32, 44, 73, 124

April 26, 1872—*Nebraska*

Near the Platte River, U.S. Cavalry forces clash with hostile Indians. Civilian Scout William F. "Buffalo Bill" Cody is later awarded the Medal of Honor for Gallantry in Action. (Some historians place the actual location of this engagement in Weld County, Colorado.) The 1916 general review board deems this award as unwarranted by the fact that Cody is a civilian and ineligible for the medal. It is revoked but reinstated in June 1989 by the U.S. Army Board of Corrections of Records. Sgt. John Foley, First Sgt. Leroy Vokes and Pvt. William H. Strayer are also awarded the Medal of Honor for Gallantry in Action. Source: 115

May 23, 1872—*Arizona*

U.S. Cavalry forces battle with Apache Indians at Sycamore Canyon. First Sgt. Richard Barrett is awarded the Medal of Honor for Gallantry in Action. Source: 115

June 19, 1872—*Texas*

The homestead of Abel Lee on the Clear Fork of the Brazos is attacked by Kiowa Indians led by White Horse. Lee is killed sitting on his front porch. His wife is killed, scalped and mutilated along with one of their three children. Source: 44, 69, 84

1872—*Texas*

A party of salt miners are attacked by Indians near present-day Strawn. Jackie Daniels, William Clayton and several others escape, but Banty Allen is killed. Source: 69

July 13, 1872—*Arizona*

Apache Indians fight the U.S. Cavalry near the Whetstone Mountains. Pvt. Michael Glynn, Pvt. John Nihill and First Sgt. Henry Newman are awarded the Medal of Honor for engaging hostile Apaches and killing several. Source: 115

1872—*Arizona*

First Sgt. Rudolph Stauffer is awarded the Medal of Honor for Gallantry in Action near Camp Hualpai. Source: 115

August 5, 1872—*Texas*

Indians attack a mail wagon near Fort Griffin but are driven off. Pvt. Franklin M. McDonald is awarded the Medal of Honor for Gallantry in Action. Source: 115. Marker: Fort Griffin Historical marker located on 1701 North U.S. 283, Albany, TX.

August 14, 1872—*Montana*

A survey party for the Northern Pacific Railroad, guarded by a large force of troops under the command of Maj. Eugene M. Baker, is attacked by over 400 Lakota and Cheyenne warriors at Pryor's Fork. The Indians and troops engage in long range sniping, and two Indians are killed. Source: 73, 87

August 27, 1872—*Arizona*

U.S. Cavalry battle hostile Indians at Davidson Canyon near Camp Crittenden. Sgt. James Brown, Company F, 5th U.S. Cavalry, is awarded the Medal of Honor for leading four men in driving off the Indians. Source: 115

August 30, 1872—*California*

When Modoc Indians led by Captain Jack (Kintpuash) fail to report to the reservation, U.S. Cavalry troops under Lt. F. A. Boutelle are sent to arrest them. Negotiations between the two sides become heated, and Boutelle thinking that he is about to be shot, opens fire on the Modoc. Both sides begin random firing, wounding quite a few, but only one soldier and one Indian are killed. The Modoc War begins. Source: 102

September 8, 1872—*Arizona*

Warned by friendly Hualapai natives that those Apaches responsible for the Wickenburg massacre are in a Date Creek Apache-Yuma camp, Lt. Col. George Crook decides to investigate. Crook and a dozen armed packers ride into the camp and are fired on. The troopers return fire, and seven warriors are killed. Apache leader Ochocama and a number of natives flee into the mountains. Sgt. Frank Hill is awarded the Medal of Honor for his actions. Source: 73, 115

September 25, 1872—*Arizona*

The 5th Cavalry under Col. J. W. Mason attacks Indians at Muchoas Canyon in the Santa Maria Mountains, killing several. Source: 87

September 29, 1872, Attack on Comanche Camp—*Texas*

Two hundred and twenty-two soldiers and twenty friendly Tonkawa led by Col. Ranald Slidell Mackenzie attack the village of Bull Bear's Comanche on McClellan Creek, killing over fifty warriors and taking 130 women and children captive. Mackenzie loses three men but captures the Indians' horses and provisions. The Tonkawa begin scalping the dead Comanche but are soon stopped by Mackenzie. Sgt. William Foster, Farrier David Larkin, Cpl. Henry McMasters, First Sgt. William McNamara, Cpl. William O'Neill, Blacksmith James Pratt, Pvt. William Rankin and Sgt. William Wilson (Wilson's second Medal of Honor) are awarded the Medal of Honor for Gallantry in Action. Source: 12, 32, 44, 67, 73, 102, 115

November 1872—*Texas*

Col. Ranald S. Mackenzie commanding the 4th Cavalry attacks Kwahadi Indians on the Staked Plains. More than 100 women and children are captured. Source: 32, 133

November 29–30, 1872—*Oregon*

After refusing to live on a reservation next to their traditional enemies the Klamath, Modoc Indians under Captain Jack (Kintpuash) leave Fort Klamath and head for their home on Tule Lake in California. Troops under Capt. James Jackson attempt to disarm them at their camp on Lost River and demand their surrender. Gunfire soon erupts; one soldier is killed and seven are wounded. One Modoc, Watchman, is killed. Jack and his people continue on their way to Tule Lake. Warriors under Hooker Jim split off and attack settlers on Tule Lake, killing seventeen. Source: 70, 73, 78, 80

DECEMBER 21, 1872—*California*

Modoc natives attack an ammunition pack train, killing two of the five escorts. Forces under Lt. J. G. Kyle arrive on the scene and drive the Indians off. Source: 70, 87

DECEMBER 28, 1872, BATTLE OF SKULL CAVE—*Arizona*

Forces under Gen. George Crook attack natives trapped at Skull Cave Canyon north of the Salt River Canyon. When the Indians refuse to surrender, troopers drop boulders down on them. Ricocheting bullets also kill and wound quite a few. These Indians are believed to be Apaches but are in fact Yavapai natives and cannot understand the repeated demands to surrender. "Twice the besieged were asked to surrender ... their only answers were yells of defiance," eyewitness John G. Bourke recalled. Over seventy-six Indians are killed and twenty women and children taken prisoner. (Skull Cave is also known as Skeleton Cave.) Source: 23, 32 [Quote 23]

> "I am very sad. I want peace, or else let the soldiers come.... Let everything be wiped out, washed out, and let there be no more blood ... I have given up now and want no more fuss. I have said yes and thrown away my country."
> — Kintpuash, Modoc, note to army commander, 1873 [Source: 88]

1873

JANUARY 2, 1873—*Arizona*

The 5th U.S. Cavalry skirmishes with Apaches at Clear Creek. Pvt. James Lenihan is awarded the Medal of Honor for Gallantry in Action. Source: 115

JANUARY 17, 1873, BATTLE OF THE LAVA BEDS—*California*

Modoc War. In a thick fog 300 to 400 soldiers under Col. Frank Wheaton attack a Modoc camp south of Tule Lake in the Lava Beds, the Modoc stronghold. Although outnumbering the Indians seven to one, the soldiers are driven back and the Modoc escape into the Lava Beds. The soldiers lose nine killed and twenty-eight wounded. Wheaton is relieved of command. Maj. John Green, 1st U.S. Cavalry, is awarded the Medal of Honor for walking up and down his line while exposed to enemy fire, thus encouraging his men. Surgeon John O. Skinner also is awarded the Medal of Honor for rescuing a wounded soldier while under fire. Source: 12, 70, 80, 102, 108, 115. Marker: Lava Beds National Monument, south of Tule Lake, CA.

JANUARY 22, 1873—*California*

Capt. R. F. Bernard sends a party to retrieve some grain, and as the party passes Scorpion Point, they are ambushed by the Modoc. The wagons and grain are destroyed by the Modoc. Source: 12, 70, 80

JANUARY 22, 1873—*Arizona*

The U.S. Cavalry under the command of Lt. Frank Michler run into an Apache war party at Tonto Creek. Pvt. George Hooker is killed leading a charge at the Apaches. Hooker is posthumously awarded the Medal of Honor for Gallantry in Action. Source: 73, 115

MARCH 1873—*Arizona*

Apaches attack Wickenburg, killing several settlers, while Gen. Crook and his soldiers are out looking for them. Source: 87

MARCH 25, 1873—*Arizona*

Sgt. Daniel Bishop, First Sgt. James Hill, and Pvt. Eben Stanley, 5th U.S. Cavalry, are awarded the Medal of Honor for Gallantry for action at Turret Mountain in a skirmish with Apaches Indians. Source: 115

MARCH 27, 1873—*Arizona*

Capt. George M. Randall and the 23rd Infantry surprise and rout Apaches atop Turret Peak, killing twenty-three Indians. Randall is assisted by a number of friendly allied Indian scouts. After their defeat at Turret Creek a number of Apache and Yavapai return to their agencies. First Sgt. William Allen, I Company, is awarded the Medal of Honor for Gallantry in Action. Source: 32, 78, 115

APRIL 11, 1873, MURDER OF GENERAL E. R. S. CANBY—*California*

Modoc War. Gen. E. R. S. Canby, Rev. Eleaser Meacham and several others meet with Modoc Sub Chief Captain Jack and discuss surrender terms. Canby has been forewarned by interpreter Frank Riddle and his Modoc wife Winima (Tobey) that Captain Jack plans to kill him. Canby dismisses this report and meets with Jack and some of his followers. After several minutes of talk, Jack pulls a gun and shoots Canby in the face, killing him. The Modocs fire on the other whites, killing Rev. Thomas and wounding several others. The death of the popular Canby enrages the army. (Gen. E. R. S. Canby is the highest-ranking soldier ever killed in the Indian Wars.) Source: 12, 32, 70, 78, 80, 108

APRIL 15–17, 1873—*California*

After the murder of Gen. Canby, Col. Alvin C. Gillem orders an offensive to punish the Modoc and bring in the guilty Indians. A large force of U.S. troops, along with friendly Warm Springs Indians under the command of Col. Jefferson C. Davis, attack the Modoc stronghold at the Lava Beds. Davis besieges the Modoc position for three days. The Modoc retreat southward. Eight soldiers and volunteers are killed and seventeen wounded. The Modoc leave behind the bodies of three of their men and eight of their women killed. Source: 73, 80

APRIL 19, 1873—*California*

Modoc War. Capt. Evan Thomas and a force of U.S. soldiers are ambushed by twenty-four Modoc, killing Thomas and twenty-three soldiers. In a complete rout, some soldiers run four miles back to camp. Source: 12, 70, 80, 108

APRIL 26, 1873, THOMAS-WRIGHT MASSACRE—*California*

The 12th Infantry along with the 4th Artillery under Col. Alvin Gillem are ambushed by Modoc south of Tule Lake near Hardin Butte. Half of the command panics and flees the battlefield. The Modoc kill Capt. Thomas Wright, Capt. Evan Thomas, Lt. George M. Harris and twenty others. (Prior to the battle Capt. Thomas had complained that many of his men were unfit for command.) Source: 32, 70, 73, 80, 87

MAY 2, 1873—*California*

Modoc War. Modoc Indians attack a supply train carrying supplies to the Scorpion Point camp, wounding several soldiers. Source: 70, 80, 87, 108

MAY 1873—*Texas*

Billy Allen and his cousin Rance Brown are attacked by Comanche while horse hunting near the Allen Ranch on the Tehuacana Creek in Frio County. Chased by the Indians, Brown is fatally wounded and falls from his horse. Allen rides to a nearby ranch where a number of the men form a group to follow the raiding Indians. Rance Brown's badly mutilated body is found later by the men. Source: 37, 96

MAY 6, 1873—*Arizona*

The 1st U.S. Cavalry skirmishes with Apache Indians near the Santa Maria Mountains in Arizona. Bugler Samuel Hoover, Company A, is awarded the Medal of Honor for Gallantry in Action. Source: 115

MAY 10, 1873—*California*

At Dry Lake the 4th Artillery under Capt. H. C. Hasbrouck is attacked by Modoc led by Captain Jack. The soldiers counterattack the Modoc, and scouts open fire on their rear guard, driving them off. Source: 70, 78, 87

MAY 17, 1873—*Mexico*

Six companies of the 4th Cavalry under the command of Col. Ranald Mackenzie cross the U.S./Mexico border under cover of darkness to attack the Apache-Kickapoo village of Remolino in Mexico. The Indian warriors fight their way out, but Mackenzie's forces capture a number of women and children. Mackenzie reports killing nineteen Indians and wounding twelve. Pvt. Peter Carrigan is mortally wounded, and three troopers are wounded. Source: 73

> "I want no more war ... My skin is red; my heart is a white man's heart; but I am a Modoc. I am not afraid to die."
> — Kintpuash (Captain Jack) Modoc
> [Source: 153]

MAY 22, 1873—*California*

The U.S. Cavalry pursues Modoc natives under Hooker Jim to Willow Creek where they surrender. Captain Jack and his followers surrender June 1. The Modoc prisoners are loaded into a wagon for transfer, but as they cross the Lost River, Joseph Hzer's volunteers stop the wagon. Two of Hzer's men fire point blank into the wagon, killing Little John, Tee-He Jack, Pony and Mooch. U.S. troops arrive on the scene and bury the Modoc dead, but no arrests are made in the murders. Source: 70, 80, 87

JUNE 1873—*Texas*

A party of men which includes Louis Harting, Fred Folk, Charles Martin and a Negro named Johnson from the Verde Creek settlement are attacked by Comanche Indians while searching for livestock. Two horses are killed. Source: 96

JULY 3, 1873—*Texas*

A trading party which includes Joe, Nick and Louis Tschirhart along with Louis Ahr is attacked by Indians at their camp close to Fort McKavett. The midnight attack results in one Indian killed. The dead Indian has among his possessions three white scalps: a woman's and two small children's. Source: 96

JULY 8, 1873—*New Mexico*

Cpl. Frank Bratling, Sgt. Leonidas S. Lytle, First Sgt. James L. Morris, Blacksmith John Sheerin and Pvt. Henry Wills are awarded the Medal of Honor for their actions near Fort Selden while skirmishing with Indians. Source: 115

AUGUST 4, 1873—*Montana*

A small advance party led by Gen. George Armstrong Custer is harassed by 300 Sioux Indians near the Tongue River. Company Veterinarian Dr. John Honsinger and Sutler Augustus Baliran are ambushed and killed a short distance from camp while going for water. Source: 7, 20, 63

August 4, 1873 — *Texas*

After a number of horses are stolen Stephen, William and Eli Moss and four other men track the Comanche raiding party into the Packsaddle Mountains. The small force charges the Indians, killing two warriors and a chief. Source: 69, 73, 96, 124, 146. Marker: Two and a half miles east of the Packsaddle Mts., near present-day Kingsland, TX.

August 5, 1873, Battle of Massacre Canyon — *Nebraska*

Four hundred Pawnees, comprised of 250 men, 100 women and 50 children, are hunting buffalo at Frenchman's Creek when they are warned by buffalo hunters of a large body of Sioux headed their way. Also accompanying the hunting party are two Indian agents, John W. Williamson and L. B. Platte. The Pawnees refuse to leave the area and proceed west of Frenchman's Fork, killing and skinning buffalo. A mounted force of 100 Sioux suddenly appears and charges in on the Pawnees while they are skinning buffalos. Sky Chief, the Pawnee chief who has refused to leave the area, is killed and scalped. The Pawnees herd their packhorses into a ravine with the women and children. The two white men attempt to talk with the Sioux but are fired on and withdraw. The two sides fight for over an hour when a second Sioux force of over 800 warriors charge the Pawnees on three sides. Gripped with panic, the Pawnees begin throwing meat and robes off their horses and endeavor to mount up their women and children. Thirty-nine women, ten children and a number of men are shot down as the Pawnees flee in terror down the Republican River with the Sioux in pursuit. After a ten-mile chase a troop of U.S. Cavalry arrives on the scene, and the Sioux withdraw. When the military detachment ascends the ravine, they find the canyon littered with the dead and mutilated Pawnees, men, women and children, some who have been piled on stacks of wood and burned alive. (The massacre has a demoralizing effect on the Pawnee, and they soon sell their reservation and agree to move to the Indian territory in Oklahoma.) Source: 70, 87. Marker: Monument is located three miles east of Trenton on Hwy. 34.

August 11, 1873 — *Montana*

Forces under Crazy Horse skirmish with Col. Stanley's troops near the mouth of the Rosebud River. The troops are accompanying a survey party for the railroad. Gen. Custer's orderly, Pvt. John H. Tuttle, is killed. Source: 1, 20, 63, 111

August 16, 1873 — *Montana*

While protecting a Northern Pacific survey party, forces under Gen. George Armstrong Custer are fired on by Indians near Pompey's Pillar. (Pompey's Pillar was named by William Clark during the Lewis and Clark Expedition for Sacagawea's infant child who Clark called "Pomp" or "Little Pomp.") Source: 33, 63. Marker: Lewis and Clark Historical site. Yellowstone County, on the south bank of the Yellowstone River, approximately one-half mile north of I-94 (U.S. 10) 28 miles northeast of Billings.

> "What white man can say I never stole his land or a penny of his money? Yet they say I am a thief ... We want no white men here. The Black Hills belong to me. If the whites try to take them, I will fight."
> — Sitting Bull
> [Source: 153]

Fall 1873 — *Texas*

Howell Walker, age fifty; his son Henry, thirteen; and Mortimer Stevens are attacked by Indians while deer hunting at Thurman's Spring on Little Salt Creek. Stevens escapes, but Walker and his son are wounded and left behind. A rescue party returns later and L. J. Valentine reports on finding the mutilated bodies. "I have just returned from one of the most revolting sights I have ever witnessed—the bodies of Howell Walker, and his son Henry ... who were killed yesterday at Thurman's Springs." Source: 44

OCTOBER 3, 1873—*Oregon*

Modoc leader Capt. Jack and several of his followers are hanged at Fort Klamath. Source: 78

DECEMBER 23, 1873—*Arizona*

Lt. Walter S. Schuyler and eleven men of Company K, 5th Cavalry, attack Apaches at Cave Creek killing nine Indians including leader Nanotz. Source: 73

1874

Fort Robinson and Ft. Hartstuff, Nebraska are established. Fort Reno is established in Oklahoma.

JANUARY 19, 1874—*Nebraska*

A Sioux raiding party takes food, furs and a cow from several settlements, including the homes of the Colbys and McClimans. A dozen men led by Charles "Buckskin Charley" White catch up with the Indians the next day as they camp on Pebble Creek. After an attempted parlay fails, both sides open fire. Marion Littlefield is killed during the skirmish. Indian casualties are three killed and several wounded. Source: 137. Marker: Two miles east of Burwell on Nebraska 91 in Garfield County, NE.

FEBRUARY 5, 1874—*Texas*

Capt. Keyes and the 10th Cavalry, Companies D and G, follow a raiding party for nine days. An engagement follows in which eleven Indians are killed and sixty-five head of cattle are captured. Source: 118

MARCH 25, 1874—*Arizona*

The 5th Cavalry under the command of Lt. Walter Schuyler strikes an Apache camp in the Superstition Mountains, killing twelve Indians and capturing two. Source: 73

APRIL 1874—*Texas*

The camp of the 10th U.S. Cavalry is attacked by Indians on the Lancaster River. Private William Hutton is wounded. Source: 118

APRIL 2, 1874—*Arizona*

Apache Indians clash with the U.S. Cavalry at Apache Creek. Sgt. George Deary, 5th U.S. Cavalry, is awarded the Medal of Honor for Gallantry in Action. Source: 115

1874—*Texas*

Indians kill Upton Blackwell at Rock Creek in Parker County. Source: 69, 124

JUNE 1874—*Texas*

Dave Dudley and John Wallace are killed at the Red River near the Canadian River. Although it appears that Wallace was killed outright, Dudley was not so fortunate. He is found propped up in sitting position, one hand staked to the ground, another stake driven through his stomach and scalped from his head down to his back. The wagons and hides have been burned. Hide hunters John "Antelope" Holmes and Blue Billy, an Englishman, are killed on a tributary of the Salt Fork of the Red River. Comanche Medicine Man Little Wolf urges an attack on whites at Adobe Walls. Source: 44, 70

JUNE 27, 1874, SECOND BATTLE OF ADOBE WALLS—*Texas*

Early in the morning of June 27, a large war party of Comanche, Cheyenne and Kiowa attack the small buffalo-hide trading post of Adobe Walls. The huge war party is led by half-breed Quanah Parker, Lone Wolf and Stone Calf. As they near the fort, they attack the wagon of Ike and Shorty Shadler, killing them and their dog; only the vigilance of saloonkeeper Jim Hanrahan saves the tiny outpost. Two massed charges on the four buildings are stopped by the accurate gunfire of the hide hunters. The Indians pull back out of range and begin long range sniping as the day comes to an end. Source: 32, 44, 70, 78, 102, 107, 108

JUNE 29, 1874—*Texas*

The siege of Adobe Walls continues, but daily reinforcements of hide hunters slip through the Indian lines bringing the defenders up to 100. Source: 32, 44, 70, 102, 107

JULY 1, 1874—*Texas*

The siege of Adobe Walls. Hide hunter Billy Dixon, armed with a Sharps forty-four rifle, shoots an Indian at an estimated 1,538 yards. Source: 32, 44, 70, 102, 107

JULY 3, 1874—*Oklahoma*

Cheyenne and Arapaho Indians attack Patrick Hennessey's wagon train on its way to the Anadarko Agency on the Darlington-Wichits road. Hennessey's body is found burned along with three of his men and his wagon. Source: 18, 73, 87

JULY 4, 1874—*Wyoming*

Shoshone scouts report an Arapaho Indian village to authorities at Camp Brown. Capt. Alfred E. Bates with sixty men of Company B, 2nd Cavalry, and twenty Shoshone Indians attack the Arapahos in the Snake Mountains. The Arapahos fire from ravines killing two soldiers and wounding three. The Shoshones fight their way into the camp, and Shoshone Chief Pe-a-quite is killed in the assault. Twenty-five Arapahos are reported killed, and three soldiers are killed. Source: 73

JULY 12, 1874—*Texas*

Twenty-six Texas Rangers led by Maj. John B. Jones and Capt. G. W. Stevens are ambushed while trailing Comanche and Kiowa Indians led by Lone Wolf at Lost Valley near the site of the 1871 Salt Creek Prairie Massacre. Rangers D. W. H. Bailey and W. A. Glass are killed. Source: 18, 73, 96, 102, 107

"I read once about how everyone who touched an Egyptian King's tomb was doomed to die a violent death. Seems to me that the Indians must have put some curse like that on the white men who first touched their sacred Black Hills."
—Sgt. Charles Windolph, 7th Cavalry
[Source: 111]

SUMMER 1874—*Kansas*

At Medicine Lodge Creek an Osage hunting party is attacked on their way back to the reservation by a party of whites, killing four Indians and taking horses, meat and robes. Source: 87

AUGUST 15, 1874—*Kansas*

Cheyenne Dog Soldiers attack and kill four Santa Fe railroad workers between Aubrey Station and Syracuse. Source: 18

AUGUST 22, 1874—*Kansas*

Troops C, E, H and L fight with over 400 Comanche and Kiowa warriors as they attempt to burn down the Wichita Agency. Source: 118

AUGUST 24, 1874—*Kansas*

Cheyenne warriors led by Chief Medicine Water attack a railroad survey party working in an area about forty-five miles southwest of Fort Dodge. In a running fight, head surveyor Oliver F. Short and five men are killed in what is known as the Lone Tree Massacre. (A nearby cottonwood tree was the site of their burial and gives its name to the incident.) Source: 18,

131. Marker: U.S. 54, one mile west of Meade, KS, roadside turnout.

September 9–11, 1874— *Texas*

Col. Nelson Miles' supply train is attacked by Indians near the Washita River. The wagon train quickly makes a circle and is almost overrun in the first charge by the Indians. Maj. Lyman and his men are soon besieged, and the Indians begin long-range sniping. The majority of the Indians pull out on the third day, but several warriors remain to fire on the wagon train. Medals of Honor are presented to Sgt. William DeArmond (KIA), Sgt. Fred Hay, Cpl. John James, Cpl. John Kelly, Pvt. Thomas Kelly, Sgt. George K. Kitchen, Sgt. John Knox, Sgt. William Koelpin, First Sgt. John Mitchell, Cpl. William W. Morris, Sgt. Frederick S. Neilon, Sgt. Josiah Pennsyl and Cpl. Edward C. Sharpless. Source: 73, 108, 115

September 1874— *Kansas*

Nine members of the John German family are attacked while en route to Fort Wallace by Cheyenne led by Medicine Water. John and Lydia German, along with their nineteen-year-old son Stephen, are killed. Taking part in the killings is Medicine Water's wife, Buffalo Calf Woman. The Germans' daughters are carried off by the Indians but are later recovered by the U.S. Army. Source: 47

September 12, 1874, Battle of Buffalo Wallow— *Texas*

On September 10, a four-man patrol leaves Col. Nelson Miles' camp with dispatches for camp supply. On the morning of September 10, the small patrol runs headlong into a Comanche war party of over 126 warriors. Taking refuge in a nearby buffalo wallow the men dig in as their horses run off. Wounded and in a bad need of water, the soldiers find the hot day unbearable, but a cloudburst at 3:00 helps ease the agony. The small detachment repels several attacks on their position throughout the day. A cold north wind at night adds to the misery. Pvt. George Smith dies during the night. At sunrise the Indians withdraw. Scout Billy Dixon sets out on foot for help and finds a patrol of the 8th Cavalry under Col. Price. Pvt. John Harrington, Pvt. Peter Roth, Pvt. George W. Smith (mortally wounded during engagement), Sgt. Zachariah Woodall, Scout Amos Chapman (leg amputated) and Scout Billy Dixon (wounded in leg) are awarded the Medal of Honor for Gallantry in Action. (Scouts Amos Chapman and Billy Dixon were civilians and not eligible for the MOH although they are presented with one. These medals were revoked in 1916 but restored by the U.S. Army Board of Corrections of Records in 1989.) Source: 70, 73, 89, 115. Marker: Buffalo Wallow Battleground, south of Canadian, TX. U.S. 83 left on Texas 277—seven miles to marker.

September 13, 1874— *Texas*

Comanche Indians, fresh from their fight at the Buffalo Wallow, run into a patrol under Col. Price and 110 of his men between Sweetwater Creek and the upper Washita. In a running battle which covers over seven miles, eight warriors are killed or badly wounded. Source: 73

September 14, 1874— *Kansas*

A Mr. Stowell and his two sons are attacked by Cheyenne Dog Soldiers while collecting buffalo bones about six miles north of Buffalo Station on the Kansas Pacific Railway. The Indians capture one of the Stowell boys and kill another. The war party then heads north and finds Charles W. Canfield driving a wagonload of hides. Canfield's body is later found with a bullet hole in the head. Source: 18

September 27, 1874 — *Texas*

At five o'clock in the morning about 300 Indians made up of Comanche, Kiowa, Cheyenne and Arapahoe fire on the camp of the 4th Cavalry. At daylight Col. Ranald Mackenzie orders a charge by Troops E and H that drives the Indians off. Pvt. Adam Paine and Corp. Edwin Phoenix are awarded the Medal of Honor. Paine is awarded the medal for Gallantry in Action for rendering "invaluable service to Colonel Mackenzie ... during engagement." Source: 70, 113, 115

September 28, 1874, Palo Duro Canyon — *Texas*

At dawn troopers of the 4th Cavalry led by Capt. Eugene Beaumont attack sleeping Kiowa, Comanche and Cheyenne in Palo Duro Canyon. The Indians flee up the northwest rim leaving all their possessions behind. Troops D, I, and K hold the Indians in check while the rest of the command pulls down the lodges and sets them afire. The soldiers then withdraw with 1,000 captured horses which are all killed on Mackenzie's orders the following day. Indian losses are estimated at fifty to sixty killed. The Indians, now divested of all their worldly goods, return to the Indian Territory and their reservations. Source: 12, 32, 70, 73, 102, 108. Marker: Located at Texas 217, Palo Duro Canyon State Park, Canyon, TX.

November 1, 1874 — *Arizona*

Sgt. Bernard Taylor is awarded the Medal of Honor for rescuing Lt. King from Indians near Sunset Pass. Source: 115

November 3, 1874 — *Texas*

U.S. troops under Col. Ranald Mackenzie skirmish with Indians at Las Lagunas Quatro. Source: 73

November 5, 1874 — *Texas*

At Staked Plains, the 4th U.S. Cavalry engages Indians. Cpl. John W. Comfort runs down and kills an Indian and is awarded the Medal of Honor. Farrier Ernest Veuve is also awarded the Medal of Honor for the "gallant manner in which he faced a desperate Indian." Source: 115

November 6, 1874 — *Texas*

While scouting for Col. Price's camp on the Washita, a twenty-eight-man patrol of the 8th Cavalry under Lt. Henry Farnsworth is attacked by over 100 Cheyenne warriors on McClellan Creek. The soldiers fight the Indians until dark when they withdraw. Farnsworth loses several killed and four wounded. Farnsworth pulls out under cover of darkness and leaves his dead unburied on the field. It is believed that two Indians are killed. Source: 73

November 8, 1874 — *Texas*

U.S. troops commanded by Lt. Frank Baldwin attack a Cheyenne camp under Grey Beard on McClellan Creek, killing over twenty warriors and rescuing two of four kidnapped girls (Adelaide and Julia German) who were taken in the Kansas raid on September 11. The troops burn the village. In a running battle Baldwin pursues the Indians over twelve miles and four hours. All four German girls are eventually reunited. Source: 48, 79, 115

November 20, 1874 — *Texas*

Near Elm Creek Indians attack Texas Rangers Scott Cooley and William Trayweek. The Austin *Daily Statesman* reports, "The Indians came within a few miles of camp, and, running in on a beef detail of two men ... opened fire upon them, when they fled to camp in hot haste, pursued by the Indians ... The boys brought some fresh scalps with them and they report that Scott Cooley ... not only cut a wounded Indian's throat, but stripped a large piece of skin from his back." Source: 53, 96 [Quote 53]

November 21, 1874 — *Texas*

U.S. Cavalry led by Lt. Dan Roberts with an escort of Texas Rangers under Major John Jones catch up with raiding Comanche in southern Menard. In a running fight five Indians are killed and one captured. Robert's command attempts to catch up with a larger raiding party, but the exhausted horses are unable to continue. Source: 73, 107

December 2, 1874 — *Oklahoma*

At Gageby Creek, Indian Territory, the U.S. Cavalry skirmishes with hostile Indians. First Sgt. Dennis Ryan is awarded the Medal of Honor. Citation: "Courage while in command of a detachment." Source: 115

December 7, 1874 — *Texas*

At Kingfisher, Seminole-Negro scouts capture thirteen Southern Cheyenne warriors and two women. Source: 118

December 8, 1874 — *Texas*

The Medal of Honor is awarded to Pvt. Frederick Bergerndahl, Pvt. John O'Sullivan and First Lt. Lewis Warrington, 4th U.S. Cavalry, for "Gallantry on this date at Staked Plains for pursuit of hostile Indians." Source: 115

December 28, 1874 — *Oklahoma*

After an eight-mile chase Seminole-Negro Scouts capture fifty-two warriors on the North Fork of the Canadian River. Source: 118

1875

April 7, 1875 — *Oklahoma*

When troopers under Lt. Keyes attempt to put shackle irons on Cheyenne warrior Black Horse, a violent confrontation breaks out at the Cheyenne Agency on the North Canadian River. The Cheyenne hold the soldiers at bay until nightfall when they escape under cover of darkness. Little Bull leads his people north hoping to reach safety of the Northern Cheyenne villages in the Powder River country. U.S. Cavalry forces are sent in pursuit. Source: 118

April 23, 1875, Sappa Creek Fight — *Kansas*

At daybreak the U.S. Cavalry catches up with Southern Cheyenne who have fled the Cheyenne-Arapaho Agency in Oklahoma on April 7. The Cheyenne Indians dig in defensively at Sappa Creek as the 6th Cavalry under Lt. Austin Henley advance up a crest firing rapidly. Little Bull asks for a parlay, and Sgt. Theodore Papier is sent out to talk with the chief but is shot dead by White Bear. The troops open fire on the Cheyenne and twenty-seven Indians are killed, including women and children. The dead also includes Little Bull, Dirty Water and White Bear. Medals of Honor are awarded to Pvt. James F. Ayers for "rapid pursuit, gallantry, energy, and enterprise in an engagement with Indians." Trumpeter Michael Dawson receives the Medal of Honor for Gallantry in Action along with Pvts. Peter Gardiner, Simpson Hornaday, James Lowthers, Marcus M. Robbins, Sgt. Frederick Platten, and Sgt. Richard Tea. Source: 79, 102, 108, 115. Marker: Lake Rd. and Second St., Lake Atwood City Park.

April 25, 1875 — *Texas*

A three-man scouting party led by Lt. John L. Bullis skirmish with over twenty-five warriors near the Pecos River. The troopers make a dash for their horses, but Lt. Bullis is cut off by the Indians. Sgt. John Ward makes dash to help Bullis while Trumpeter Issac Payne and Pvt. Pompey Factor lay down a covering fire. Ward is awarded the Medal of Honor along with Trumpeter Payne and Pvt. Factor. Source: 73, 113, 115

May 8, 1875 — *Texas*

After Indians raid the Loving Ranch and steal of a number of horses, Rangers led by Maj. Jones pursue them. After a five-mile pursuit the Rangers catch up with the Indians and kill five in a running fight. Maj. Jones wrote: "One of those killed was a squaw ... another was a half-breed ... was quite fair, and had curly auburn hair." Source: 73, 107 [Quote 107]

June 2, 1875 — *Oklahoma*

Chief Quanah Parker, last of the diehard Comanche, surrenders at Fort Sill. Source: 32, 36, 99

July 9, 1875 — *Montana*

In action at the Big Horn River, Pvt. James Bell carries dispatches through Indian lines to General George Crook and is awarded the Medal of Honor for his actions. Source: 115

1876

February 1–7, 1876, Reservation Deadlines — *Washington, D.C.*

Secretary of the Interior Zachariah Chandler notifies Secretary of War Alphonso Taft that the January time limit given the Sioux Nation and its allied tribes in the Montana territory to report to reservations has expired and that the U.S. Army should move against said "hostiles" in the Montana territories. General Phil Sheridan is authorized to begin military actions against those Indians who have not reported to the reservations, consisting of forcible roundup and placement on reservations. Source: 7, 12, 20, 70

March 17, 1876, Battle of Powder River — *Montana*

Gen. George Crook sends Col. Joseph J. Reynolds and a force consisting of the 3rd Cavalry and six companies of the 2nd Cavalry to attack an Indian village located on the Powder River in the southeast corner of Montana. Reynolds strikes the village at dawn but is soon driven back and finally orders a full withdrawal, leaving his dead on the field. After being court-martialed for questionable behavior, including leaving the dead unburied, he retires the following year. The Medal of Honor is awarded to Hospital Steward William C. Bryan and Pvt. Jeremiah Murphy for helping two comrades to safety while under fire. Source: 7, 12, 20, 47, 102, 108, 115. Marker: The Powder River Battlefield is located 35.8 miles southwest of Broadus, Montana, on Moorhead Road paralleling the Powder River.

April 28, 1876 — *Nebraska*

Sioux warriors clash with a detachment of civilians and three troopers led by Second Lt. Charles H. Heyl on Grace Creek twelve miles from Fort Hartstuff. First Sgt. Dougherty is killed along with one Sioux. Second Lt. Heyl, Cpl. Jeptha L. Lytton and Cpl. Patrick T. Leonard are awarded the Medal of Honor. Citation: "Though outnumbered, the three charge the enemies strong defensive position while under fire." Source: 73, 115, 137. Marker: Located at Elyria, NE, in Valley County.

May 17, 1876 — *North Dakota*

U.S. military forces commanded by Brig. Gen. Alfred Terry leave Fort Abraham Lincoln as part of a planned military expedition against hostile Sioux and Cheyenne. Leading the 7th Cavalry is Lt. Col. George Armstrong Custer. Source: 7, 20, 102

May 29, 1876 — *Wyoming*

Gen. George Crook leaves Fort Fettermen with fifteen companies of cavalry and five companies of infantry, totaling 1,002 men and 47 officers. A number of civilian packers and teamsters also join. At Clear

Creek sixty-five miners also join the expedition to roundup Sioux and Cheyenne who have not reported to the reservations. Source: 7, 20, 70

June 8, 1876—*Montana*

Gen. Crook receives word that a large party of Shoshone allies from the Wind River Reservation are on the way to join his force. (The Shoshone are traditional enemies of the Sioux.) Source: 7, 20

June 9, 1876—*Wyoming*

Gen. George Crook, in command of 1,100 troops, establishes a base camp on Goose Creek on June 7. Two days later a large force of Sioux Indians appear on the surrounding hills and fire into camp, killing several mules and horses. Troops quickly attack the fleeing warriors, driving them off and killing two Indians. Source: 7, 20, 70

June 14, 1876—*Montana*

One hundred and seventy-six well-armed and well-mounted Crow Indian allies join Crook's forces. Eighty-six Shoshone allies also arrive in Crook's camp. Indian allies now total 262. Crook's entire force now numbers about 1,300. Source: 7, 20, 70

June 17, 1876, Battle of the Rosebud—*Montana*

While in camp at the head of the South Fork of the Rosebud River, Crook's forces are attacked by over a thousand Sioux and Cheyenne warriors. The Crow Indians battle the attacking warriors for over twenty minutes, giving the soldiers valuable time for defense. Much of the fighting is hand-to-hand. After over six hours of fighting the hostiles withdraw. Crook retires to his base camp on Goose Creek and goes fly fishing, neglecting to send word to Custer that he had been engaged by a major force of Indians. (The general disorganization of the campaign against the Sioux during this period led to so many mistakes that commanding officers involved were criticized for years.) First Sgt. Michael A. McGann, First Sgt. Joseph Robinson, First Sgt. John Shingle, and Trumpeter Elmer A. Snow are awarded the Medal of Honor for Gallantry in Action. Source: 7, 8, 12, 20, 70, 73, 81, 102, 108, 115. Marker: The Rosebud Battlefield is located twenty-four miles south of Busby on Montana 314 and one mile west of the highway.

June 25, 1876, Battle of the Little Big Horn—*Montana*

On the morning of June 25, scouts for Gen. George Armstrong Custer report a large Indian village in the valley of the Little Big Horn River. Custer divides his command into three battalions. Capt. Frederick Benteen is directed to scout to the left while Custer proceeds toward the valley with the rest of the 7th Cavalry. As dust rises up in the valley, Custer orders Maj. Marcus Reno to cross the Little Big Horn River and advance down the valley and engage the Indians. Reno crosses the swift moving river and advances toward the large Indian village as hundreds of warriors rush out to meet him. Reno's assault grinds to a halt, and he assumes a defensive position in the timber as the warriors attack, firing into his small force. With no support in sight, he leads a retreat back across the river with the warriors charging after. Fighting his way up the bluffs he digs in for an assault as forces under Capt. Benteen arrive. Meanwhile Custer leads his forces along the high bluffs looking for a way into the village as warriors pour out to meet him. Several companies under Lt. James Calhoun are directed to stop the advancing Indians at Custer's rear but are overrun and killed. Indians swarm up the ridges, and the situation becomes critical as the Indians overrun and kill men of Capt. Myles

Keogh's command. Minneconjou Warrior Standing Bear: "There were so many of us that I think we did not need guns. Just the hoofs would have been enough." Some survivors flee to Custer Hill where the remnants of the command shoot their horses for barricades. The Sioux and Cheyenne warriors work their way up the ridge killing all of Custer's command. Over 215 soldiers are killed. Source: 7, 8, 12, 15, 20, 50, 70, 73, 81, 102, 108, 111 [Quote 81]. Marker: The Little Big Horn Battlefield is a National Park run by the National Park Service, Crow Agency Montana, located on I-90 at Garryowen, MT.

> "I do not think the fight lasted long. The country was not one in which a prolonged resistance was possible; his [Custer] position was on a ridge; there was no way to protect himself."
>
> — Lt. George D. Wallace, 7th Cavalry [Source: 39]

JUNE 26, 1876, LITTLE BIG HORN — *Montana*

Battle of the Little Big Horn. Soldiers under Maj. Marcus Reno and Capt. Frederick Benteen are besieged by Sioux and Cheyenne warriors. From their position on the high bluffs Reno and Benteen see no sign of Custer's command. Indians and troopers skirmish all day. Water runs low, and soldiers make several trips to the river under fire; the men are all awarded the Medal of Honor: Pvt. Abram B. Brant, Pvt. Thomas J. Cable, Sgt. Benjamin C. Criswell, Cpl. Charles Cunningham, Pvt. Frederick Deetline, Pvt. John Georgian, Pvt. Theodore W. Goldin, Sgt. Richard Hanley, Pvt. David Harris, Pvt. William Harris, Pvt. Henry Holden, Sgt. Rufus D. Hutchinson, Blacksmith Henry Mechlin, Sgt. Thomas Murray, Pvt. James Pym, Sgt. Stanislaus Roy, Pvt. George D. Scott, Pvt. Thomas W. Stivers, Pvt. Peter Thompson, Pvt. Frank Tolan, Saddler Otto Voit, Sgt. Charles H. Welch and Pvt. Charles Windolph. (Windolph writes *I Fought with Custer* and is the last living white participant of the battle, dying in 1950.) Source: 7, 8, 12, 20, 73, 81, 102, 108, 111, 115. Marker: Reno Battlefield marker located at the Little Big Horn Battlefield, Crow Agency, Montana.

JUNE 27, 1876 — *Montana*

Battle of the Little Big Horn. Lt. J. H. Bradley rides up to report finding a number of bodies four miles away. The dead are the men of Custer's command. Reports Sgt. Charles Windolph, "Most of the troopers had been stripped of clothing and scalped. Some of them had been horribly mutilated." Owing to a lack of shovels and the rancid condition of the bodies, very few of Custer's men are buried. Source: 7, 8, 12, 20, 70, 73, 81, 102, 108, 111 [Quote 111]

JULY 1876 — *Wyoming*

After he wanders off from his companions, Herman Ganzio is attacked by a war party, shot twice and is set upon by a warrior who scalps him. Ganzio survives, and a surgeon shaves off what is left of his hair to prevent infection. Source: 20

JULY 7, 1876 — *Wyoming*

Over 300 Sioux and Cheyenne warriors attack a scouting party commanded by Second Lt. Frederick Sibley. The soldiers are chased deep into the Big Horn Mountains where they abandon their horses and climb over the rugged mountains. Cheyenne Chief White Antelope is killed in the fight. Source: 8

JULY 9, 1876 — *Montana*

Pvt. William Evans and Pvt. Benjamin F. Stewart are awarded the Medal of Honor after carrying dispatches to Brig. Gen. George Crook through country swarming with Sioux Indians. Source: 115

July 17, 1876, Fight at Warbonnet Creek—*Nebraska*

A band of Cheyenne fleeing the Red Cloud Agency are intercepted by Col. Wesley Merritt and the 5th Cavalry at Warbonnet Creek. Shots are fired, but the warriors are driven back toward the agency. Scout Buffalo Bill Cody shoots and kills Yellow Hand, a Cheyenne sub chief. Source: 7, 73, 102. Marker: Warbonnet Creek State Historic Site, NE.

August 2, 1876—*Montana*

A small force commanded by Orlando H. Moore, consisting of the 6th and 17th Infantry is attacked by Sioux and Cheyenne warriors at the Powder River Depot. The Indians are driven off by shots from a twelve-pounder. Scout Wesley Brockmeyer is killed. Source: 47, 87, 115. Marker: Graves of Brockmeyer and trooper William George who died aboard the steamer *Far West* are located northeast of Miles City off I-94 on the Powder River Road on U.S. 10 near the Powder River Railroad Bridge.

August 7, 1876—*Wyoming*

George Powell Hay, a civilian contractor, arrives in Cheyenne with the news that thirty Indians attacked the wagon train of A. H. Reel loaded with government supplies. The Indians scalp George Thrastle the wagon master, wound a teamster, kill four horses and ten cattle and burn three wagons. Source: 71

September 9, 1876, Slim Buttes—*South Dakota*

The 3rd Cavalry under Capt. Anson Mills attacks a Sioux camp belonging to the Minneconjou Sioux American Horse at Slim Buttes. The Indians hold the high ground and fire down on the troops all day. The warriors finally withdraw, and the troops burn the village. Among the booty found in the village are relics from the Custer fight. American Horse is mortally wounded. Sgt. John Kirkwood and Pvt. Robert Smith are awarded the Medal of Honor for dislodging some Indians secreted in a ravine. Source: 7, 12, 20, 102, 108, 115. Marker: The Slim Buttes Battlefield is located 20 miles east of Buffalo on South Dakota 20.

October 21, 1876, Cedar Creek—*Montana*

After talks between Col. Nelson Miles and Sitting Bull break down, the Indians begin setting fire to the tall dry grass. The Sioux rapidly abandon their villages; both sides exchange gunfire. Two soldiers are wounded, and five Indians are killed. Like Slim Buttes, the village contains relics from Little Big Horn. The Medal of Honor for Gallantry in Action of October 21, 1876 to January 8, 1877 is awarded to Musician John Baker, Pvt. Richard Burke, Sgt. Dennis Byrne, Pvt. Joseph A. Cable, Pvt. James Calvert, Sgt. Aquilla Coonrod, Pvt. John Donelly, Pvt. Christopher Freemeyer, Cpl. John Hadoo, First Sgt. Henry Hogan, Cpl. David Holland, Pvt. Phillip Kennedy, Cpl. Edward Johnston, Pvt. Michael McCormick, Pvt. Owen McGar, Pvt. John McHugh, Sgt. Michael McLoughlin and Sgt. Robert McPhelan. Source: 47, 102, 115. Marker: Take Prairie County 253 north from Terry, MT 16 miles, turn on Cedar Creek Road, and follow the signs approx. 10 miles to site.

October 15, 1876—*Montana*

Indians attack a ninety-four-wagon supply train near Spring Creek but are driven off by the troopers. Source: 47

November 25, 1876, Dull Knife Battlefield—*Wyoming*

A force under the command of Col. Ranald S. Mackenzie attacks Dull Knife's Cheyenne village at dawn on November 25, in freezing weather. The Indians are driven back into the high rugged hills west of camp. Over thirty Indians and six enlisted men are killed, including First Lt. John A. McKinney. Eleven Indian babies exposed to frigid weather without shelter freeze to death during the night. Sgt. Thomas H. Forsyth rescues his commanding officer who has been shot down and is awarded the Medal of Honor. Source: 12, 20, 47, 102, 108, 115. Marker: Located west of Kaycee on the Red Fork of the Powder River. Take Wyoming 190 west of Kaycee to the hamlet of Barnum, then north following the signs to site.

December 7, 1876—*Montana*

Three 5th Infantry companies led by Lt. Frank Baldwin attack Sitting Bull's camp on Ash Creek. The Indians flee, and over 122 lodges are burned. No casualties are reported, but the Indians' shelter and food supply is destroyed. Source: 47, 73, 87. Marker: The Ash Creek Battlefield is 7.3 miles beyond the Cedar Creek Battlefield on private property.

December 24, 1876—*Texas*

Isaac Kountz, a young sheep herder, is killed by Indians in Kimble County. Source: 69, 124

1877

January 8, 1877, Battle of Wolf Mountain—*Montana*

Troops under Col. Nelson Miles attack Sioux and Cheyenne Indians at Battle Butte Creek. Indians under Crazy Horse and Big Crow hold off the soldiers while the women and children escape up the Tongue River in a blizzard. Big Crow, a Cheyenne, is killed while Oglala Sioux and Northern Cheyenne losses are only three; but the loss of their winter camp and supplies is a severe blow. Crazy Horse and his followers are convinced surrender is inevitable. Medals of Honor for Gallantry in Action of October 21, 1876, to January 8, 1877, are presented to Capt. Edmond Butler, Capt. James S. Casey, Pvt. Fred Hunt, First Sgt. Wendelin Kreher, First Lt. Robert McDonald, Musician John McLennon, Cpl. George Miller, Pvt. Charles Montrose, First Sgt. David Roche, Pvt. Henry Rodenbury, Pvt. Edward Rooney, Pvt. David Ryan, Pvt. Charles Sheppard, Sgt. William Wallace, Pvt. Patton G. Whitehead and Cpl. Charles Wilson. Source: 7, 47, 87, 102, 108, 115. Marker: Wolf Mountains Battlefield, 4.8 miles from Birney, MT.

January 9, 1877—*New Mexico*

The 6th Cavalry led by Lt. John Rucker track and attack Chiricahua Indians who have stolen horses in the area. Gunfire from Jack Dunn and several of his scouts drive the Indians toward Rucker's position. Rucker reports ten Indians killed and captures an Indian identified as a nephew of Geronimo. Source: 73

January 13, 1877—*Wyoming*

At Elkhorn Creek a scouting party of the 3rd U.S. Cavalry is ambushed by Indians. The four-man scouting party suffers two wounded but holds its position. Corp. Charles A. Bessey is among the four men ambushed by Indians. Although wounded, Bessey goes to the aid of his comrades and is later awarded the Medal of Honor. Source: 115

January 22, 1877—*Wyoming*

The 3rd U.S. Cavalry skirmish with Indians near Bluff Station. Sgt. William B. Lewis is awarded the Medal of Honor for, "bravery in skirmish." Source: 115

January 24, 1877—*New Mexico*

The 9th Cavalry attempts to persuade a renegade party of Apaches to surrender. Corp. Clinton Greaves and several men advance toward the Apaches but are suddenly attacked. Greaves and his men fight hand to hand with the warriors and make their way out. Corp. Greaves is awarded the Medal of Honor. Source: 113, 115

FEBRUARY 27, 1877—*Texas*

Comanche Indians led by Chief Nigger Horse attack the camp of Bill Devins, killing Marshall Seawall. A tracking party is formed and begins pursuit of the Comanche war party. Source: 17

MARCH 18, 1877—*Texas*

A number of Comanche are given permission to hunt off their Oklahoma reservation and soon several hide hunters are killed and several are missing. After the killing of Marshall Seawall on February 27, a tracking party led by Big Hank Campbell and guided by Jose Tafoya locates the Comanche camp at Yellow House Canyon. The 45-man party of hide hunters is no match for over 300 Comanche and Apache warriors, and a number of them are wounded. Campbell and his men set fire to the grass and the Indians withdraw, carrying off a number of dead warriors. Source: 17, 73

APRIL 22, 1877—*Texas*

Eighteen-year-old Joe Wilton is killed by Indians on his way to religious services near present-day Devine. Source: 96

MAY 6, 1877, SURRENDER OF CRAZY HORSE—*Nebraska*

Crazy Horse brings his band of over 800 Lakota Sioux into Fort Robinson and surrenders. Source: 12, 47, 88, 101, 108. Marker: Camp Robinson and Red Cloud Agency, NE.

MAY 7, 1877, BATTLE OF LAME DEER—*Montana*

Col. Nelson Miles traps Lame Deer's village on Muddy Creek, and his troops drive off the pony herd. Lame Deer approaches Miles to talk but is shot and killed by a young trooper as fighting breaks out on both sides. Sixteen Lakota Sioux are killed. This battle marks the end of the Great Sioux War. Cpl. Harry Garland, Pvt. William Leonard, Pvt. Samuel D. Phillips and First Sgt. Henry Wilkens are awarded the Medal of Honor for Gallantry in Action against hostile Sioux. (This battle is also known as the Battle of Muddy Creek.) Source: 12, 47, 102, 108. Marker: Lame Deer Battlefield, Lame Deer Northern Cheyenne Indian Reservation, MT.

JUNE 16, 1877—*Idaho*

A Nez Perce raiding party which includes Big Dawn, Two Moons and Yellow Bull raid Benedict's Saloon on lower White Bird Creek and kill over a dozen settlers. Source: 3

JUNE 17, 1877, BATTLE OF WHITE BIRD CANYON—*Idaho*

One hundred and ten soldiers led by Capt. David Perry attack Nez Perce Indians under Chief Joseph in White Bird Canyon. The well-positioned Indians kill thirty-four soldiers, including Trumpeter John Jones and Lt. Edward K. Theller. First Lt. William R. Parnell is awarded the Medal of Honor for rescuing a soldier who had been left behind in the retreat when his horse was killed. Source: 3, 78, 102, 108, 115. Marker: Marker designates fort site built in 1877 to protect the area from the Nez Perce is on SR 12, 6 miles west of Lolo, MT.

JULY 4, 1877—*Idaho*

Gen. Oliver O. Howard and U.S. troops attack Nez Perce under Looking Glass near the Cottonwood Ranch at the southeastern tip of the Nez Perce Reservation. Twelve soldiers and a scout are killed. Source: 3, 87, 108

JULY 5, 1877—*Idaho*

Seventeen civilian volunteers led by D. B. Randall are attacked by Nez Perce

Indians, and several are killed, including Randall. After watching the volunteers battle the Indians for over twenty-five minutes, troops from a nearby post lead a forty-two-man relief party to rescue the men. Source: 3, 73

JULY 11, 1877—*Idaho*

Nez Perce and U.S. troops clash along the Clearwater River. One hundred warriors hold the 500-man force of soldiers and civilians off until dark when the natives withdraw. Thirteen soldiers are killed and twenty-seven are wounded. Six Nez Perce warriors are believed killed. First Lt. Charles Humphrey is awarded the Medal of Honor. Citation: "Voluntarily and successfully conducted, in the face of a withering fire ... recovered possession of an abandon howitzer and 2 Gatling guns." Source: 3, 78, 87, 108, 115. Marker: Nez Perce National Historical Park, U.S. 95, Spalding, ID.

AUGUST 9, 1877—*Montana*

At Big Hole, U.S. forces clash with Nez Perce Indians. Pvt. Lorenzo D. Brown, Pvt. Wilfred Clark, First Sgt. William Edwards, Sgt. Patrick Rogan and Sgt. Milden H. Wilson are awarded the Medal of Honor for Gallantry in Action. Source: 3, 87, 102, 108. Marker: The Big Hole National Battlefield, Wisdom, MT.

AUGUST 13, 1877—*Idaho*

Nez Perce Indians kill William Flynn, W. S. Montague and James W. Smith at the Montague-Winters Ranch and steal its horses. A settler named William Farnsworth is killed nearby. Source: 3, 108

AUGUST 15, 1877, BIRCH CREEK MASSACRE—*Idaho*

Nez Perce Indians capture seven men, eight wagons, plus a wagon full of guns, ammunition and whiskey. After getting drunk they kill Jim Hayden, Al Green, Dan Combs, two unnamed white men and two Chinese passengers. Albert Lyons escapes and is rescued by cowboys. Source: 3, 87

AUGUST 20, 1877, BATTLE OF CAMAS MEADOW—*Idaho*

Nez Perce Indians attack the camp of Gen. Oliver Howard and his men, stampeding horses and mules. Troops chase the Indians for over eight miles. Bugler Bernard Brooks is killed and eight wounded. The Medal of Honor is awarded to Capt. James Jackson and Farrier William Jones for Gallantry in Action. Source: 3, 102, 108, 115. Marker: White Bird Battlefield and Camas Prairie marker is located on U.S. 95 south of Grangeville, ID.

AUGUST 23, 1877, FLIGHT OF THE NEZ PERCE—*Wyoming*

Prospector John Shivley and the Radersburg party are captured by Nez Perce Indians in Yellowstone National Park. August 24: The Cowan party, a group of tourists visiting Yellowstone, are captured by Chief Joseph's band as they flee government authorities. August 26: The Weikert Party, a group of men from Helena, Montana, are captured by Nez Perce Indians in Yellowstone. August 31: Nez Perce Indians kill Helena musician Richard Dietrich at the hotel in Yellowstone. James McCartney and Andrew Weikert are fired on but escape. Bart Henderson's ranch is burned by the raiders. Source: 3, 12, 57, 87, 88, 108. Marker: Radersburg marker is located within Yellowstone National Park.

SEPTEMBER 5, 1877, DEATH OF CRAZY HORSE—*Nebraska*

A rumor spreads that Crazy Horse is planning an uprising among the Indians at Fort Robinson. Authorities are sent to arrest him but trouble breaks out when Crazy Horse resists arrest. Crazy Horse is bayoneted by a private named William Gentles and dies that night. His parents remove his body and bury it at an undisclosed site. Source: 12, 20, 102, 108. Marker: Death site marker, 3 miles west of Crawford, NE, on Hwy. 20.

SEPTEMBER 13, 1877—*Montana*

U.S. troops led by Col. Samuel D. Sturgis overtake some 700 Nez Perce north of the Yellowstone at Canyon Creek. Long-range fighting kills three soldiers, and the Nez Perce escape. Source: 3, 87, 108

SEPTEMBER 23, 1877—*Montana*

Nez Perce Indians approach the Cow Island depot on the Missouri River but are told by Sgt. William Moelchert to keep their distance. Moelchert gives them some bacon and hardtack. A short time later they shoot and kill a Pvt. Person and begin long-range sniping. Two enlisted men and one civilian are killed. Source: 73

SEPTEMBER 30, 1877, BATTLE OF BEAR PAW MOUNTAIN—*Montana*

In a cold freezing rain which turns to snow, U.S. troops under Col. Nelson Miles attack Nez Perce Indians under Chief Joseph at Bear Paw Mountain. Joseph and his followers hold the army off for some time but finally surrender. "From where I stand I will fight no more forever." Joseph's War Chief, Looking Glass, is killed along with Joseph's brother Ollokot. Capt. Owen Hale and Lt. J. W. Biddle are killed. Medals of Honor go to Maj. and Surgeon Henry R. Tilton, Capt. Edward S. Godfrey, First Lt. George W. Baird, First Lt. Carter Mason, First Sgt. Henry Hogan (second Medal of Honor), Second Lt. Oscar Long, Second Lt. Edward J. McClernand, Capt. Myles Moylan and First Lt. Henry Romelyn (Romelyn will later write *The Capture of Chief Joseph and the Nez Perce*). Source: 3, 8, 102, 108, 115

[Quote 3]. Marker: Bear Paw State Monument, CR 240, 16 miles south of U.S. 2, Chinook, MT.

SEPTEMBER 30, 1877—*Arizona*

The U.S. Cavalry clash with Apache Indians at Simon Valley. Sgt. James Brogan is awarded the Medal of Honor for single-handedly engaging two Indians until his horse is killed. Source: 115

1878

1878—*Texas*

Capt. Malcom Van Pelt and his son Joe are attacked by Indians near Uvalde but manage to outrun the Indians. The Indians circle back and kill a Mexican herder they had passed. A tracking party later catches up with the raiders and recapture a Negro boy and a little white girl. Source: 96

1878—*Texas*

Indians attack and kill the children of James Dowdy while they watch their father's sheep. The dead Dowdy children are Fanny, twenty; Alice, eighteen; Rilla, fifteen; and James, twelve. Their bodies are discovered after they fail to return home. Source: 96

JUNE 8, 1878—*Idaho*

Forces led by Col. Robbin track and locate Bannock Indians on Clark's Fork. Capt. Harper and twenty volunteers engage the Bannock Indians led by Buffalo Horn. The volunteers retreat after the Bannock open fire on them, killing four. Buffalo Horn, chief of the Bannock, is shot from his horse and killed. Source: 70, 87

JUNE 23, 1878—*Oregon*

Four companies of the 1st Cavalry under the command of Brevet Col. Rueben Frank Bernard attack Bannock Indians at Silver Creek in south-central Oregon. Source: 78

July 8, 1878, Fight with Bannocks—*Oregon*

Troops under Gen. Oliver Howard attack and rout Bannock and Northern Paiute Indians at Birch Creek. The Indians flee to the Umatilla Reservation where they are attacked by the Umatilla Indians who are now aligned with the whites. Source: 70, 78, 102

July 11, 1878—*Oregon*

Umatilla Indians aligned with whites convince Bannock led by Chief Egan that they want to come over and join them against the whites. The Umatilla suddenly open fire on the Bannocks, killing Chief Egan. The Umatilla cut the chief's head off and take it to the Indian agency. Source: 70, 73

July 20, 1878—*Oregon*

The 1st Cavalry commanded by Gen. James Forsythe drives the Bannocks from their canyon stronghold, ending the Bannock War. One band attempts to reach Sitting Bull's camp in Canada but are cut off in the mountains east of Yellowstone, driven back toward their homeland and captured. Source: 70, 102

August 5, 1878—*New Mexico*

Capt. Henry Carroll is sent to Dog Canyon to round up a small party of Apaches. The Apaches fire down on the soldiers and roll rocks down on them. Carroll orders his men to climb up the steep slopes only to find the Indians have withdrawn. Source: 73

September 7, 1878, Dull Knife's Raid—*Kansas*

Cheyenne Indians led by Dull Knife and Little Wolf leave their Oklahoma reservation against government orders and head north, killing several settlers and cowboys along the way. A dispute between the two chiefs splits the fugitives. Dull Knife takes his band and heads for Fort Robinson to surrender while those with Little Wolf head for the Yellowstone Valley. Source: 7, 12, 102, 108. Marker: The Last Indian Raid Museum is located on S. Penn Ave. in Oberlin, KS.

September 27, 1878—*Kansas*

U.S. Cavalry from Fort Dodge skirmish with Northern Cheyenne led by Chief Dull Knife near present-day Scott City. Col. William H. Lewis is fatally wounded and six troopers are wounded. (This engagement is sometimes referred to as Squaw's Den Battleground.) Source: 73, 131, 144. Marker: U.S. 83, 10.5 miles north of Scott City, roadside turnout.

October 11, 1878—*Texas*

Kiowa Chief Satanta commits suicide by jumping out a second story window of the Huntsville prison hospital. Source: 108

October 23, 1878—*Nebraska*

Dull Knife and his Northern Cheyenne followers, on the run since September 7, surrender to a cavalry patrol near Fort Robinson. (Dull Knife resists all efforts to make him and his people return to the Oklahoma territory agency and attempts another breakout on January ninth.) Source: 7, 102, 108, 137

1879

Fort Assinniboine is built in Montana.

January 9, 1879—*Nebraska*

Confined at Fort Robinson, Cheyenne Indians led by Dull Knife attempt an escape after shooting two guards. The Cheyenne retreat toward a line of bluffs, but mounted troops soon overtake them and kill over half the warriors plus women and children. Thirty-eight escape but twenty-nine are hunted down and killed. The Cheyenne dead are buried in a mass grave near the post sawmill. Source: 7, 12,

78, 102, 137. Marker: Fort Robinson State Park in Dawes County, NE.

1879—*Idaho*

U.S. military track Shoshone Indians after the killing of five Chinese miners and two ranchers at Oro Grande. Source: 87

MARCH 17, 1879—*Colorado*

Nathan C. Meeker, Indian agent at the White River Agency, writes the commandant of Fort Steele, Wyoming, that agency Indians are buying up a large amount of ammunition. He requests immediate help. (Trouble erupts at the agency on September 29.) Source: 12, 108

MARCH 27, 1879—*Montana*

Little Wolf and his Cheyenne fugitives surrender to U.S. troops under Lt. William Philo Clark on the Little Missouri River in southeast Montana. Source: 12, 102, 108

APRIL 10, 1879—*Montana*

The 2nd U.S. Cavalry clashes with a Sioux war party at Mizpah Creek. Sgt. T. B. Glover is awarded the Medal of Honor for Gallantry in Action. Source: 115

MAY 29, 1879—*New Mexico*

For his action on this date at the Mimbres Mountains and for his actions on September 27, 1879, Sgt. Thomas Boyne is awarded the Medal of Honor. Source: 115

AUGUST 20, 1879—*Idaho*

Sheepeater Indians attack troops led by Col. Reuben Bernard at Soldier Bar on Big Creek. One soldier is killed. Source: 78

SEPTEMBER 4, 1879—*Arizona*

After a skirmish with Company E of the 9th Cavalry under Captain Hooker Apaches led by Victorio kill and stake to the ground several troopers. Killed are Sgt. Silas Chapman and Pvts. Lafayerre Hoke, William Murphy, Silas Graddon and Alvrew Percival. Source: 118

SEPTEMBER 4, 1879—*New Mexico*

The 9th Cavalry (Buffalo Soldiers) under Capt. Ambrose Hooker is attacked by Apaches led by Victorio at Las Animas Creek. Eight soldiers are killed, and the Indians make off with over forty-six cavalry horses. Source: 73

SEPTEMBER 18, 1879—*New Mexico*

The 9th U.S. Cavalry clashes with Indians at Las Animas Canyon. Second Lt. Matthias W. Day, Sgt. John Denny, and Second Lt. Robert Temple are awarded the Medal of Honor. Source: 113, 115

SEPTEMBER 29, 1879, SIEGE OF MILK CREEK/MEEKER MASSACRE—*Colorado*

Ute Indians grow increasingly angry at Agent Nathan Meeker's reservation policies. The Utes are accustomed to spending the summers in the high, cool mountains and rebel against the agency's harsh farming policies which they consider degrading. To make matters worse, delays in government delivery of clothes, provisions and food make matters dangerous. Meeker sends for troops to protect the agency but is murdered along with eleven other agency employees before the army arrives. On the morning of the twenty-ninth, a force of 140 troops under the command of Maj. Thomas T. Thornburg arrives near the agency and are fired on by Ute natives. A number of soldiers are wounded, and Major Thornburg is killed. At this point a full-scale battle begins along Milk Creek. Capt. John Payne takes command and orders the supply wagons burned, and the soldiers take a defensive position inside a nearby corral. The Ute make several ferocious charges at Payne and his men but are driven back by heavy gunfire. At dusk a large body of Indians attack the dug-in troopers but are repulsed. A relief force of forty men led by Capt. Francis Dodge rides all night and arrives at Milk Creek in the morning. Nine soldiers win the Medal of Honor for valor: Capt. Dodge, Sgt. Edward Grimes, Sgt. John Lawler, Sgt. John Merrill, Cpl. George Moquin, Blacksmith Wilhelm O. Philipsen, Sgt. John Poppe, Cpl. Hampton Roach and First Sgt. Jacob E. Widmer. Source: 12, 70, 73, 78, 102, 108, 115. Marker: The Meeker Museum is located at 1324 9th Ave., Meeker, CO. The White River Museum is located at 265 Park Ave., Meeker, CO.

September 30, 1879—
Colorado

Milk Creek. Ute Indians open fire early in the morning on Capt. Payne and his men who are now well entrenched at Milk Creek. Source: 70, 102

October 1, 1879—Colorado

Milk Creek. Payne's water supply begins to run critically low, and several men are fired on making a dash for water. Source: 70, 102

October 3–5, 1879—
Colorado

Milk Creek. Payne's rations begin to run low, and the stench from the dead animals is suffocating. Source: 70, 102, 108

October 6, 1879—Colorado

Milk Creek. Capt. Payne's besieged army is rescued when troops under Gen. Wesley Merritt arrive. The Ute withdraw. Agent Meeker and eleven others are found dead at the agency. Mrs. Meeker, her daughter and Mrs. Shadrick Price are found alive but have been violated by a number of warriors. Sgt. Henry Johnson, Company D, 9th U.S. Cavalry, is awarded the Medal of Honor for bringing water to the wounded while under fire. Source: 70, 102, 108, 113, 115

October 1879—Texas

Canyon del Marranos. Capt. George Baylor and a force of nine Texas Rangers plus ten volunteers are fired on by Apaches, killing Sgt. Swilling's horse. Heavy fire from the Rangers drives the Apaches deep into the canyon where the fighting is finally called off after two days because of a lack of water. Source: 38

1880

Fort Niobrara is built in Nebraska.

January 12, 1880—
New Mexico

After being chased into Mexico by U.S. troops Apache leader Victorio returns in January. Major Albert Morrow receives the news that the Apaches are located in the Black Range and moves against them on January 12. Morrow catches up with them on upper Percha Creek. Sgt. D. J. Gross and another enlisted man are killed in the engagement. Indian casualties are unknown. Source: 73

January 29, 1880—Texas

Texas Rangers under Capt. George W. Baylor with Pueblo scouts ambush an Apache war party in bitter cold weather in the Devil Mountains. One Indian woman and two children are captured along with seven mules and two Winchester rifles. Three Apache warriors, three squaws and two children are killed. Supplies taken from troops killed at Ojo Caliente are recovered. Source: 58

February 9, 1880—
New Mexico

Searching for Victorio's Apaches in the San Andres Mountains, the 9th Cavalry under Capt. Louis Rucker runs into Apaches camped in a canyon. Both sides are caught totally by surprise. The Apaches fire first driving the soldiers down the canyon and scattering their supplies. Source: 73

FEBRUARY 12, 1880—
Montana

Lakota Indians kill three hay cutters on the Powder River and flee the area. After a sixty-five-mile chase troopers led by Sgt. T. B. Glover catch up with the Indians at Pumpkin Creek. One Indian is killed and two are wounded. Source: 73

APRIL 1, 1880—*Montana*

Hostile Indians clash with the 2nd U.S. Cavalry at O'Fallon's Creek. Second Lt. Lloyd M. Brett and Capt. Eli Huggins are awarded the Medal of Honor for cutting off the Indians' pony herd. Source: 115

APRIL 8, 1880—*Arizona*

Capt. Henry Carroll and three battalions of Buffalo Soldiers run headlong into Victorio's Mescalero at a water hole in Hembrillo Canyon. The Apaches' gunfire pins Carroll's men down; only the arrival of Col. Hatch's troops saves Carroll's forces from annihilation. Source: 23, 68, 102

APRIL 16, 1880—
New Mexico

About 309 Apaches come to the Mescalero Agency to surrender but refuse to give up their firearms. Seven hundred men of the 6th, 9th and 10th Cavalries under Cols. Benjamin Grierson and Edward Hatch oversee the surrender. Capt. Charles Steelhamer and Company G of the 15th Infantry attempt to disarm the Mescalero, but a general melee breaks out. Gunfire leaves 14 Indians dead, and the rest flee to the Guadulupe Mountains. Source: 73

MAY 12, 1880—*Texas*

Eight Mescalero Apaches attack a wagon train, killing two settlers and wounding two. Capt. Carpenter and the 10th Calvary, Company H and W, pursue the warriors to the Rio Grande. Source: 73, 87

> "He ordered the boys to dismount ... Capt. Roberts and Sgt. Hawkins were the only ones who had ever been in an Indian fight and I suppose the hearts of all beat a little faster."
> — James B. Gillett, Texas Ranger [Source: 38]

MAY 14, 1880—*New Mexico*

A twenty-five-man force of the 9th U.S. Cavalry is attacked by over 100 Indians near Fort Tularosa. The troopers led by Sgt. George Jordan repel the attack. For his actions on this day and August 12, Sgt. Jordan is awarded the Medal of Honor. Source: 115

MAY 23, 1880—*Arizona*

Apache scouts led by Henry Parker track Apaches under Victorio into a canyon on the Palomas River. At daybreak the scouts open fire, and a day-long battle begins. At the end of the day over thirty Apaches lay dead. Parker's men run out of ammunition and water and have to withdraw before they can finish the Apaches off. Source: 68, 102

JUNE 5, 1880—*New Mexico*

Maj. Albert P. Morrow and four troops of the 9th Cavalry attack Apaches in Cooke's Canyon. One of the dead is said to be Victorio's son Washington. Source: 74

JULY 26, 1880—*Oklahoma*

Cherokees raid the Negro settlement of Marshalltown which they believe is responsible for stolen cattle. Source: 87

AUGUST 6–11, 1880, BATTLE OF RATTLESNAKE SPRINGS—*Texas*

Col. Benjamin Grierson has the waterhole at Rattlesnake Springs staked out by troops in hopes that Victorio's Apaches will show up. On the morning of August 6, Capt. Viele with Company C and G ambush the Apache raiders as they approach the springs. The Apaches make several charges to reach the water but are driven back by heavy gunfire from the troops. No casualties are reported on either side, but Victorio and his men escape and are pursued by the troopers. On August 11, U.S. troops locate Victorio and his men but are unable to capture them. Victorio and his men cross the Rio Grande River into Mexico. Source: 102, 108, 118

September 1880—*New Mexico*

Apaches attack a stagecoach sixteen miles west of Fort Cummings, killing driver Alexander LeBeau and passengers Emery S. Madden and Isaac Roberts. Source: 74

October 14, 1880—*Mexico*

Mexican troops under Col. Joaquin Terrazas attack Apaches under Victorio in the Tres Castillos Mountains. Victorio, along with sixty warriors and eighteen women and children, is killed. Source: 68, 102, 107, 119

1881

January 1881—*Texas*

Apaches attack a stagecoach in Quitman Canyon and kill the driver Morgan and a gambler named Crenshaw. Texas Rangers under Maj. John Jones begin a pursuit of the raiding party. On January 29, the Rangers catch up with the raiding Apaches at their camp near the Diablo Mountains. An early morning attack kills four warriors, two women and two children. Source: 107

July 19, 1881—*North Dakota*

Sitting Bull and his followers surrender at Fort Buford. Source: 20, 108. Marker: From Williston, U.S. 2 seven miles to North Dakota 1804, sixteen miles to Fort Buford Historic site.

August 5, 1881— *South Dakota*

Brule Sioux Chief Spotted Tail, chief of all Dakota Sioux agencies and uncle of Crazy Horse, is shot and killed by Crow Dog on the Rosebud Agency. Source: 20, 108

August 12, 1881— *New Mexico*

At Carrizo Canyon the 9th U.S. Cavalry is attacked by a large force of hostile Indians but drives them off. Sgt. George Jordan and Sgt. Thomas Shaw are awarded the Medal of Honor for holding the enemy back while being in an exposed position. Source: 115

August 16, 1881— *New Mexico*

The 9th U.S. Cavalry engages Apache Indians in the Cuchillo Negro Mountains. Second Lt. George R. Burnett saves the life of a dismounted soldier by riding to his rescue under fire. Second Lt. Burnett is awarded the Medal of Honor along with Pvt. Augustus Walley and First Sgt. Moses Williams for Gallantry in Action. Source: 115

> "I don't want to run over the mountains anymore: I want to make a big treaty ... I will keep my word until the stones melt ... God made the white man and God made the Apache, and the Apache has just has much right to the country as the white man."
> — Delshay [Tonto Apaches]
> [Source: 153]

August 30, 1881, White Mountain Apache Rebellion—*Arizona*

White Mountain Apache medicine man Nochedelklinne is arrested by Col. Eugene

Carr of the 6th Cavalry at Cibecu Creek, but the medicine man's followers crowd the camp and a gun battle breaks out. Carr orders his men to shoot Nochedelklinne who is wounded in the thighs and unable to walk. A trooper then puts a gun in the medicine man's mouth and fires while another soldier hits him in the head with an axe. Over eighteen Apaches are killed in the incident. Brevet Lt. Col. Edmund C. Hentig rounds up the Indian survivors and takes them to the San Carlos Agency. First Lt. William H. Carter, Pvt. Richard Heartery and Sgt. Alonzo Bowman are awarded the Medal of Honor for rescuing wounded soldiers while under fire. Source: 23, 68, 78, 87, 108, 115

September 1, 1881—
Arizona

Apaches attack Fort Apache in eastern Arizona in retaliation for the arrest and killing of Nochedelklinne two days before. Source: 68. Marker: Arizona 73 east from Carrizo, 22 miles from turnoff.

September 11, 1881—
Arizona

U.S. Cavalry skirmishes with Indians. Pvt. First Class Will C. Barnes is awarded the Medal of Honor for bravery in action. (Barnes will later write a number of books including the popular *Arizona Place Names*.) Source: 23, 115

1881—*Utah*

After killing a rancher a party of Indians is tracked by a posse near Moab where they ambush the posse, killing eight. Source: 87. Marker: Pinhook Battleground in the Manti–La Sal National Forest, UT.

1882

April 19, 1882—*Texas*

While playing with her children in the garden, Mrs. John McLauren is attacked by Indians at Cherry Creek near the town of Leakey. She attempts to flee with her children but is shot over four times. Her fourteen-year-old son is shot dead, and her six-year-old daughter Maud runs for help to a nearby home. A party of neighbors with the help of a Seminole guide tracks the marauding Indians for five days into Mexico. The men ambush the raiding party and kill several, including a chief. This attack is one of the last Indian attacks in Texas. Source: 96

April 19, 1882—*Arizona*

An Apache war party under Juh, Nachez, Geronimo, Chihuahua and Chato attack the Camp Goodwin sub-agency, killing Police Chief Albert D. Sterling. (Sterling's successor is killed July 6.) Source: 68, 102

April 23, 1882—*Arizona*

At Horseshoe Canyon, U.S. troops fight an engagement with hostile Indians. Wagoneer John Schnitzer and First Lt. Wilber E. Wilder are awarded the Medal of Honor. Source: 102, 115

July 6, 1882—*Arizona*

About sixty White Mountain Apache led by Natiotish ambush and kill J. L. "Cibicu Charley" Colvig near the Camp Goodwin sub-agency. (Colvig had been appointed agent after the murder of Albert D. Sterling on April 19.) Source: 23, 102, 108

July 17, 1882—*Arizona*

At Canyon Diablo Apaches open fire on two companies of cavalry led by Maj. A. W. Evans and Maj. A. R. Chaffee but are soon driven off. The soldiers recapture seventy horses. Second Lt. George Morgan is awarded the Medal of Honor. Citation: "Gallantry ... held his ground at a critical moment and fired on the advancing enemy until he was shot." First Lt. Frank West is awarded the Medal of Honor for rallying his troop and leading it against the Indians' position. Second Lt. Thomas Cruse is awarded the Medal of Honor: "Gallantly charged hostile Indians." Source: 23, 108, 115

AUGUST 31, 1882—
Arizona

Miner Tom Johnson is killed by Apaches on the Sonora Road outside of Tombstone while trying to catch up with two friends who have ridden ahead of him. Source: 85

1883

MARCH 21, 1883—
Arizona

Apaches led by Chatto, Chihuahua and Bonito kill four white men at a charcoal camp near the Huachuca Mountains. In a 400-mile raid they kill over twenty-six people. Source: 68, 87

1885

JUNE 8, 1885—*Arizona*

Apaches led by Chihuahua ambush the 4th U.S. Cavalry led by Capt. Henry W. Lawton at Guadalupe Canyon, killing five soldiers and stealing two horses and five mules. Source: 87

JUNE 10, 1885—*Arizona*

Bill Daniels is reported killed by Apaches near Bisbee. Source: 85

DECEMBER 1, 1885—
Arizona

Sheriff Crawford of Graham County and two other men are killed by Apaches. Source: 85

DECEMBER 9, 1885—
New Mexico

Apaches led by Ulzana (Josanie) are attacked by the 8th U.S. Cavalry near Alma but escape. Source: 68, 87

DECEMBER 19, 1886—
New Mexico

The 8th Cavalry led by Lt. Samuel W. Fountain is ambushed by Apaches in the Mogollon Mountains near Alma. Privates Wisehart and Gibson are killed along with Asst. Surgeon Thomas J. C. Maddox. A blacksmith named Collins is mortally wounded and dies later. Navajo scouts arrive on the scene and drive the Apaches off. Source: 73

1886

JANUARY 10, 1886—
Mexico

U.S. forces led by Capt. Emmet Crawford cross into Mexico and skirmish with Apaches led by Geronimo and Natchez in the Sierra Madre Mountains. Capt. Crawford is killed. First Lt. Marion P. Maus is awarded the Medal of Honor for Gallantry in Action. Source: 68, 78, 108, 115

MARCH 25, 1886—*Mexico*

Geronimo and his lieutenants meet with Gen. George Crook at Canyon de los Embudos to negotiate surrender terms, but Geronimo changes his mind and slips away in the night with thirty men, women and children. Source: 68, 78, 108

MARCH 3, 1886—*Mexico*

The 10th Cavalry crosses into Mexico and engages Apaches in the Pinito Mountains. Second Lt. Powhatan H. Clarke rushes to the assistance of a wounded soldier and is awarded the Medal of Honor. Source: 108, 115

APRIL 27, 1886—*Arizona*

Apaches led by Geronimo raid a number of ranches near Casita, killing over thirty people. The wife and one of the children of A. L. Peck are killed. Peck and Thomas Watson are captured while branding cattle. Watson is killed trying to escape, but Peck escapes later. One of Peck's young daughters is later recovered by Mexicans. Source: 68, 73

May 3, 1886—*Mexico*

After the raids on the ranches near Casita and the killing of Mrs. Peck, the 10th Cavalry led by Capt. Thomas C. Lebo follows Geronimo's Apaches into Mexico. Lebo tracks the Apaches into the Pinito Mountains. The Apaches first volley kills Pvt. Hollis and wounds Cpl. Scott. Lt. Powhatan Clark pulls Scott to safety and later is awarded the Medal of Honor. Source: 73, 115

May 15, 1886—*Mexico*

The 4th U.S. Cavalry pursues Apaches into Mexico where they clash in the Santa Cruz Mountains. Sgt. Samuel H. Craig is awarded the Medal of Honor. Source: 115

May 19, 1886—*Arizona*

Apaches kill Fred Lutley and one other man at Granite Springs. Source: 85

June 5, 1886—*Arizona*

W. C. Davis' brother is killed by Apaches near Walter Harvey's Ranch. Source: 85

August 7, 1886—*Arizona*

First Lt. M. W. Day and his scouts surprise Geronimo's camp thirty miles north-northeast of Nacor, killing three warriors, one squaw, a boy and a girl and capturing fifteen squaws and children. Source: 23

September 6, 1886, Geronimo Surrenders—*Arizona*

Geronimo surrenders to U.S. authorities. The Apaches are taken to Fort Bowie where a train is dispatched to take them to prison in Florida along with the Apache scouts who have tracked Geronimo for the army. One Apache, Ma-si, escapes, and a massive manhunt begins for his capture. Source: 12, 23, 68, 88, 108

1887

November 5, 1887—*Montana*

Crow Indians raid and steal a number of horses from Piegan Indians on the Crow Agency in southern Montana. Agency Director Henry E. Williamson sends police to arrest the Crows, led by Sword Bearer. Soldiers engage the Crows killing seven and wounding two. Sword Bearer flees the agency and is later shot in the back and killed by Crow policeman Fire Bear. Source: 73, 91

1888

June 1, 1888—*Arizona*

Several Apache tribal police at the San Carlos Reservation are ordered to surrender their guns after getting drunk on duty, but gunfire erupts hitting the chief of scouts Al Sieber. Several Indians flee the area, but the Apache Kid is accused of firing the shot. A massive manhunt begins for him. Source: 23, 68

1890

March 7, 1890—*Arizona*

The 4th and 10th U.S. Cavalry fight an engagement with Apache Indians. This fight is the last engagement of the Apache Wars. Sgt. James T. Daniels, Sgt. William McBryar and Sgt. Rowdy, an Indian scout, are awarded the Medal of Honor. Source: 115

December 1890— *South Dakota*

Col. H. M. Day and ten soldiers clash with a party of Sioux Indians near Phinney's Ranch. Source: 87

December 15, 1890, Death of Sitting Bull—*South Dakota*

Near the Grand River on the Standing Rock Reservation Sitting Bull is killed at his home while resisting arrest. Source: 12,

20, 54, 103, 108. Marker: Reinterred in 1953 on the west side of Lake Oahe, off U.S. 12 near Mobridge, SD.

DECEMBER 29, 1890, WOUNDED KNEE MASSACRE—*South Dakota*

The Nebraska militia arrives at the Pine River Reservation to reinforce soldiers under Col. George A. Forsyth after rumors of impending trouble arise. After attempting to flee the reservation Big Foot and his followers are cut off by Maj. S. M. Whiteside and four troops of the 7th Cavalry. That night, camp is made on the west side of Wounded Knee Creek, and the teepees are pitched in a semicircle. The next morning as the temperature hovers well below zero, troops begin the search for weapons, but trouble begins. Yellow Bird, a medicine man, calls for resistance: "When I throw up a handful of dust ... kill." A gunshot rings out and both sides open fire. Capt. George Wallace goes down shot in the leg. Father Kraft is stabbed as the 7th Cavalry answers with a volley of gunfire. Springfield and Hotchkiss guns soon join in as both Indians and soldiers frantically attempt to escape. Shot and shell tear through the Indian ranks. Soldiers begin indiscriminate firing into women and children as they flee toward nearby ravines, and a number of Indian wounded are shot and killed as they lie in the snow. The dead lie in frozen heaps as a blizzard hits late in the day, making burial of the dead impossible. Although exact casualties will never be known, it is believed that some 300 Indians are killed. Col. Forsyth is court-martialed but later exonerated. Medal of Honor winners: Sgt. William G. Austin, Musician John E. Clancy, Pvt. Mosheim Feaster, First Lt. Ernest Garlington, First Lt. John Gresham, Pvt. Mathew Hamilton, Pvt. Joshua Hartzog, Second Lt. Harry Hawthorne, Pvt. George Hobday, Pvt. Marvin Hillock, Sgt. George Loyd, Sgt. Albert W. McMillan, Farrier Richard J. Nolan, Pvt. Thomas Sullivan, First Sgt. Frederick E. Toy, First Sgt. Jacob Trautman, Sgt. James Ward, Cpl. Paul H. Weinert and Pvt. Herman Ziegner. Source: 12, 56, 70, 78, 102, 103, 108, 115 [Quote 13]. Marker: Wounded Knee Battlefield, Wounded Knee, SD.

> "The soldiers had followed ... and murdered them in there. Sometimes they were in heaps because they had huddled together ... bunches of them had been killed and torn to pieces where the wagon guns hit them."
> — Black Elk, Oglala Sioux, on Wounded Knee
> [Source: 81]

DECEMBER 30, 1890— *South Dakota*

U.S. troops skirmish with Indians at White Clay Creek. Capt. Charles Varnum and First Sgt. Theodore Ragnar are awarded the Medal of Honor for Gallantry in Action. Source: 115

1891

JANUARY 1, 1891— *South Dakota*

The U.S. Cavalry clashes with a force of 300 Brule Sioux warriors attempting to leave the Pine River Agency at the White River. The Indians are turned back toward the agency. Six Indians are killed or wounded. Capt. John B. Kerr, Second Lt. Robert L. Howze, Sgt. Joseph F. Knight, Sgt. Fred Myers, and Cpl. Cornelius C. Smith are awarded the Medal of Honor for Bravery in Action. Source: 103, 115

JANUARY 7, 1891— *South Dakota*

Lt. Edward W. Casey is shot and killed while talking with some Indians on the Pine River Reservation. (Plenty Horses, who fired the shot, says at his trial, "I shot the lieutenant so I might make a name for myself among my people. Now I am one of them. I shall be hung and the Indians will bury me as a warrior. They will be proud of me. I am satisfied." The judge rules that Plenty Horses acted as a combatant during a state of war, and he is found not guilty and released.) Source: 103

1898

October 5, 1898—
Minnesota

Battle of Sugar Point. Eighty armed troopers are sent to the Lake Leech Reservation to arrest fugitive Chief Old Bug who is wanted for illegally selling alcohol on the reservation. Gunfire soon breaks out, and six soldiers including Maj. Melville Wilkinson are killed. The number of Indians killed and wounded is unknown. Pvt. Oscar Burkard is awarded the last Medal of Honor issued during the Indian Wars. Citation: "For distinguished bravery in action against hostile Indians." Source: 87

1901

December 3, 1901—
Tennessee

The Memphis *Appeal* reports, "Today 100 Indians of the Choctaw tribe will pass through Memphis in special railroad cars. They will be en route from the vicinity of Meridian, Miss., to the Indian Territory to claim their allotments of Government land." Source: 71

Appendix: American Indian Wars After 1890

For the most part, the Indian wars ended at Wounded Knee in 1890 although sporadic resistance occurred for several more years. The years of European-Indian struggle cost more than just human lives. The Pequot War, King Philip's War, and the French and Indian War resulted in the destruction of possibly millions of dollars in property and livestock for both sides in New England. Numerous towns in Massachusetts were burned repeatedly for over one hundred years. The Comanche raid led by Chief Buffalo Hump in August 1840 did more than $300,000 worth of destruction in south central Texas, and the town of Linnville, Texas, burned in the raid, never recovered and was abandoned. Army and militia raids resulted in the total destruction of hundreds of Indian settlements and villages from Tennessee to Arizona.

Why didn't the tribes unite to fight the French, English and Spanish invaders? Great numbers of tribes chose to fight *with* the invaders rather than join their long-standing enemies. Around 1809 Shawnee Chieftain Tecumseh made an attempt to unify the tribes against the white invaders, but put together only a fragile coalition. Years of hatred and bitterness among tribes defeated any consolidations. While many tribes went to war against the invaders, some tribes saw no advantage in fighting the European forces and aligned themselves with the advancing tide of civilization. As a result many tribes and tribal alliances were split forever. In the southern woodlands Lower Creeks joined with whites to fight Upper Creeks. Apache fought Apache as the struggle migrated into the southwest. These tribal feuds continued long after most tribes were shipped to the Indian territory in present-day Oklahoma. The Civil War further widened the chasm between many tribes in the Indian territory.

The number of Indian lives lost in the over 400 years of warfare can never be known although white casualties were slightly better documented. Whooping cough, smallpox and cholera took untold numbers of Native Americans. Indian mortality rates by disease and war are unknown, and the numbers of Indians killed in battle were usually greatly exaggerated. For example, after defeating the Maubila Indians on October 18, 1540, Spanish commander Pedro Mendez Marquez reported over 3,000 of the enemy killed. Given the primitive firearms of the time and European battle tactics, Marquez's 950-man army would have probably been routed and overrun in fighting 3,000 experienced woodland warriors. The general consensus of the day was that the Native Americans' fighting skills were no match for European military minds. Yet in battle after battle, American Indians proved an equal foe to organized military might.

The 1862 Sioux uprising in Minnesota alone resulted in 644 white civilians being killed. According to historian Greg Michno, Arizona counted over 4,340 white and Indian casualties in the Southwest Indian Wars of the 1800s. The years 1863 and 1864 produced over 1,712 Indian and white battle casualties. Most were the product of the Sully and Sibley campaigns against the Lakota Nation. Definitive casualty records from 1500 through 1700 are not as well documented. In addition to Indian lives lost, numerous slaves were killed through the years. Many were killed in attacks on white settlements, but others were killed fighting alongside the Native Americans. Huge numbers of slaves sought refuge among Native Americans; this was especially true during wars in Florida where many fugitive slaves fought with the Seminole warriors. These slaves married into the tribe and were known as black Seminoles. Large numbers of slaves also found sanctuary with the southeast Cherokees and fought as Indians against the whites.

Attempts to subjugate or civilize the Native Americans lasted for centuries. What may be called the first Indian reservation, the town of Natick, was founded in Massachusetts in 1651 for "Christian Indians." In 1830 the U.S. Congress passed the Indian Removal Act, calling for the relocation of all eastern tribes to an Indian territory west of the Mississippi River. A legal challenge to the Removal Act by Georgia Cherokees resulted in an 1832 ruling by the Supreme Court in their favor. The ruling was the first in their favor but was soundly ignored by President Andrew Jackson. The removal continued. Tennessee and Alabama Cherokees, Mississippi Choctaws, and Florida Seminoles along with other tribes were rounded up and began a long and deadly journey westward. Hundreds died on the Trail of Tears.

Many Indians resisted removal long after other tribes had been sent to reservations or the Indian territory. Apaches led by Geronimo fought the longest and finally surrendered in 1886 and were sent to prison in Florida. The Modocs of California may have been the most successful in resistance fighting against the U.S. Army and militias. The 160-odd Indians routed and killed more of the enemy than their own total strength. They also managed to kill the highest ranking officer killed in the Indian wars, General E.R.S. Canby.

The Indians' refusal to accept reservation life resulted in a number of reservation insurrections in the latter part of the nineteenth century. Reservation lands also dwindled in size through the years as the government gave land away in allotment programs. In 1901 the Snake Indians violently resisted the allotment of their lands in Oklahoma to Negroes. Theodore Roosevelt signed executive orders transferring 2.5 million acres of reservation land to national forests in 1909. Indian resentment and anger continued to grow, and in 1968 the American Indian Movement was founded at the height of the Vietnam War. AIM was a radical and militant organization founded to protest the Indians' plight. The group took over part of the Pine River Reservation at Wounded Knee, South Dakota, in 1973, and a violent standoff began, leading to one AIM member being killed in a shootout with FBI agents and local law enforcement officers. In 1969, Red Power activists took over Alcatraz

Island in San Francisco Bay to bring attention to the plight of the American Indian. This time the protest was ignored by the government. Red Power activists later abandoned the island.

As the twentieth century dawned the federal government and some states began reconciliation efforts toward Indians. In 1909, the government allowed the Modocs to return to their Yainax reservation in California. In 1972, Washington State returned over 21,000 acres to the Yakima tribe. In 1990, Congress passed the Native American Repatriation Act, providing protection for American Indian graves and the repatriation of Indian remains and cultural artifacts to tribes. All 547 federally recognized American Indian and Alaska tribes were invited to the White House by President Bill Clinton in 1994. The Indian wars have long since ended, but the lords of the woodlands and plains have survived. While the gaming industry has helped resurrect a number of Native American tribes, most struggle to keep their identities in today's world. Henry Red Cloud, a Winnebago Indian and founder of the Society of American Indians, wrote that American Indians possess a "great history, and great thoughts, and great ideas and inspirations in our hearts."

Bibliography

Books and Publications

1. American Automobile Association. *AAA Tour Book Series*. N.p.: 1997
2. Anderson, Gary Clayton, and Alan R. Woolworth, eds. *Through Dakota Eyes*. St. Paul: Minnesota Historical Society Press, 1988.
3. Beal, Merrill D. *"I Will Fight No More Forever": Chief Joseph and the Nez Perce War*. Seattle: University of Washington Press, 1991.
4. Beckham, Stephen Dow. *Requiem for a People: The Rogue Indians and the Frontiersman*. Norman: University of Oklahoma Press, 1971.
5. Boone, Floyd E. *Florida Historic Markers & Sites*. Moore Haven, FL: Rainbow Books, 1988.
6. Bourne, Russell. *The Red King's Rebellion: Racial Politics in New England 1675–1678*. New York: Atheneum, 1990.
7. Brady, Cyrus Townshend. *The Sioux Indian Wars*. New York: Indian Head Books, 1992.
8. Brininstool, E. A. *Troopers with Custer*. Harrisburg: Bison Books, 1988.
9. Broome, Jeff. "The 1864 Hungate Family Massacre." *Wild West Magazine*, June 2006, p. 48.
10. _____. "Death at Summit Springs: Susanna Alderice and the Cheyennes." *Wild West Magazine*, October 2003, p. 24.
11. _____. "Libbie Custer's Encounter with Tom Alderice." *Custer and His Times: Book Four*. LaGrange Park, IL: Little Bighorn Associates, Inc., 2002.
12. Brown, Dee. *Bury My Heart at Wounded Knee*. New York: Bantam Books, 1972.
13. _____. *Fort Phil Kearney*. New York: G. P. Putnam's Sons, 1962.
14. Calloway, Colin G., ed. *Dawnland Encounters: Indians and European in Northern New England*. Hanover, NH: University Press of New England, 1991.
15. Carruth, Gorton. *The Encyclopedia of American Facts & Dates*. New York: Harper & Row, 1987.
16. Casey, Powell. *Louisiana at the Battle of New Orleans*. N.p: Eastern National, 2002.
17. Cashion, Ty. *A Texas Frontier: The Clear Fork Country*. Norman: University of Oklahoma Press, 1996.
18. Chalfant, William Y. *Cheyennes at Dark Water Creek: The Last Fight of the Red River War*. Norman: University of Oklahoma Press, 1997.
19. Church, Colonel Benjamin. *Diary of King Philip's War*. Chester, CT: The Pequot Press, 1975.
20. Connell, Evan S. *Son of the Morning Star*. New York: Promontory Press, 1984.
21. Cottrell, Steve. *Civil War in the Indian Territory*. Gretna: Pelican Publishing, 1988.
22. Cox, Mike. *Texas Ranger Tales, Stories That Need Telling*. Plano: Republic of Texas Press, 1997.
23. Cozzens, Peter. *Eyewitnesses to the Indian Wars 1865–1890*, Volume One. Mechanicsburg, PA: Stackpole Books, 2001.
24. Crane, Verner W. *The Southern Frontier 1670–1732*. Ann Arbor: University of Michigan Press, 1956.
25. Dowd, Gregory Evans. *War under Heaven*. Baltimore: Johns Hopkins University Press, 2002.
26. Drake, Samuel Adams. *The Border Wars of New England*. 1897. Reprint, Williamstown, MA: Corner House Publishers, 1973.
27. Drake, Samuel G. *Five Years French and Indian War in New England and Parts Adjacent*. Freeport, NY: Books for Libraries Press, 1970.
28. Drimmer, Frederick, ed. *Captured by the Indians: 15 Firsthand Accounts, 1750–1870*. New York: Dover Publications, 1961. Reprint, New York: Coward-McCann, 1985.
29. Dunlay, Tom. *Kit Carson & the Indians*. Lincoln: University of Nebraska Press, 2000.
30. Eckert, Allan W. *That Dark and Bloody River*. New York: Bantam Books, 1995.
31. Every, Dale Van. *A Company of Heroes: The American Frontier 1775–1783*. New York: William Morrow, 1962.

Bibliography

32. Fehrenbach, T. R. *Comanches: The Destruction of a People.* New York: Alfred A. Knopf, 1971.
33. Ferris, Robert, ed. *Lewis and Clark.* Washington, D.C.: United States Department of the Interior National Park Service, 1975.
34. Fleming, Paula Richardson, and Judith Luskey. *The North American Indians in Early Photographs.* New York: Barnes & Noble Books, 1992.
35. Flint, Timothy. *The First American Frontier.* New York: Arno Press & *The New York Times*, 1971.
36. Gibson, Arrell M. *The Oklahoma Story.* Norman: University of Oklahoma, 1978.
37. Gildea, A. M. "Indian Raids in Frio County." *Frontier Times Magazine* 23, no.12 (1946): p. 226.
38. Gillett, James B. *Six Years with the Texas Rangers.* 1925. Reprint, Lincoln: Bison Books, 1976.
39. Graham, W. A. *The Reno Court of Inquiry.* 1954. Reprint, Mechanicsburg, PA: Stackpole Books, 1995.
40. Gunnerson, Dolores A. *The Jicarilla Apaches: A Study in Survival.* DeKalb: Northern Illinois University Press, 1973.
41. Haefeli, Evan, and Kevin Sweeney. *Captors and Captives: The 1704 French and Indian Raid on Deerfield.* Amherst: University of Massachusetts Press, 2003.
42. Hafen, LeRoy R., ed. *Mountain Men & Fur Traders of the Far West.* Glendale: Arthur H. Clark Co., 1965.
43. Halbert, H. S., and T. H. Ball. *The Creek War.* Tuscaloosa: University of Alabama Press, 1969.
44. Hamilton, Allen Lee. *Sentinel of the Southern Plains, Fort Richardson and the Northwest Texas Frontier 1866–1878.* Ft. Worth: Texas Christian University Press, 1988.
45. Hamilton, Virginia Van de Veer. *Alabama: A Bicentennial History.* New York: W. W. Norton, 1977.
46. Hauptman, Laurence M. *Between Two Fires: American Indians in the Civil War.* New York: The Free Press, 1995.
47. Hedren, Paul. *Traveler's Guide to the Great Sioux War.* Helena: Montana Historical Press, 1996.
48. Hoig, Stan. *Tribal Wars of the Southern Plains.* Norman: University of Oklahoma Press, 1993.
49. Horowitz, David. *The First Frontier.* New York: Simon & Schuster, 1978.
50. Hoyt, Edwin P. *America's Wars & Military Excursions.* New York: McGraw-Hill, 1987.
51. Hubbard, William Rev. *The History of the Indian Wars in New England.* 1864. Reprint, New York: Kraus Reprint Co., 1969.
52. Jennings, Francis. *Empires of Fortune: Crowns, Colonies & Tribes in the Seven Years War in America.* New York: W. W. Norton, 1988.
53. Johnson, David. "Scott Cooley — A Byword for Terror." *National Association for Outlaw and Lawmen History [NOLA]* XXXVII, no.2 (2003): p. 5.
54. Johnson, Dorothy M. *The Bloody Bozeman: The Perilous Trail to Montana's Gold.* New York: McGraw-Hill, 1971.
55. Johnson, Randy, and Nancy P. Allen. *A Dispatch to Custer: The Tragedy of Lieutenant Kidder.* Missoula, MT: Mountain Press Publishing Co., 1999.
56. Josephy, Jr., Alvin M. *500 Nations: An Illustrated History of North American Indians.* New York: Alfred A. Knopf, 1994.
57. _____. *The Nez Perce Indians and the Opening of the Northwest.* New Haven: Yale University Press, 1965.
58. Kelly, Fanny. *Narrative of My Captivity Among the Sioux Indians.* Chicago: R. R. Donnelley & Sons, 1990.
59. Leach, Douglas Edward. *Flintlock and Tomahawk: New England in King Philip's War.* New York: Macmillan, 1958.
60. Lehman, Herman. *9 Years Among the Indians.* Albuquerque: University of New Mexico Press, 1927.
61. Lepore, Jill. *The Name of War.* New York: Alfred A. Knopf, 1998.
62. Libby, Orin G., ed. *The Arikara Narrative of Custer's Campaign and the Battle of the Little Bighorn.* Norman: University of Oklahoma Press, 1998.
63. Liddic, Bruce, and Paul Harbaugh, eds. *Walter Camp's Notes on the Custer Fight.* Lincoln: University of Nebraska Press, 1998.
64. Lincoln, Charles H. *Narratives of the Indian Wars.* New York: Barnes & Noble Books, 1913.
65. Mahon, John K. *History of the Second Seminole War 1835–1842.* Gainesville: University of Florida Press, 1967.
66. _____. *The War of 1812.* Gainesville: University of Florida Press, 1972.
67. Mayhall, Mildred P. *The Kiowas.* Norman: University of Oklahoma Press, 1962.
68. McChristian, Douglas G. *Fort Bowie, Arizona.* Norman: University of Oklahoma Press, 2005.
69. McConnell, Joseph Carroll. *The West Texas Frontier.* Jacksboro, TX: privately published, 1933.
70. Members of the Potomac Corral of the Westerners. *Great Western Indian Fights.* Lincoln: Bison, 1966.
71. Memphis *Appeal.* December 3, 1901. "Mississippi Choctaw Removal." Memphis, 1901.
72. Michno, Gregory F. *Custer and His Times,*

Book Four: "The Mild West or the Wild West." LaGrange Park, IL: The Little Bighorn Associates, Inc., 2002.
73. _____. *Encyclopedia of Indian Wars: Western Battles and Skirmishes, 1850–1890*. Missoula, MT: Mountain Press Publishing Co., 2003.
74. _____. "Treacherous Track Through Cook's Canyon." *Wild West Magazine*, October 2005, p. 46.
75. Michno, Susan. "The Box Family, The Custers & The Last Bullet." *Research Review. The Journal of the Little Big Horn Associates*, 2006, p. 2.
76. Milling, Chapman J. *Red Carolinians*. Chapel Hill: University of North Carolina Press, 1940.
77. Missall, John, and Mary Lou Missall. *The Seminole Wars*. Jacksonville: University of Florida Press, 2004.
78. Monaghan, Jay, ed. *The Book of the American West*. New York: Simon & Schuster, 1963.
79. Monnett, John H. *Massacre at Cheyenne Hole*. Boulder: University Press of Colorado, 1999.
80. Murray, Keith A. *The Modocs and Their War*. Norman: University of Oklahoma Press, 1959.
81. Neihardt, John G. *Black Elk Speaks*. Lincoln: University of Nebraska Press, 1961.
82. Nelson, George. *The Alamo: An Illustrated History*. San Antonio: Aldine Books, 1998.
83. Nester, William R. *The Arikara War: The First Plains Indian War*. Missoula, MT: Mountain Press Publishing Co., 2001.
84. Nye, W. S. *Carbine & Lance: The Story of Old Fort Sill*. Norman: University Of Oklahoma Press, 1943.
85. Parsons, George Whitwell. *The Private Journal of George Whitwell Parsons*. Tombstone, AZ: Cochise Classics, 1997.
86. Peithmann, Irvin M. *Broken Peace Pipes: A Four Hundred Year History of the American Indian*. Springfield, IL: Charles C. Thomas, 1964.
87. Rajtar, Steve. *Indian War Sites*. Jefferson, NC: McFarland & Co., 1999.
88. Reader's Digest Publications. *Through Indian Eyes*. Pleasantville, NY: Reader's Digest, 1995.
89. Reading, Robert S. *Arrows Over Texas*. San Antonio: The Naylor Company, 1960.
90. Remini, Robert. *Andrew Jackson and His Indian Wars*. New York: Viking, 2001.
91. Rickey, Jr., Don. *History of Custer Battlefield*. Fort Collins, CO: Old Army Press, 1967.
92. Russell, Osborne. *Journal of a Trapper*. 1955. Reprint, Lincoln: First Bison Printing, 1965.
93. Schultz, Eric B., and Michael J. Tougias. *King Philip's War*. Woodstock, VT: The Countryman Press, 1999.
94. Slotkin, Richard, and James K. Folsom, eds. *So Dreadful a Judgment: Puritan Responses to King Philip's War 1676–1677*. Middletown, CT: Wesleyan University Press, 1978.
95. Snell, Tee Loftin. *The Wild Shores: America's Beginnings*. Washington, D.C.: The National Geographic Society, 1974.
96. Sowell, A. J. *Texas Indian Fighters*. Austin: State House Press, 1986.
97. Tennessee Historical Society. Nashville: Tennessee Historical Society, 1918.
98. Time Life Books editors, eds. *The European Challenge*. Alexandria, VA: Time Life Publishing, 1992.
99. Time Life Books editors. *The Mighty Chieftains*. Alexandria, VA: Time Life Publishing, 1993.
100. Time Life Books editors. *The Reservations*. Alexandria, VA: Time Life Publishing, 1995.
101. Time Life Books editors. *War for the Plains*. Alexandria, VA: Time Life Publishing, 1994.
102. Utley, Robert M. *Frontier Regulars: The United States Army and the Indian 1866–1891*. New York: Macmillan, 1974.
103. _____. *The Last Days of the Sioux Nation*. New Haven, CT: Yale University Press, 1963.
104. Wallace, Anthony F. C. *The Death and Rebirth of the Seneca*. New York: Alfred A. Knopf, 1970.
105. Walton, George. *Fearless & Free: The Seminole Indian War 1835–1842*. Indianapolis: Bobbs-Merrill, 1877.
106. Ware, Captain Eugene F. *The Indian War of 1864*. Lincoln: University of Nebraska Press, 1994.
107. Webb, Walter Prescott. *The Texas Ranger: A Century of Frontier Defense*. Austin: University of Texas Press, 1935.
108. Wellman. Paul. *Indian Wars of the West*. New York: Indian Head Books, 1992.
109. Willbarger, J. W. *Indian Depredations in Texas*. 1889. Reprint, Austin: Eakin Press, 1985.
110. Williams, Samuel Cole. *Tennessee During the Revolutionary War*. Nashville: University of Tennessee Press, 1944.
111. Windolph, Charles. *I Fought with Custer: The Story of Sergeant Windolph*. 1954. Reprint, Lincoln: University of Nebraska Press, 1947.
112. Withers, Alexander Scott. *Chronicles of Border Warfare*. Parsons, WV: McClain Printing Company, 1970.

Internet Sources

113. *www.9thcavalry.com* History of the Ninth Cavalry/Buffalo Soldiers.
114. *www.ah.dcr.state.nc.us/Sections/hs/bath/tuscarora.htm* Tuscarora War.
115. *www.army.mil/cmh-pg/mohind.htm* The Medal of Honor page.
116. *www.avenue.org/nrhs/histaught.htm*
117. *www.bozemanonline.com/history.php* Montana history.

Bibliography

118. *www.buffalosoldier.net* History of the Buffalo Soldiers.
119. *www.cr.nps.gov/history* Military-Indian wars.
120. *www.cviog.uga.edu/projects/gainfo/search.php* Search Georgia.
121. *www.dickshovel.com/win.html* Winnebago Indians history.
122. *www.earlyamerica.com/review/1998/scalping.html* New York Mercury, June 18, 1759.
123. *www.earlyamerica.com/review/1998/scalping.html* New York Mercury, July 9, 1759.
124. *www.forttours.com*
125. *freepages.history.rootsweb.com/~familyinformation/transcripts/indiandeaths.html* Tennessee Indian depredations.
126. *genforum.genealogy.com/jinggeorgeswar/messages/29.html*
127. *http://home.att.net/~ftmimsdar/* Fort Mims, Alabama.
128. *www.indianatravler.com* Fort Harrison State Park.
129. *www.in.gov/dnr/parklake/* Prophets State Park.
130. *www.iowagreatlakes.com* Spirit Lake Massacre.
131. *www.kshs.org* Kansas State Historical Society.
132. *www.kentucky.gov* Kentucky Historical Society.
133. *www.lapahie.com/Timeline_Spanish_1651_1699.cfm* Spanish southwest timeline.
134. *www.louisianahistory.org/timelines* Louisiana history.
135. *www.musketoon.com/2005/01tule-river-war-1856.html* Tule River War.
136. *www.natchezbelle.org* Mississippi/Natchez Indians.
137. *www.nebraskahistory.org* Nebraska State Historical Society.
138. *www.ngeorgia.com/people/ridge.html* About North Georgia.
139. *www.nps.gov/arpo/found/chap5d.htm* Fort Carlos/Arkansas Post.
140. *www.nyhistory.net/~drums/stockade.htm* New York history.
141. *http://politicalgraveyard.com/death/indians.html* Political figures killed in Indian wars.
142. *www.olemiss.edu* Mississippi writers page.
143. *www.sevierlibrary.org/genealogy/indians/cherokee.htm* Indian Wars/East Tennessee.
144. *www.swcenter.fortlewis.edu/FLC_guide/LewisBio.htm* Squaw's Den Battleground.
145. *www.tamu.edu/ccbn/dewitt/glassanthony.htm* Anthony Glass.
146. *www.texasbeyondhistory.net* Texas history.
147. *www.thehistorynet.com/we/blalderice/index1.htm* Battle of Elephant Rock.
148. *www.tsha.utexas.edu/handbook/online* Texas history.
149. *www.uark.edu/depts/contact/explorers.html* Mississippi Valley explorers.
150. *www.washingtonwars.net* Washington State Indian wars.
151. *www.waymarking.com* Historical markers.
152. *www.wiyot.com/history.htm* Wiyot Massacre.
153. *www.wovoca.com/native-american-quote.htm* Native American quotes.
154. *www.Wyomingtalessandtrails.com* Wyoming history.

INDEX

Abenaki Indians 15, 16, 20, 21, 23, 25, 29, 32, 41
Acoma Indians 5, 24
Acoma Pueblo 8, 13, 22, 24
Addison's Fort 93
Agawam Indians 16
Ais Indians 5, 6
Alabama 6, 25, 26, 52, 61, 65–69, 71, 72, 77
Alabama River 66, 67
Alalachino Indians 11
Alamo (El) 30, 31, 76
Albany, N.Y. 33
Alden, Lt. 89
Algonquin Indians 9, 18
Alibamon Indians 26
Allegheny River 40
Alligator, Chief 75, 78
Almouchiquois Indians 9
Amauskeeg, NH 36
Anawan Indians 21
Androsoggin Indians 21
Apaches 24, 29, 30, 31, 32, 37, 43, 47, 53, 58, 80, 81, 87, 88, 90, 95, 99-102, 105-107, 109, 112, 114, 118, 119, 121, 123–128, 130–132, 134, 147–154; Chiricahuas 100, 123, 128; Coyotero 100; Lippan 72, 80, 87, 118; Jicarilla 37, 87, 88, 90; Mescalero 90, 101; Natage 31, 32; Plains 8; White Mountain 151, 152
Apalachee Indians 6, 24- 28
Apalachicola River 6, 24, 69
Apple River fort 73
Aquascogoc settlement, NC 8
Arapaho Indians 62, 79, 80, 84, 107, 111, 135, 137, 138
Arickara (Arikara) Indians 70, 71, 104, 107, 122, 124
Arizona 5, 24, 62, 71, 87, 88, 97, 99–102, 106, 112, 114, 115, 118, 119, 121–132, 134, 137, 146, 148, 150–154
Arkansas 56, 71, 101
Arkansas River 71, 97, 107
Armstrong, Col. John 41

Arnold, Maj. Lewis 93
Arredondo, Gen. Jose Joaquin de 66
Arrowsic Garrison 21
Ashley, Gen. W.H. 70
Ashuelot River 36
Attacks: Ft. Michilimackinac 45; Fowltown, Ga. 69; Lancaster, Ma. 17; Linnville, Tex. 83; Mobile, Ala. 26
Augusta, S.C. 43
Austin, Stephen 70
Austin, Tex. 85
Ayubale Mission 25

Bacon, Nathan 20
Bacon's Rebellion 20
Bakersfield, Cal. 88
Bankhead, Lt. Col. James 79
Bannock Indians 99, 101, 102, 110, 146, 147
Barboncito, Chief 99, 106
Barnett, Dr. George Washington 87
Barnwell, Col. John 26- 28
Bath Town, N.C. 26
Battle of Adobe Walls: first 109; second 134, 135
Battle of Apache Pass 102
Battle of Ash Creek 107
Battle of Bad Axe River 73
Battle of Bandera Pass 84
Battle of Bear Paw Mountain 146
Battle of Bears River 104
Battle of Black Point 75
Battle of Bloody Island 88
Battle of Blue Licks 56
Battle of Blue Water (Ash Hollow) 91
Battle of Boyd's Creek 53
Battle of Brushy Creek 81
Battle of Brushy Run 46
Battle of Buffalo Wallow 136
Battle of Cabin Creek 108
Battle of Camas Meadow 145
Battle of Canyon De Chelly 106
Battle of Chucalissa 31
Battle of Dunlawton 76

Battle of Emuckfau 67
Battle of Enitachopco 68
Battle of Escanachala 67
Battle of Fallen Timbers 61
Battle of Four Lakes and Spokane Plains 97
Battle of Horseshoe Bend 68
Battle of Island Flats 48
Battle of Killdeer Mountain 108
Battle of Lame Deer 144
Battle of Little Big Horn 140, 141
Battle of Little Wichita 125
Battle of Locust Grove 101
Battle of Loxahatchee 79
Battle of Massacre Canyon 133
Battle of Mobile (Maubila) 6
Battle of Neches River 81
Battle of Negro Fort 69
Battle of New Orleans 68
Battle of New Ulm 102
Battle of Newton 52
Battle of Okeechobee 79
Battle of Pea Ridge 101
Battle of Peace River Swamp 94
Battle of Pensacola 54
Battle of Plum Creek 83
Battle of Point Pleasant 47
Battle of Poison Springs 101
Battle of Rattlesnake Springs 150
Battle of Sandy Creek 68
Battle of South Deerfield 15
Battle of Summit Springs 123
Battle of Taliwa 40
Battle of Talladaga 67
Battle of Tallushatchee 67
Battle of the Lava Beds 130
Battle of the Rosebud 140
Battle of the Washita 121
Battle of Tieconderoga 42
Battle of Tippecanoe 63
Battle of To-Hoto-Nim-Me 97
Battle of Tongue River 111
Battle of Turner's Falls 19
Battle of Victoria 82
Battle of White Bird Canyon 144
Battle of Whitestone Hill 106
Battle of Wolf Mountains 143
Battle of Wood Lake 103

165

Index

Beasley, Maj. Daniel 66
Beecher Island 120
Beers, Capt. Richard 15
Beers' Ambush 15
Belknap, Maj. William 84
Bent, Gov. Charles 86
Bent Massacre 86
Bent's Fort 99
Beothuk Indians 9
Bienville, Jean Baptiste de 25, 28
Big Cypress Swamp 93, 94, 96
Birch Creek Massacre 145
Black Hawk 68, 72–74
Black Kettle 109, 121
Black Point Garrison 21
Blackfeet 63, 70, 72, 74, 75, 80, 106, 108, 114
Blackfeet, Piegans 70, 124
Black's Fort 69
Blackstone River 14
Block Island, Conn. 10
Bloody Brook Massacre 15
Blue Jacket 58–61
Boise River 89
Bonaparte, Pres. (Texas), Mirabeau 81
Boone, Daniel 47, 48, 50, 55, 56, 83
Bory Indians 26
Boston, Mass. 15, 17, 20, 32, 37
Bouquet, Col. Henry 45
Bozeman, John 114
Bozeman Trail 111, 114
Bowlegs (Boleck), Chief Billy 64, 69, 84, 92, 93, 95, 96
Bowles, Chief 81
Braddock, Gen. Edward 40
Braddock's Defeat 40
Bradford, Maj. William 20
Bradstreet, Col. John 41
Brant, Joseph 46, 50
Brazos River 101, 108
Bridgman's Fort 34, 37
Broadhead, Col. Daniel 52, 54
Bruce, Maj. James 91
Buchanan, Capt. Robert C. 93, 94
Buffalo Hump, Chief 82, 83
Bull's Garrison, R.I. 17
Burleson, Gen. Edward 81
Burnt Corn Creek 66

Cabot, John 5
Cabot, Sebastian 5
Cachupin, Gov. Tomas Velez 39
Caddo Indians 72, 97
Caddoan, Red River 43
Cadillac, Gov. Lamotte 28
California 48, 54, 80, 83, 85, 86, 88, 89, 92, 93, 98, 129–132
Call, Gen. Richard 78
Caloosahatchee River, FLA 82, 92
Calusa Indians 5, 6, 7
Camp Grant Massacre 126
Canada 5, 25, 34, 37, 38, 44, 72, 147

Canadian River 84, 96, 109
Canasatego 31
Canby, Gen. E.R.S. 99, 131
Canonchet 18
Canonchet's Fort 17
Canyon de Chelly, AZ 62, 106
Captain Jack (Kintpuash) 129–132, 134
Caranchua Indians 74
Carlton, Lt. Alderman 94
Carrington, Col. Henry B. 113
Carson, Kit 75, 85, 86, 90, 98, 104, 106, 109
Catawba Indians 26, 27
Caughnawaga Indians 25, 40
Cayuga Indians 47, 51
Cayuse Indians 86, 87, 91, 92, 94
Cedar Creek 142
Chacatos Indians 24, 25
Chakaika 83
Chama River 39
Champlain, Samuel de 9
Chaoucha Indians 30
Charles Town (Charleston), SC 22, 43
Charlotte Harbor 5
Chattahoochee River 77
Cherokees 22, 24, 26, 27, 31, 39, 40, 43, 44, 53, 55–57, 60–62, 68, 69, 79–81, 101, 106–108, 111, 150; Middle 27; Northern 39
Chesapeake Bay 7
Chetco River 90, 93
Cheyenne Indians 62, 79, 80, 85, 95, 107–111, 114, 115, 119, 120, 122, 123, 129, 134–143, 147
Chickahominie Indians 11
Chickamauga Indians 51, 54, 57, 60–62
Chickasaw Indians 7, 25, 29, 31, 39, 44, 53, 54, 68, 101, 105
Chinookan Indians 93
Chippewa Indians 30, 39, 44, 54, 57, 65, 72
Chitimacha 26
Chivington, Col. John 101, 107, 109
Choctaw Indians 30, 32, 54, 61, 68, 72, 101, 105, 111, 156
Chowan River 26
Chucalissa 31
Chumash 71
Church, Col. Benjamin 14, 20
Civil War 100, 105, 110
Claiborne, Gen. Ferdinand 67
Clark, Brig. Gen. George Rogers 53, 56
Clarkson, Col. James J. 102
Clermont, Chief 69
Clinch, Lt. Col. Duncan L. 69
Clinch River, GA 69
Coacoochee 76, 82
Cochise, Chief 100, 102, 123–125, 127
Cochiti Pueblo 9
Cody, Buffalo Bill 123, 128, 142

Coeur d'Alene Indians 87, 97
Coffee, Gen. John 67
Colorado 28, 52, 74, 99, 107, 109, 110, 120, 122, 123, 148, 149
Colorado River 71, 80, 83, 88
Columbia River 91
Columbia Valley 93
Columbus, Christopher 5
Comanche Indians 28, 34, 37, 39, 42–44, 53, 55, 56, 58, 72, 74, 76, 79–88, 93–96, 98, 99, 108, 109, 115, 118, 126–129, 131–139, 144
Comanches, Panateka 82
Combahee River 29
Concho River 84, 95
Confederacy 99–102, 104–108, 110
Congaree Indians 26
Connecticut 10, 11, 16, 18
Connecticut River 10, 25
Connor, Col. Patrick 104, 111
Contoocook Indians 32
Cooke, Lt. Col. Philip St. George 90
Coquille Indians 89, 90
Coquille River 89
Cor Indians 26
Cordova Rebellion 81
Cornstalk (Hokolesqu) 47
Coronado, Francisco Vasquez de 5, 6
Council House Fight 82
Coweto 68
Crazy Horse 5, 133, 143, 144, 145
Creek Indians 22, 25, 27, 28, 31, 39, 40, 53, 54, 56, 60, 62, 68–70, 76, 77, 85, 101, 105, 107; Tuckabatchee 41, 66
Creeks, Lower 24, 65, 67, 68, 70, 77
Creeks, Upper (Red Sticks) 65–70, 77
Crockett, David (elder) 49
Crockett, David (younger) 49, 76
Crook, Gen. George. 127, 129, 130, 139, 140, 141, 153
Crow Indians 140, 154
Curaca 7
Custer, Gen. George Armstrong 115, 120, 121, 132, 133, 139–141

Dade Massacre 75
De Aviles, Pedro Menendez 7
De Bonilla, Francisco Leyva 8
Deerfield, Ma. 15, 24, 25, 32, 35
Deerfield, Massacre 25
De Gourgues, Dominique de 7
Delaware Indians 10, 41, 47, 51, 54, 55, 59, 64, 65, 79, 85, 102, 104
De Leon, Ponce 5, 6
De Narvaez, Gov. Panfilo 6
Deschutes River 87
De Soto, Hernando 7
De Vaca, Cabeza 6
Dinwiddie, Lt. Gov. Robert 39

Index

Doeg Indians 14
Dodge, Col. Henry 73, 74
Dodge, Henry L. 95
Donaldson, Maj. A. 68
Douglas, Gen. K.H. 81
Dragging Canoe 47, 48, 50, 51, 54, 56
Drake, Sir Francis 8
Dull Knife, Chief 142, 147
Dull Knife Battle 142
Dull Knife's Raid 147
Dunmore, Gov. John Murray 47

Edisto River 28
Eel River 17
El Paso, del Norte 22
Eliot, John 16
England 9
Escamacu Indians 7
Esopus Indians 13
Eustis, Brevet Brig. Gen. Abraham 76, 77
Everglades 84, 92

Fancher Party 96
Fetterman, Capt. William 113, 114
Fetterman Massacre 113
Fight at Warbonnet Creek 142
First Seminole War 69
Five Crows, Chief 87
Flathead Indians 73
Flint River 31
Floyd, Gen. John 67, 68
Florida 5, 6, 7, 11, 24–26, 28, 29, 31, 39, 49, 54, 64, 65, 69, 70, 75, 76–80, 82–85, 87, 92–96
Ford, Rip 96
Forsyth, Maj. George "Sandy" 120, 155
Fort Abercrombie 95
Fort Abraham Lincoln 128, 139
Fort Alabama 77
Fort Alden 50
Fort Apache 124, 152
Fort Apalachicola (Blount's Fort, Negro Fort) 69
Fort Arbuckle 117
Fort at No. Four 31
Fort Atkinson 88
Fort Barnwell 77
Fort Belknap 88
Fort Bellingham 92
Fort Belmont 98
Fort Benton 86, 106
Fort Berthold 104, 122, 124
Fort Bidwell 110
Fort Bliss 87
Fort Boggy 82
Fort Boonesborough 48, 50, 51, 52, 54
Fort Bowie 101, 102, 123, 127, 128, 154
Fort Bridger 84
Fort Brooke 75
Fort Brooks 84
Fort Buford 111, 151

Fort Bull 41
Fort Carillion 42
Fort Caroline 7
Fort Caspar 111
Fort C.F. Smith 113, 114, 116
Fort Chadbourne 89
Fort Concho 114
Fort Crittenden 127
Fort Cummings 112, 151
Fort D.A. Russell 114
Fort Dade 80
Fort Dallas 92
Fort Davis 89
Fort Dearborn 62, 64
Fort de Chartres 28
Fort Defiance 77, 95, 97, 99
Fort Denaud 92
Fort Detroit 44, 64
Fort Dodge 110, 112, 135, 147
Fort Douglas 101
Fort Downer 110
Fort Drane 77, 78
Fort Dummer 37, 38
Fort Duquesne 40, 42
Fort Edwards 41
Fort Fetterman 114, 124, 139
Fort Francis de Pupa 31
Fort Fredericia 31
Fort Frederick 41
Fort George 32
Fort Gibson 71, 108
Fort Graham 87
Fort Grant 128
Fort Granville 41
Fort Grenville 58
Fort Griffin 129
Fort Hall 74
Fort Hallack 105, 111
Fort Hamer 92
Fort Hand 51
Fort Harker 110
Fort Harmer 59
Fort Harrison 64
Fort Hartstuff 134, 139
Fort Hayes 110, 118
Fort Henrietta 91, 93
Fort Henry 47, 56
Fort Herkimer 50
Fort Hill 9
Fort Houston 80
Fort Inglish 78
Fort Jefferson 58
Fort Jupiter 79
Fort King 75, 82
Fort Klamath 134
Fort LaBoeuf 45
Fort Lane 91, 93
Fort Laramie 74, 90, 110, 112, 124
Fort Larned 97
Fort Lauderdale 79
Fort Laurens 51
Fort Leaton 87
Fort Lemhi 96
Fort Lincoln, NM 104
Fort Lincoln, TX 114
Fort Ligonier 45

Fort Louis 24
Fort Lyon 114
Fort Mandan 62
Fort Marion 127
Fort Marlin 75
Fort Mason 88
Fort Massachusetts 33, 34, 35
Fort Massachusetts Massacre 35
Fort McCord 41
Fort McIntosh 87
Fort McKavett 89, 132
Fort McRae 105
Fort Meade 94
Fort Meigs, Oh. 65, 66
Fort Mellon 78
Fort Miami, Fla. 22
Fort Miamis, Oh. 29
Fort Michilimac (Michilimackinac) 27, 45
Fort Mims 66
Fort Mims Massacre 66, 67
Fort Mitchell 106
Fort Mobile 25
Fort Mojave 115
Fort Murrah Massacre 108
Fort Myers 95
Fort Mystic 11
Fort Nashborough 51, 54, 59
Fort Neoheroka 27
Fort Niagara 42, 43
Fort Ninety-Six 43
Fort Niobrara 149
Fort Nisqually 74, 85
Fort Omaha 118
Fort Ontario 41
Fort Orleans, Mo. 30
Fort Oswego 41
Fort Ouiantenon 28, 45
Fort Phantom Hill 88
Fort Phil Kearney 112, 113, 116
Fort Pierce 87
Fort Pitt, Penn. 45
Fort Pitt, WV 42
Fort Polk 86
Fort Pontchartrain 24
Fort Presidio San Saba 39
Fort Prince George 43, 44
Fort Prudhomme 22
Fort Pulaski 72
Fort Rankin 110
Fort Recovery 58
Fort Richardson 127
Fort Ridgley 89, 103
Fort Riley 89
Fort Robinson 134, 144, 145, 147
Fort Rosalie 28, 30
Fort Rosalie Massacre 30
Fort Royal 27
Fort St. Francis 28
Fort St. Louis, Texas 22
Fort St. Jean Baptiste 27
Fort St. Pierre 28, 30
Fort St. Stephens 27
Fort San Juan 7, 8
Fort Sandusky 31
Fort Santa Elena 7

Index

Fort Saraghota 37
Fort Savannah 47
Fort Saybrook 10
Fort Scott 84
Fort Sedgewick 123
Fort Selden 110
Fort Shaw 114
Fort Sill 121, 125, 127
Fort Sinquefield 67
Fort Sisseton 106
Fort Stanton 90
Fort Stephenson 66
Fort Stockton 96, 97
Fort Sumner 106, 115
Fort Totten 114
Fort Toulouse 27
Fort Townshend 92
Fort Towson 71
Fort Umpqua 89
Fort Union, ND 71
Fort Union, NM 88
Fort Vancouver 71
Fort Vasquez 74
Fort Verde 110
Fort Yuma 87
Fort Wacahoota 84
Fort Walker 84
Fort Walla Walla 92, 96, 97
Fort Wallace 115, 120, 136
Fort Washakie 118
Fort Washington 14
Fort Whipple 114
Fort William Henry 41
Fort Wingate 86
Fort Worth 87
Fox Indians 30, 73
France 44
Franciscans 11
Freemont, John C. 85, 86
French and Indian War 41

Gaines, Gen. Edmund P. 72, 76
Garrison Number Four, Mass. 32–34, 36–38
Gatienoude 33
Georgia 5, 8, 22, 24, 31, 39–41, 43, 56, 60, 62, 65, 66, 69, 70, 72
Geronimo 102, 152, 153, 154
Gibson, Col. John 42
Gila River, NM 47
Gilliam, Col. Cornelius 87
Girty, Simon 55
Glass, Anthony 63
Gonzales Wagon Train 128
Gorham Town 32
Goshute Indians 104, 105
Grande Ronde River 94
Grattan, Lt. John 90
Grattan Massacre 90
Great Sioux War 102
Greenwood, Chief 72
Grey Eagle, Chief 87
Grey Eyes, Chief 71
Gros Ventres Indians 73

Haida Indians 95
Haller, Maj. Granville O. 90, 91
Hancock's Fort, NC 26, 27
Harding, Capt. Samuel 20
Harney, Lt. Col. William 79, 82, 84, 91
Harney Massacre 91
Harrison, Gen. William Henry 66
Havanna, Cuba 31
Havasupai Indians 115
Hawikuh Pueblo 6
Hawks, Sgt. John 33, 35
Hayes, Capt. John (Jack) Coffee 83–85, 99
Hayfield Fight 116
Hegone, Chief Mugg 21
Hidatsa Indians 104, 122, 124
Hill, Col. Edward 12
Hillabee Indians 67
Hillabee Massacre 67
Hinsdale's Fort 38
Hitchitis Indians 68
Hokolesqua 40
Hood, J.B., Lt. 95
Hoosic (Hoosick) River 16
Hopi Indians 24
Houston, Sam 68
Hudson, Henry 9
Hudson's Bay Company 71, 72
Humboldt Bay Massacre 98
Huron Indian 9, 44, 54
Huston, Gen. Felix 83

Idaho 74, 80, 89, 90, 98, 99, 102, 104, 110, 112, 144–146, 148
Illinois 28, 30, 46, 53, 54, 62–64, 72, 73
Illinois Indians 30
Illinois River, Ill. 30
Illinois River, Or. 90, 93
Indian Territory 72, 79
Indiana 28, 45, 51, 57, 58, 63, 64, 71
Inkpaduta 95, 105
Iowa 95
Iroquois 12, 33, 34, 40, 42, 43

Jackson, Andrew 67–70
Jacob, Chief 41
James River 11, 12
Jamestown Massacre 9
Jamestown, Va. 9, 20
Jano Indians 24
Jefferson, Thomas 51
Jemez Indians 9, 12, 23, 24
Jesuits 23, 29
Jesup, Gen. Thomas S. 78, 79
Jicarilla River 37
Jocelyn's Garrison 21
Jocome Indians 24
Jugeant, Maj. Pierre 68

Kansa (Kansas) Indians 98
Kansas 69, 72, 84, 87–89, 98, 104, 105, 114–123, 127, 135, 136, 138, 147

Karankawa Indians 22, 71
Kelawtset Indians 71
Kelly, Fanny 106, 108
Kelly, Lt. Col. James 91
Kennebeck River 20
Kentucky 48, 49, 50, 52–60
Kentucky Massacre 53
Keresan Indians. 23
Kickamuit River 13
Kickapoo Indians 30, 45, 62–64, 72, 104, 110, 118
Kickapoo River 73
Kidder Massacre 115
Kieft, Gov. William 11
King George's War 31
King Philip (Metacom) 9, 13, 16, 19, 20
King Philip (Seminole) 79
Kingfisher, Chief 40
Kiowas 79, 80, 84, 97–99, 108, 109, 112, 114, 124–128, 134, 135, 137
Kiskiack Indians 7
Klamath Indians 85, 86
Klamath Lake 85, 86
Klickitat Indians 93
Kwahadi Indians 129

Lake Apopka (Ahapopka), Fla. 78, 85
Lake Champlain 9, 38, 42
Lane, Gov. Ralph 8
Leavenworth, Gen. Henry 70
Lee, Capt. Fitzhugh 98
Lee, Maj. Henry A.G. 87
Lee, John D. 96
Lehman, Herman 125
Lewis, Meriwether 63
Lewis and Clark 62, 63, 133
Lincoln, President Abraham 57, 73, 104
Lindsay, Col. William 76
Lisa, Manuel 63
Little Buffalo 108, 109
Little Crow, Chief 102, 103, 105
Little Eagle 42
Little Turtle 58, 59
Little Turtle's Victory 58, 59
Little Wolf 147, 148
Livingston, Lt. Henry B. 98
Louisiana 26, 27, 30, 68
Lyon, Brevet Capt. Nathaniel 88
Lyttleton, Gov. William Henry 43

Mackenzie, Col. Ranald Slidell 129, 132, 137, 142
Macouten Indians 27, 30
Mad Buffalo 71
Maine 9, 15, 16, 20–23, 25, 29, 31–39
Malatchi 39
Manakato Mass Execution 104
Manatee River 93
Mandan Indians 104, 122, 124
Mangas Coloradas 100–102

Index

Manhattan Indians 9
Manhattan Island 11, 15
Manuelito, Chief 99
Marmusekit Indians 26
Marquez, Pedro Menendez 7
Maryland 41
Mason, Capt. John 11
Massachusetts 9, 10, 13–21, 23–26, 32–39
Massacre Cave, Attack on 62
Massacre Rocks 102
Matoonas, Chief 14
Mattapoisett Indians 14, 17
Maubila (Mobile) 6, 26
Maubila Tribe (Mobilian) 6, 26
Maumee River Ambush 58
McIntosh, William 65, 70
Meeks, Joe 75
Mellon, Capt. Charles 78
Melvin, Capt. Eleazer 35, 38
Mendizabal, Gov. Bernardo Lopez de 12
Mendoza, Don Juan Dominguez 12, 13, 14, 21, 22
Menominees 73
Mexia, Capt. Ruis 25
Mexico 7, 80, 81, 132, 151, 152, 153
Miami Indians 39, 54, 58, 64, 71
Micanopy 78
Miccosukee (Mikauski) Indians 75, 84, 95
Michigan 22, 24, 27, 44–46, 64, 65
Miles, Col. Nelson 136, 142, 143, 144, 146
Miltmore Massacre 98
Mimac Indians 9, 34
Mingo Indians 42, 47, 51, 54, 58
Minnesota 9, 56, 102–105, 156
Minnesota River 102
Mississippi 6, 7, 28, 30–32, 72
Mississippi River 6, 30, 31, 32, 44, 73
Missouri 30, 52
Missouri Fur Company 70
Missouri River 70, 108
Missouria Indians 27, 30
Missouria Massacre 30
Mitchigami Indians 12
Mobile River 66
Mobilian (Mobila) Indians 6, 26
Modoc Indians 86, 89, 129–132
Mohawk Indians 9, 11, 16, 19, 25, 29, 35, 40, 50, 52
Mohawk River 42
Mohegans 11, 14, 18
Mojave Indians 71, 97
Monoco (One-eyed John) 15, 17
Montana 63, 70, 78, 86, 112–114, 116, 124, 129, 132, 133, 139, 141–146, 148, 150, 154
Moore, Gov. Col. James 25, 27
Moore, Col. John H. 81, 83, 84
Moore's Fort 71
Mormons 90, 96

Moseley, Capt. Samuel 15, 16
Moulton, Capt. Jeremiah 29
Mountain Meadows Massacre 96
Mutt(a)wamp 15, 16, 18

Naakewoin Indians 54
Namble Pueblo, NM 24
Nansemond Indians 11
Narrangansett Indians 14, 16–20
Narshatowey, Chief 85
Nashaway Indians 15
Nasomah Indians 89
Natchez Indians 6, 28, 30
Navajo Indians 12, 13, 14, 21, 22, 62, 95, 97, 99, 106, 115
Nebraska 28, 70, 91, 107, 108, 110, 111, 114, 116, 117, 119, 120, 122, 125, 128, 133, 134, 139, 140, 142, 144, 145, 147
Negro Fort (Fort Apalachicola, Blount's Fort) 69
Nevada 99, 105
New England 25, 32, 37–39
New Hampshire 23, 29, 31–38
New Mexico 5, 6, 8, 9, 11–14, 21–24, 31, 34, 37, 39, 44, 46, 47, 86–88, 90, 98, 100, 101, 104, 105, 107, 112, 132, 143, 147–151, 153
New Orleans, LA 30, 68
New York 9, 11–13, 16, 22, 24, 29, 32, 33, 35–42, 46, 49–52, 65, 68
News Tribe 26
Nez Perce Indians 73, 87, 90, 97, 144, 145, 146
Niantic Indians 18
Nipmuc Indians 14, 16–18
Nisqually Indians 92
Nocona's Raid 99
Norridgewack Indians 32
Norse explorers 5
North Carolina 8, 26, 27, 43, 44, 48, 106
North Dakota 70, 71, 104–106, 108, 122, 124, 139, 151
Northfield (Squakaeg), Ma. 15, 32, 36–38
Norwottck Indians 15
Nova Scotia, Canada 35
Nueces River 98

Oatman Massacre 88
Ogden, Peter Skene 86
Ogelthorpe, Gen. James 31
Ohio 29, 31, 39, 44, 47, 51–56, 58–61, 64–66
Ohio River 47
Ohio Territory 41
Ojibway Indians 57
Okefenokee Swamp 79
Oklahoma 43, 69, 79, 81, 96, 101, 102, 105–108, 111, 121, 124, 125, 127, 135, 138, 139, 147, 150
Oneida Indians 68
Oneko 14

Onondaga Indians 9, 22, 24, 31, 51
Opechancanough 9
Opotheyohola, Chief 101
Ord, Capt. E.O.C. 93
Oregon 71, 85–94, 129, 134, 146, 147
Oregon Trail 102, 108
Osage Indians 43, 63, 69, 71, 80, 87, 105
Osceola, Chief 75
Ottawa Indians 39, 42, 44, 54, 57, 61, 65, 72
Otter Wagon Train 99
Oyster River Massacre 23

Pahvan Indians 96
Paiutes 89, 96, 112, 147
Palentine Indians 26
Pallis Indians 63
Palo Duro Canyon 137
Palouse Indians 96, 97
Pamptego Indians 26
Pamunkey Indians 11
Parilla, Col. Don Diego Ortiz 43
Parker, Cynthia Ann 77
Parker, Quanah 77, 135, 139
Parker's Fort 77
Passaconaway 12
Pawnee Indians 29, 69, 70, 79, 84, 107, 133
Pawnee Killer 115
Pawtuxet River 20
Pecatonica River 73
Pecos, NM 34, 47
Pend d' Oreilles Indians 87
Pennsylvania 39–42, 45, 46, 50–52, 55, 57, 59
Penobscot Indians 32
Pensacola (Panzacola) Indians 6, 26
Peopeomoxmox, Chief 92
Pequot Indians 9, 10, 11, 18
Pequot War 9, 10
Perier, Gov. Etienne de 30
Phips, Lt. Gov. Spencer 32
Picuris Pueblo, NM 22
Pierre's Hole 73, 78
Pierre's Hole Fight 73
Pike, Gen. Albert 101
Pima Indians 9, 24, 112, 119
Placido, Chief 83
Platte River 109
Pluggy (Plukkemehnotee), Chief 49, 50
Plymouth, Ma. 10, 13, 17, 19–21
Pocumtuck 15
Pokanoket Indians 13, 20
Pomo Indians 88
Pontiac, Chief 44–46
Pope (Popay) 22, 23
Potuck, Chief 20
Potwawatomi Indians 12, 27, 30, 41, 42, 44, 54, 61–65, 72, 73
Powder River 112
Powder River Expedition 111

Index

Powhatan Indians 9–11
Prairie du Chien (fort) 68
Providence, RI 18
Pueblo Indians 8, 9, 11–13, 21–23, 86
Puget Sound 92
Pumham, Chief 20
Putnam, Maj. Benjamin A. 76
Pyramid Lake 99

Quapaw Indians 30, 31
Quebec, Canada 34
Quechan Indians 88
Quigualtam, Chief 6

Rabal, Gov. Joaquin Codallos y 37, 39
Rains, Capt. Gabriel J. 82, 91
Raritan Indians 11
Rechahecrian Indians 12
Red Cloud, Chief 112
Red Cloud Agency 111, 142
Red Eagle 66, 67
Red River 43, 71, 108
Rhode Island 13, 14, 16–18, 20
Rio Grande River 12
River Raisin Massacre 65
Roanoke Indians 8
Roanoke River 26
Rogers, Col. S. St. George 96
Rogers, Maj. Robert 42
Rogue Indians 88, 89, 91–94
Rogue River 88, 89, 93
Rogue Valley, Ca. 89
Rowlandson, Mary 17, 19
Rusk, Gen. T.J. 80
Russell, Osborne 74, 80

Sac Indians 30, 73
Sadekanaktie 22
Sagoyewatha (Red Jacket) 8
Saint-Cosme Mission 26
St. George's Fort 33
St. Katherine's Island (Santa Catalina), GA 22
St. Pierre, Canada 37
St. Simons Island, GA 31
Sakonnet Indians 20
Salish Indians 85
San Antonio River 71
San Antonio, TX 29–31, 71, 76, 80, 82, 83, 86
San Cristobal Pueblo 24
San Ildefonso Pueblo 24
San Saba Mission 42, 43
San Saba River 42
Sand Creek Massacre 107, 109, 110
Sandusky River 66
Santa Anna, Jose Lopez de 76
Santa Clara Indians 22
Santa Cruz Pueblo, NM 22
Santa Fe Mission, FL 24
Santa Fe, NM 23, 29, 39, 72, 88
Santa Ynez Mission 71
Santee Indians 26
Sappa Creek Fight 138

Saratoga Garrison 33
Sassacus 11
Sassamon, John (Wussausmon) 13
Satank 114, 126, 127
Satanta 112, 114, 124–126, 147
Saulk Indians 32, 53, 72, 73
Savannah Indians 28, 39, 40
Saxapahaws Indians 26
School House Massacre 115
Scott, Winfield 76
Seloy Indians 7
Seminole Indians 62, 68, 70, 75–80, 82–85, 87, 92–96, 101, 107
Seminole-Negro Scouts 127, 138
Seneca Indians 40, 42, 47, 51, 52, 54, 55, 71
Serna, Capt. Cristobal de la 28
Seven Years' War 41
Sevier, John 56, 62
Shasta Indians 89, 92
Shawnee Indians 40, 47, 52, 53, 56–61, 67, 68, 79, 104
Sheepeater Indians 148
Sheepscot River 39
Sheridan, Gen. Phil 139
Sherman, Gen. William T. 127
Shirley, Gov. William 32, 35
Shoshone Indians 63, 85, 89, 90, 98, 99, 102, 104, 135, 148
Sibley, Gen. Henry H. 101, 103–106
Siege of Detroit 44
Siege of Ft. Niagara 42
Siege of Ft. William Henry 41
Siege of Milk Creek/Meeker Massacre 148, 149
Siggenauk Indians 54
Sioux: Lakota 62, 70, 72, 85, 90, 91, 95, 103, 106–108, 110, 111, 113, 115, 119, 122, 124, 129, 132–134, 139–141, 150; Oglala 100, 107, 112, 143
Sitting Bull 133, 142, 143, 147, 151
Slim Buttes 142
Smith, Jedediah 70–72
Smith, Capt. John 9
Smith, Capt. Kirby 97
Smith's Garrison, RI 16
Snake Indians 100
Snake River 74, 80, 85, 97
Sobaipuri Mission (Santa Cruz de Quiburi) 24
Solomon River 95
South Carolina 7, 8, 22, 25, 27–29, 39, 40, 43, 44, 48, 55
South Dakota 62, 70, 103, 112, 142, 151, 154, 155
Spain 7
Spirit Lake, Iowa 95
Spirit Lake Massacre 95
Spokane Indians 96
Squandro Indians 21
Squannakonk Swamp 21
Squanto (Squando) 20, 21
Standish, Miles 10
Steptoe, Maj. William J. 96, 97

Stillman, Maj. Isaiah 72
Stockbridge Indians 37
Stremmel, Lt. Phillip 87
Stuart, J.E.B., Lt. 95, 99
Sublette, Milton 73
Sully, Gen. Alfred H. 106, 108
Susquehannock Indians 14, 20
Sutter's Fort, CA 80
Suwanee River 6, 70, 85
Swiss Indians 26

Tahome Indians 26
Talcott, Maj. John 19–21
Talcott Massacre 19
Taliwa 40
Tallapoosa Indians 26
Tallushatchee 67
Taos Indians 22
Taos Pueblo 22, 24, 28, 44, 86
Taovayas 43, 78, 79
Tar River 27
Taunton River 20
Taylor, Gen. Zachary 79
Tecumseh 64, 65, 68
Tenino Indians 87
Tennessee 22, 29–31, 44, 48, 49, 51, 53, 54, 56, 57, 59–62, 156
Tenskwatawa 67
Terry, Brig. Gen. Alfred 139
Texas 22, 29–31, 39, 42, 43, 47, 53, 55, 56, 58, 63, 66, 70–72, 74–80, 82–90, 93–101, 104–115, 116, 118–120, 123–129, 131–140, 143, 144, 146, 147
Tewa Pueblo 23, 28
Tewas Indians 22
Texas Rangers 70, 76, 80, 81, 84, 85, 96, 99, 126, 135, 137, 138, 149, 151
Thesaotin, Chief 32
Thompson, Gen. Wiley 75
Tiloukait, Chief 86
Timecho Indians 22
Timucuans Indians 7, 24
Tispaquin (Tisaquin), Sachem 13
Tlaxcaltecan Indians 43
Tolowa 89
Toluca Indians 76
Tomasito, Chief 86
Tonkawa Indians 43, 81, 83, 96, 97, 118, 119, 127, 129
Tookabatchee Indians 67, 68
Totoson, Chief 14, 17
Totutni Indians 92
Touchet River 92
Trail of Tears 79, 81
Train attacked by Cheyenne 117
Treat, Maj. Robert 16, 18
Treaty of Dancing Rabbit Creek 72
Treaty of Paris 44, 56
Trent Indians 26
Trevino, Gov. Juan Francisco 13, 14
Tulare Indians 88
Tule Lake 89, 93

Index

Tule River 93
Turner, Capt. William 18
Tuscaloosa, Chief 6
Tuscaroras 26, 27
Tustenuggee, Chief Oscen 92, 94
Twiggs, Maj. David 69

Umatilla Indians 90, 147
Umpqua Indians 71, 72
Uncas, Chief 11
Underwood, Lt. Charles N. 88
U.S. Corp of Engineers 89
Upper Ashuelot Garrison, NH 32, 33
Uriz, Capt. Francisco Romo 24
Utah 89, 96, 104, 105, 121, 152
Utes 28, 31, 39, 83, 88, 89, 98, 105, 109, 148, 149
Utinas Indians 6

Van Dorn, Capt. Earl 97
Vargas, Don Diego Jose de 23, 24
Vaudreuil, Gen. Rigauld de 35
Vermont 34, 35
Victorio 148, 149, 150, 151
Villasur, Gen. Don Pedro de 28, 29
Virginia 7, 9, 10–12, 14, 20, 43, 47, 61, 110

Waco Indians 71, 85, 97
Wagon Box Fight 116
Waldron, Maj. Richard 21
Walker, Col. Tandy 101
Walla Walla Indians 87, 91, 92, 94
Wampanoag Indians 13, 14, 16, 18, 19
Wappinger Indians 11
Ward, Nancy 40
Ward Wagon Train Massacre 90
Ware, Capt. Eugene F. 109
Warren, Col. John 75, 78
Warren Wagon Train Massacre 126
Washington 72, 74, 85, 90–93, 95–97
Washington, George 40
Washington, Col. John 14
Wateree Indians 26
Watie, Chief (General) Stand 101, 102, 106–108, 111
Waxhaw Indians 26
Wayne, Gen. "Mad" Anthony 61
Weatherford, William 66
Weetamoo (Squaw Sachem) 20
Wells Fort 81
Welsh, Paddy 66
West Virginia 40, 42, 47, 49, 50, 53, 56–58
Westo Indians 22
Wetock Indians 26
Weyanock Indians 11
Wheeler's Capt. Thomas 14
Wheeler's Surprise 14
White Mountain Apache Rebellion 151, 152
White River 91
Whitman, Dr. Marcus 86
Whitman Mission 86, 92
Whitman Mission Massacre 86
Wichita Indians 43, 53, 56, 104
Willard, Maj. Josiah 32, 37
Winnebago Indians 63, 71, 73, 74
Wisconsin 12, 28, 30, 68, 71, 73
Withlacoochee River 75–78, 80
Wounded Knee Massacre 155
Wright, Col. George H. 93, 97
Wyandot Indians 47, 50–52, 55, 57, 58, 61
Wynkoop, Capt. Eugene F. 109
Wyoming 72–75, 84, 85, 90, 100, 101, 105, 107, 110–113, 116, 117, 124, 135, 139, 140–143, 145

Yakima Indians 90, 91, 93
Yakima River 90
Yamacrow Indians 31
Yamasee Indians 5, 8, 22, 26–29, 31
Yavapai Indians 88, 131
Yazoo River 30
Yellow Wolf 85
Yokut Indians 93, 94
Young, Brigham 96
Ypandi Indians 31
Yuchi, Billy 79
Yuchi Indians 24, 26–28
Yuma Apaches 127

Zia Indians 14, 23, 24
Ziaguan Indians 30
Zuni 5, 6

www.ingramcontent.com/pod-product-compliance
Lightning Source LLC
Chambersburg PA
CBHW081600300426
44116CB00015B/2946